John Dawson
Jung-Hee Lee
Editors

International Retailing Plans and Strategies in Asia

International Retailing Plans and Strategies in Asia has been co-published simultaneously as *Journal of Global Marketing*, Volume 18, Numbers 1/2 2004.

More pre-publication
REVIEWS, COMMENTARIES, EVALUATIONS . . .

"**I**NVALUABLE READING FOR ACADEMICS AND PROFES- SIONALS interested in global retail- ing. Asia is the land of hope and glory for large retail corporations working to expand their markets. However, dif- ferences in retail culture, both within Asia and between Asia, Europe, and the United States are substantial. This collection, written by well-known schol- ars in retail research, documents strat- egies of internationalization, and their successes and failures."

Harry Timmermans
Director
European Institute of Retailing
and Service Studies

"**A** WELCOME ADDITION TO THE LITERATURE. I usually do not like edited books because they lack the consistency of thought development that comes from one author. However, this book is an exception. Every chapter author has extensive experience in Asia and is able to bring this valuable exper- tise to the table. This is the first book on Asian retailing I have read that presents primary data and sophisticated research. Most books dealing with retailing in Asia report the same old dreary govern- ment statistics: number of stores, sales per square foot, etc.–information that does not help us understand the system. In contrast, this book provides some very rich original information ranging from behavioral relationships in Japa- nese channels to sophisticated econo- metric modeling of the effects of retail liberalization in Korea."

Brenda Sternquist, PhD
Professor
International Retailing
Michigan State University

International Business Press®
An Imprint of The Haworth Press, Inc.

New York • London • Victoria (AU)
www.HaworthPress.com

International Retailing Plans and Strategies in Asia

International Retailing Plans and Strategies in Asia has been co-published simultaneously as *Journal of Global Marketing,* Volume 18, Numbers 1/2 2004.

Monographic Separates from the *Journal of Global Marketing*

For additional information on these and other Haworth Press titles, including descriptions, tables of contents, reviews, and prices, use the QuickSearch catalog at http://www.HaworthPress.com.

International Retailing Plans and Strategies in Asia

John Dawson
Jung-Hee Lee
Editors

International Retailing Plans and Strategies in Asia has been co-published simultaneously as *Journal of Global Marketing*, Volume 18, Numbers 1/2 2004.

International Business Press®
An Imprint of The Haworth Press, Inc.

New York • London • Victoria (AU)
www.HaworthPress.com

Published by

International Business Press®, 10 Alice Street, Binghamton, NY 13904-1580 USA

International Business Press® is an imprint of The Haworth Press, Inc., 10 Alice Street, Binghamton, NY 13904-1580 USA.

International Retailing Plans and Strategies in Asia has been co-published simultaneously as *Journal of Global Marketing,* Volume 18, Numbers 1/2 2004.

The development, preparation, and publication of this work has been undertaken with great care. However, the publisher, employees, editors, and agents of The Haworth Press and all imprints of The Haworth Press, Inc., including The Haworth Medical Press® and The Pharmaceutical Products Press®, are not responsible for any errors contained herein or for consequences that may ensue from use of materials or information contained in this work. Opinions expressed by the author(s) are not necessarily those of The Haworth Press, Inc.

Cover design by Kerry E. Mack

Library of Congress Cataloging-in-Publication Data

International retailing plans and strategies in Asia / John Dawson and Jung-Hee Lee, editors.
   p. cm.
   "International retailing plans and strategies in Asia has been co-published simultaneously as Journal of global marketing, Volume 18, numbers 1/2 2004."
   Includes bibliographical references and index.
   ISBN–13: 978-0-7890-2888-4 (hard cover : alk. paper)
   ISBN–10: 0-7890-2888-3 (hard cover : alk. paper)
   ISBN–13: 978-07890-2889-1 (soft cover : alk. paper)
   ISBN–10: 0-7890-2889-1 (soft cover : alk. paper)
   1. Retail trade–Asia. 2. International trade–Asia. 3. Strategic planning–Asia. 4. Corporate culture–Asia. I. Dawson, John A. II. Lee, Jung-Hee, 1961-
HF5429.6.A75I577 2005
658.8'7'0095–dc22

2004026733

Indexing, Abstracting & Website/Internet Coverage

This section provides you with a list of major indexing & abstracting services and other tools for bibliographic access. That is to say, each service began covering this periodical during the year noted in the right column. Most Websites which are listed below have indicated that they will either post, disseminate, compile, archive, cite or alert their own Website users with research-based content from this work. (This list is as current as the copyright date of this publication.)

Abstracting, Website/Indexing Coverage . . . . Year When Coverage Began

- *ABI/INFORM. Contents of this publication are indexed and abstracted in the ABI/INFORM database, available on ProQuest Information & Learning
  <http://www.proquest.com>* 1992

- *ABI/INFORM Global. Contents of this publication are indexed and abstracted in the ABI/INFORM Global database, available on ProQuest Information & Learning
  <http://www.proquest.com>* 1992

- *Business Periodicals Index (BPI) produced by The H W Wilson company. Periodical coverage includes the leading business magazines and a broad array of trade & research journals.
  <http://www.hwwilson.com>* 1999

- *Business Source Corporate: coverage of nearly 3,350 quality magazines and journals; designed to meet the diverse information needs of corporations; EBSCO Publishing
  <http://www.epnet.com/business/bsourcecorp.asp>* 1987

- *Business Source Elite: coverage of scholarly business, management and economics journals; EBSCO Publishing
  <http://www.epnet.com/academic/bussourceelite.asp>* 1987

(continued)

(continued)

(continued)

Special Bibliographic Notes related to special journal issues
(separates) and indexing/abstracting:

- indexing/abstracting services in this list will also cover material in any "separate" that is co-published simultaneously with Haworth's special thematic journal issue or DocuSerial. Indexing/abstracting usually covers material at the article/chapter level.
- monographic co-editions are intended for either non-subscribers or libraries which intend to purchase a second copy for their circulating collections.
- monographic co-editions are reported to all jobbers/wholesalers/approval plans. The source journal is listed as the "series" to assist the prevention of duplicate purchasing in the same manner utilized for books-in-series.
- to facilitate user/access services all indexing/abstracting services are encouraged to utilize the co-indexing entry note indicated at the bottom of the first page of each article/chapter/contribution.
- this is intended to assist a library user of any reference tool (whether print, electronic, online, or CD-ROM) to locate the monographic version if the library has purchased this version but not a subscription to the source journal.
- individual articles/chapters in any Haworth publication are also available through the Haworth Document Delivery Service (HDDS).

International Retailing Plans and Strategies in Asia

CONTENTS

ABOUT THE EDITORS

John Dawson is Professor of Marketing at University of Edinburgh, Visiting Professor at ESADE, Barcelona and Distinguished Professor, UMDS, Kobe. He is presently participating in a European-Japanese project on international retailing. He is co-editor of the International Review of Retail, Distribution and Consumer Research.

Jung-Hee Lee is a Professor in the department of Industrial Economics at Chung-Ang University, Republic of Korea. His researches have mainly focused on changes in food marketing distribution system and globalization in retail market.

Introduction:
International Retailing in Asia

John Dawson

Jung-Hee Lee

The expansion of retailers beyond their domestic markets is a major feature of twenty first century commerce. Whilst the international operation of retailers has a long history there has been a surge in activity over the last two decades. International activity has become a significant element of strategy for many of the world's large retailers. From being a peripheral aspect of retailer strategy, international activity has become much more important to the continuing growth of retailers. The role of international activity has therefore changed as it has taken up a more central position in the strategic development of retailers.

Not only has the amount and significance of international activity changed so also has the location of such activity. The entry of American and European retailers into Asia marks a new phase in international activity. Previously, the focus of European retailers was mainly moves into other European countries with a small number of entries into North America, often with limited success. The opening of Central Europe after 1989 provided new European markets into which European retailers expanded. Retailers from the USA in these earlier phases tended to move into other parts of North America and Central America with a few moves, again often of limited success, into Europe. Whilst trans-Atlan-

---

[Haworth co-indexing entry note]: "Introduction: International Retailing in Asia." Dawson, John, and Jung-Hee Lee. Co-published simultaneously in *Journal of Global Marketing* (International Business Press, an imprint of The Haworth Press, Inc.) Vol. 18, No. 1/2, 2004, pp. 1-4; and: *International Retailing Plans and Strategies in Asia* (ed: John Dawson, and Jung-Hee Lee) International Business Press, an imprint of The Haworth Press, Inc., 2004, pp. 1-4. Single or multiple copies of this article are available for a fee from The Haworth Document Delivery Service [1-800-HAWORTH, 9:00 a.m. - 5:00 p.m. (EST). E-mail address: docdelivery@ haworthpress.com].

Digital Object Identifier: 10.1300/J042v18n01_01

1

tic flows of know-how were common there were only modest inter-continental moves for operational purposes. The moves of major retailers from both Europe and USA into Asia and the international moves within Asia of large Asian based retailers, since the late 1990s, has introduced a new dimension into the concept of the global spread of retailing. The gradual relaxation of governmental constraints on development in China is providing a similar stimulus for retailers to that of the privatisation of Central Europe post-1989.

Academic research into international retailing is extensive and, as might be expected, has tended to focus on European and American experiences. Only in the last few years, as the retail activity has increased, has internationalisation in Asia begun to generate a body of research. The issues that are now coming to the fore not only replicate the experiences of Europe and North America but also are new and particular to the retail cultures present in Asia.

The contrasts in retail culture within Asia are greater than within Europe or North America. Retailers entering Asia therefore are faced with not only a consumer and retail culture very different from their own but ones that are very different depending on the country of entry. Thus, for example, entry into Japan presents very different issues to entry into China. In both cases the previous experiences and knowledge gained from international expansion within Europe or North America may be of limited value. Retail internationalisation in Asia is generating new managerial and academic issues not previously addressed by managers or academics.

The papers in this special volume begin to address some of these new issues in retail internationalisation. The papers result from a workshop held in Chung-Ang University in Seoul in November 2003. The workshop was sponsored by the Society for Asian Retailing and Distribution, and involved presentations of early versions of several of the papers provided here, and discussions that have stimulated other papers in this volume. The original papers have been re-worked in the light of debate and discussion. They provide some new insights into the ways that retail internationalisation is progressing in Asia.

The investments by foreign retailers in Asian countries have implications for many aspects of channel relationships. The foreign retailers introduce different, sometimes new, ways of operating the supply chain. This can have implications for local suppliers to whom the new methods mean new forms and structures to previously established patterns of relationship between retailers and suppliers. SeongMu Suh reports a survey and analysis of the suppliers' views of trading relationships with the main foreign retailers in Korea. He shows significantly different perceptions by suppliers of the levels of trust in these relationships and he points to the importance of incorporating some local cultural values into the trading relationships of foreign firms. Yoshinobu Sato's study of success and failure of foreign retailers in Japan also emphasises the need of foreign retailers to incorporate local cultural values into channel relationships and store operations if they are to succeed in Japan.

Nobukazu J. Azuma explores some of the conceptual issues that international fashion retailers face as they develop in foreign markets. From his study it is clear that many traditional perspectives need to be re-considered if we are to understand fully the moves of fashion clothing retailers into Asian markets. The experience of European fashion retailers in becoming more international is relevant in this connection and expertise may be transferable as the same retailers move into Asia. John Dawson also explores how the bases of success of European retailers in Europe may be transferred into an Asian context. By analysing the factors behind the successful strategies in Europe it is possible to consider how these might be transferred to Asia. Nonetheless, although the knowledge base may be of value, adaptation of trading methods in the new market is still required.

The amount of international retail activity in Asia is increasing steadily. Roy Larke describes how Japanese retailers are investing in China. This study is of particular interest being the first account of the increasing trend of internationalisation in Asia by Asian based retailers. It seems likely that over the next decade Japanese retailers will expand much more into China and there appears to be considerable potential for them to explore other Asian markets in a substantial way. Korea has already begun to receive some investment from Japan, notably in convenience stores. Jung-Hee Lee and Sang-Chul Choi review in detail the evolution of foreign investment in Korea in the superstore sector. They point to the different strategies of the firms involved and explore the competitive relationships with local firms.

The issues of local competition and the need for foreign firms to adapt to local consumer cultures is further analysed in Verena Schmekel's study of Metro in Asia and Jungyim Baek's study of the adaptation of the sales methods of Toys "R" Us and Carrefour as they have become established in Japan. The extent to which foreign retailers learn about the market and so adapt to it is a recurring feature of analyses of international retailer success. The issue of adaptation to the changes in the commercial environment is important for wholesalers as well as retailers. Junji Nishimura explores some of these adaptation issues in Japanese wholesalers as they respond to new entrants at the retail level.

The papers in this special volume are concluded by Masao Mukoyama who reviews some themes in international retail research as applied to Asia and suggests possible future directions for study. He highlights the need for research on the ways that adaptation takes place not only in terms of changes in vertical relationships in the supply chain but also changes in format and formula of the international retailers as they enter new markets and as they become established in those markets. The increase in the amounts of international activity in Asia by retailers from within and outside Asia provides a unique opportunity to gain a much fuller understanding of the process by which retail concepts get transferred between different commercial cultures. It is hoped that these papers resulting from the workshop sponsored by the Society for Asian and Retail Distribution will stimulate future research in this area.

The editors wish to express their thanks to Lynn Walford who has worked on the papers to bring them into an appropriate style. They also wish to thank the Executive Committee of SARD, the University of Marketing and Distribution Science, Kobe and Chung-Ang University, Seoul for their sponsorship of the original workshop out of which this collection of papers has sprung.

Fairness and Relationship Quality Perceived by Local Suppliers: In Search of Critical Success Factors for International Retailers

SeongMu Suh

SUMMARY. This study compares the perception of local suppliers on fairness and relationship quality towards the top five hyper-market retailers in Korea. The study specifically addresses the factors leading to the relatively poor performance of Wal-Mart and Carrefour in Korea. Results show that the business model of Tesco based on joint-venturing with a local partner proves more successful than that of Wal-Mart or Carrefour based on expatriate CEO leadership. Causal relationship analysis on these measures reveals that procedural fairness exerts most influence on the commitment level of local suppliers in a channel relationship. *[Article copies available for a fee from The Haworth Document Delivery Service: 1-800-HAWORTH. E-mail address: <docdelivery@haworthpress. com> Website: <http://www.HaworthPress.com> © 2004 by The Haworth Press, Inc. All rights reserved.]*

KEYWORDS. Retail-supplier relationships, hypermarkets, international retailing, Korea, fairness, commitment

SeongMu Suh is Professor of Marketing, College of Social Sciences, Chung-Ang University, Ansungsie, Kyungkido, Korea 456-756 (E-mail: smsuh@cau.ac.kr).

[Haworth co-indexing entry note]: "Fairness and Relationship Quality Perceived by Local Suppliers: In Search of Critical Success Factors for International Retailers." Suh, SeongMu. Co-published simultaneously in *Journal of Global Marketing* (International Business Press, an imprint of The Haworth Press, Inc.) Vol. 18, No. 1/2, 2004, pp. 5-19; and: *International Retailing Plans and Strategies in Asia* (ed: John Dawson, and Jung-Hee Lee) International Business Press, an imprint of The Haworth Press, Inc., 2004, pp. 5-19. Single or multiple copies of this article are available for a fee from The Haworth Document Delivery Service [1-800-HAWORTH, 9:00 a.m. - 5:00 p.m. (EST). E-mail address: docdelivery@haworthpress.com].

INTRODUCTION

Since the opening of the Korean local market in 1995, the leading retailers including Wal-Mart, Carrefour, and Tesco have expanded their store networks to exploit the fast growing opportunity. Between 1996 and 2003, the three companies opened approximately seventy-eight hypermarkets or super-centers and contributed to rapid change of the Korean retail industry. Many experts predicted that the foreign retailers would take complete control over the industry in a short period of time because their management and economic resources far exceeded that of the local retailers. Furthermore, the Korean retail industry was fragmented and merchandise management systems were unsophisticated. The leading retail format in Korea in 1995 was department stores in the metropolitan areas. Those department stores delegated most of their merchandising activities to tenants and concentrated mostly on customer services and tenant management. They overlooked the importance of accumulating merchandising know-how and developing sophisticated management information systems, both of which are critical to retail success.

Ten years later, many experts are surprised by the competitive structure of the Korean retail industry. The two most powerful retailers, Wal-Mart and Carrefour, are still striving to prove their reputations in Korea while a local firm, E-mart, and Homeplus, a joint venture of Samsung and Tesco, are growing in competitive power. Table 1 shows that E-mart leads total sales followed by Lotte and Homeplus. In sales per unit of space, Wal-Mart and Carrefour lag behind the other three retailers, implying that the two may be experiencing difficulty in their operation. Such performance figures raise an interesting question; why are the two most powerful international retailers trailing relatively inexperienced local retailers and a smaller international Tesco in Korea? From an economic perspective, Wal-Mart and Carrefour should far surpass their competitors; they have the financial resources, sourcing and operational know-how, international experience, and brand equity. Furthermore, the Korean legal environment is not hostile toward foreign retailers. In fact, the Korean retail industry is almost completely open to foreign capital, and regulations regarding location, size, or business hours are relatively flexible. This indicates that differences in performance, if any, may be due to managerial expertise rather than resources or business environment.

Levy and Weitz (2001) list location, customer relationships, vendor relationships, operations, human resource management, merchandise management, and store management as the seven sources of sustainable competitive advantage in retail management. Among these, location is

TABLE 1. The Five Largest Hyper-Market Firms in Korea

		LOTTE	Carrefour	E-Mart	Homeplus	Wal-Mart
Established in		1998	1996	1993	1997	1996
Number of stores	2001	24	22	41	14	9
	2002	32	25	49	21	15
	[1] (2003)	(42)	(28)	(61)	(32)	(17)
Annual Sales (billion won)		12,743	11,490	34,300	12,562	5,697
Floor Space (pyung)		70,059	79,397	116,512	47,102	33,500
Daily Sales per Store (million won)		181.9	145.1	232.4	249.3	175.8
Daily Sales per Unit Space (thousand won per pyung)		62.3	40.2	818	74.1	47.2

[1]Estimate
Sources: Adapted from Korea Chamber of Commerce and Industry (2002); Ban JeeMyung (2003).

often considered the most important due to its monopolistic nature. However, if the number of stores of the competitors is large as it is in most chain operations, the difference in location between competitors may become negligible because poor locations may be compensated by other good locations. One company is unable to monopolize all the good locations. In this regard, the five hypermarket retailers in Korea seem to be comparable in terms of location quality. Most stores are located near heavily populated major cities. Wal-Mart has seventeen stores, the least among the five retailers, but has enough well located stores to compensate for those in poor locations.

In addition to location, it is difficult to discriminate amongst the five retailers in terms of customer service policies, operation systems, merchandise assortments, and store layouts. The stores are large, averaging about ten thousand square meters, well maintained and run by sophisticated information systems. They provide a wide variety of products including fresh food corners. It could be said that the source of distinction among the five retailers is most likely related to the social aspects of their management: supplier relationships and corporate culture. Unsuccessful retailers are the most likely to experience difficulty in dealing with suppliers and those experiencing difficult relationships with suppliers are likely to have more limited success. Supplier relationships are a critical aspect of strategic management and operational effectiveness, particularly in the case of foreign retailers. Marketing channel literatures provide ample evidence in investigating the impact of behavioral and social aspects of dyadic relationship between the supplier and reseller. This study will focus on the relationship quality perceived by local suppliers. In the following section, related theoretical backgrounds will be discussed.

BEHAVIORAL PERSPECTIVE

Studies on retail internationalization during the past ten years are mainly taken from an economic perspective. As evident in Dawson (2003), most research has focused on the motives of retail internationalization, choice of country, and entry methods. Dawson's recommendations for future research also stay in the economic tradition. Topics such as resource transfer, diffusion of new practices, and their impacts on the origin and the host countries are characterized as economic issues. A new perspective may be needed to broaden our understanding of internationalization in retailing.

The store is a living system that constantly interacts with various constituencies of its environment. Support from its main constituencies is critical for survival as explained by the behavioral theories of the firm (Anderson 1982) and the institutional environmental theory (Grewal and Dharwadkar 2002). In particular, collaboration from local suppliers may be crucial for retail formats such as hypermarkets when entering foreign countries where significant cultural distance exists (Dupuis and Prime 1996). Local suppliers are not familiar with the demands of international retailers regarding price, promotion, returns, and other trade practices. In countries where retailing is not developed, many suppliers have a more powerful position in negotiations. In the case of food and general merchandise retailing, suppliers make demands of retailers, unlike the U.S. and Europe where a few retailers dominate. In this regard, international retailers may experience difficulty in applying their business practices in foreign countries due to the resistance of local suppliers. International retailers will have to be tactful in handling these issues. Otherwise, they may not be able to secure cooperation and commitment from the local community. As a result, a lot more than rational thinking is required of an international retail manager. Human skills for doing business in foreign countries are very important. This is particularly evident for western retailers who do business in countries like Korea where the Confucian culture still exerts much influence. For example, aspects of the Confucian culture emphasize respect for elder people, saving the other party's face in relationships, and human networks or Guanxi (Lovett, Simmons and Kali 1999, Fock and Woo 1998).

RELATIONSHIP QUALITY

A marketing manager aims for long-term relationships with customers and suppliers. Maintaining such relationships demands commitment from suppliers in which trust and good social association play an important role (Dwyer, Schurr, and Oh, 1987). In reality, however, many supplier-reseller relationships are full of coercion, broken promises and opportunism and result in distrust and conflict. The more asymmetrical the dyadic relationship, the more likely the stronger business partner will be perceived as exploiting the weaker one.

The behavioral aspects of channel relationship have been discussed extensively in marketing. Ever since the introduction of the political economies paradigm by Stern and Reve (1980), concepts such as power, conflict and satisfaction in channel relationships were extensively discussed in the context of the powerful supplier and its weak resellers. Studies in the behavioral research stream (Dwyer, Shurr and Oh 1987, Celly and Frazier 1996) attempt to focus on relationship quality and on explaining its determinants and consequences. There seems to be no consensus on the definition of relationship quality. However, it is safe to conclude that the concept encompasses three aspects of conflict, trust and commitment.

In most channel studies, conflict is defined as hostility, frustration, and anger toward a channel partner that produces behavioral responses such as open expression of disagreements or overt attempts to prevent the other from achieving its goals (Brown, Lusch, and Smith 1991). Trust is conceptualized to encompass honesty and benevolence. A trustful partner stands by their word (Anderson and Narus 1990) and is interested in the welfare of the other party (Rempel, Holmes, and Zanna 1985). In the meantime, commitment involves the intention to stay in and develop the dyadic relationship (Scheer and Stern 1992). Geyskens, Steenkamp, and Kumar (1999) believe that the three aspects of relationship quality are in a causal relationship; conflict affects trust, and trust in turn leads to commitment. Their model implicitly assumes that a positive relationship will bring profitable results.

FAIRNESS

A partner's perception on fairness toward its strong business partner enhances trust (Dwyer, Schurr, and Oh 1987, Anderson and Weitz 1989), and thus the relationship of the two parties is strengthened. Based on the literature on organizational and social justice, Kumar,

Scheer, and Steenkamp (1995) classify fairness into procedural fairness and distributive fairness. Procedural fairness contains six elements:

- bilateral communications,
- impartiality,
- refutability,
- explanation,
- knowledgeability, and
- courtesy.

On the other hand, distributive fairness is the perception that the actual outcome of a firm is fair compared to what the firm actually deserves. A firm may be satisfied with the distributive fairness but not notice the procedural fairness. Kumar et al. (1995) find that procedural fairness exerts a stronger effect on relationship quality even if the effect is mediated by the outcome of the given alternatives and environmental uncertainties. In an organizational context, Kim and Mauborgne (2003) find that procedural fairness enhances trust and commitment from employees and in turn stimulates voluntary cooperation.

RESEARCH QUESTIONS

This study explores the success factors for international retailers from a behavioral perspective. The findings shed light on an interesting question; why are the world's two most powerful retailers lagging their competitors in Korea? As a first step, this study compares the local suppliers' perceptions on fairness and relationship quality toward the top five hypermarkets in Korea: E-Mart, Homeplus, Lotte-Mart, Wal-Mart, and Carrefour.

Retail managers attempt to influence suppliers and achieve management objectives in the course of interactions with suppliers. During this process, a retail manager's communication skills and attitude may influence the supplier's perception on procedural fairness. The slightest difference can trigger misunderstanding and cause tension. According to an executive of a local supplier, important meetings in Homeplus are held in Korean, even in the presence of CEO and other Tesco managers from headquarters who are non-Korean speakers, in order to prevent possible miscommunication between the supplier and buyer. Even if the majority of employees in international companies command good English, it is quite likely that foreign CEOs and managers may have problems communicating with local employees. This, in turn, may impair bilateral communication with suppliers and result in poor perception of procedural fairness.

A firm's culture may influence a retail buyer's attitude toward suppliers. A business culture that emphasizes short-term goal attainment and has an individual merit system may encourage employees to be aggressive in business relationships. If the business partners feel that they are being treated unfairly, anger and distrust result. In this case, it would be hard to expect the spontaneous cooperation and commitment that are important in maintaining a business relationship. In this regard, it is likely that each of the five hypermarket retailers have distinct business cultures owing to their different origins and the characteristics of their CEOs.

The second question is to clarify the causal relations between fairness and the concept of relationship quality. Geyskens, Steenkamp, and Kumar (1999) show a theoretical framework where sub-concepts of relationship quality such as conflict, trust, and commitment are related with the use of power and economic/non-economic satisfactions. They define non-economic satisfaction as "a channel member's positive affective response to the non-economic, psychosocial aspects of its relationship, in that interactions with the exchange partner are fulfilling, gratifying, and easy." Economic satisfaction is described as "a channel member's positive affective response to the economic rewards that flow from the relationship with its partner, such as sales volume and margins" (p. 224). In a meta-analysis of the previous studies on relationships, Geyskens et al. (1999) show the negative influence that conflict has on trust and its impact on commitment. Trust is also positively influenced by non-economic satisfaction. They argue that non-economic satisfaction is dependent on conflict. However, the opposite argument may also be true: non-economic satisfaction induces conflict. Therefore, the relation between non-economic satisfaction and conflict requires further investigation.

SAMPLE AND DATA COLLECTION

A list of suppliers was provided by one of the five retailers. Since the main purpose of this study was to compare the supplier perceptions on the five hypermarket retailers, the list was narrowed to 307 companies believed to deal with the five retailers. Three questionnaires along with a reference letter from the CEO of the cooperating retailer were mailed to each supplier during July 2003. The survey requested the independent answers of three managers in different levels. Twenty-eight suppliers replied during the first wave of responses, less than 10 percent of the total requests. In an effort to increase the response rate, the suppliers were contacted individually through telephone by the researchers and by the buyers of the cooperating retailer. Maximum caution was paid to prevent possible selection bias. The final number of responses was 99 companies. Incomplete responses and suppliers that do not trade with all five retailers were excluded, and as a result, 147 responses from 49 suppliers (3×49) were used for the analysis.

MEASURE DEVELOPMENT

The items used to measure the five concepts were developed by reference to Kumar, Scheer, and Steenkamp (1995). Since the original items were translated into Korean, it was necessary to confirm the validity of the measurements through a series of factor analysis. Each of the five scales was confirmed to have one component and Cronbach's alphas ranging from 0.84 to 0.92.

Distributive fairness was assessed using the following five items in a 7-point Likert scale.

1. Compared to the effort and investment that we have made to the (retailer) our earnings are (fair/unfair);
2. Compared to the roles and responsibility requested by the (retailer), our earnings are (fair/unfair);
3. Compared to what other suppliers in our industry earn, our earnings from (retailer) are (fair/unfair);
4. Compared to what (retailer) gets through our relationship, our earnings are (fair/unfair);
5. Compared to the contributions we make to the (retailer's) marketing effort, our earnings are (fair/unfair).

Cronbach's alpha for this scale is 0.89.
Procedural fairness was assessed in a 7-point scale (agree/disagree);

1. The (retailer) sometimes alters its policies in response to supplier objections;
2. The (retailer) seriously considers a supplier's objections to its policies and programs;

3. The (retailer) presents valid reasons for any changes in policies affecting the suppliers;
4. The (retailer) is knowledgeable about the situations faced by the supplier;
5. The (retailer) takes pains to learn the situations under which the supplier operates.

Cronbach's alpha for this scale is 0.85.

Conflict was measured by the following four items with a 5-point scale (agree/disagree).

1. With the (retailer), we feel (strong/weak) anger;
2. With the (retailer), we feel (strong/weak) frustration;
3. With the (retailer), we feel (strong/weak) resentment;
4. With the (retailer), we feel (strong/weak) hostility.

Cronbach's alpha is 0.92.

Trust was assessed by eight items with a 7-point scale (agree/disagree). The items are:

1. Even when (retailer) gives us a rather unlikely explanation, we are confident that they are telling the truth;
2. Whenever (retailer) gives us advice on our business operations, we know they are sharing their best judgment;
3. Our company can count on (retailer) to be honest;
4. Though circumstances change, we believe that (retailer) will be ready and willing to offer us assistance and support;
5. When making important decisions, (retailer) is concerned about our welfare;
6. When we share our problems with the supplier, we know that (retailer) will respond with understanding;
7. In the future we can count on (retailer) to consider how its decisions and actions will affect us;
8. When it comes to matters that are important to us, we can depend on (retailer).

Cronbach's alpha is 0.90.

Commitments included the following six items in a 7-point scale (agree/disagree):

1. Even if we could, we would not disconnect our relationship because we like doing business with (retailer);

2. We want to remain a member of (retailer's) suppliers, because we genuinely enjoy our relationship with them;
3. Our positive feelings towards (retailer) are a major reason we continue working with them;
4. We expect our relationship with (retailer) to continue for a long time;
5. We are willing to put more effort and investment in building our business with (retailer);
6. In the future we will work to link our firm with (retailer) in the customer's mind.

Cronbaha's alpha is 0.87.

RESULTS

Table 2 shows the supplier perceptions on fairness and relationship quality toward the five retailers with Scheffe's multiple comparison test results. One interesting result is that E-mart, the industry leader and most financially successful firm, ranks second in four measures of distributive fairness, procedural fairness, trust and commitment, and ranks fourth in conflict. Homeplus is perceived most favorably in all five measures despite the fact that its differences in distributive fairness and conflict are statistically insignificant from E-mart and Wal-Mart respectively. Carrefour is perceived unfavorable throughout all of the five measures. However, its differences from Lotte-Mart in distributive and trust measures are statistically insignificant. Wal-Mart is in the middle group; it is behind Homeplus and better than Carrefour in the five measures. Concerning perceived conflict, the suppliers feel less constrained with Wal-Mart than Lotte-Mart, Carrefour, and E-mart. In commitment, Wal-Mart is behind Homeplus and E-mart. Lotte-Mart, which is second in the number of stores owned, is in the middle group close to Wal-Mart who has the least number of stores. To summarize the multiple comparisons: Homeplus, a foreign retailer that has a local CEO, consistently scores highest while Carrefour, another foreign retailer with an expatriate CEO, is perceived as least favorable. Wal-Mart and Lotte-Mart are in the mid-range while E-mart falls in the higher range near Homeplus.

When the samples are broken down to food versus non-food suppliers, overall results are similar. The only noticeable difference is that Wal-Mart tends to be perceived more favorably by food suppliers than by non-food suppliers and the differences from Homeplus in distributive fairness, procedural fairness, conflict and trust become statistically

TABLE 2. Supplier Perceptions of Fairness and Relationship Quality Toward Five Retailers

Retailers	N	Distributive Fairness			Procedure Fairness			Conflict			Trust			Commitment		
		Mean[1]	Rank	Difference[2]	Mean[1]	Rank	Difference[2]	Mean[3]	Rank	Difference[2]	Mean[4]	Rank	Difference[2]	Mean[5]	Rank	Difference[2]
Lotte-Mart (L)	146	17.64	4	E,H	17.88	4	C,H	12.66	3	C,H	26.57	4	H	26.55	3	C,E,H
Carrefour (C)	146	15.72	5	E,H,W	15.58	5	L,E,H,W	14.55	5	L,E,H,W	23.65	5	E,H,W	23.21	5	L,E,H,W
E-mart (E)	146	20.18	2	L,C	18.50	2	C,H	13.10	4	C,H,W	28.11	2	C,H	29.27	2	L,C,H,W
Homeplus (H)	146	22.09	1	L,C,W	21.05	1	L,C,E,W	10.81	1	L,C,E	31.91	1	L,C,E,W	31.82	1	L,C,E,W
Wal-Mart (W)	146	18.47	3	C,H	18.27	3	C,H	11.57	2	C,E	28.04	3	C,H	26.26	4	C,E,H
Total	730	18.82			18.26			12.54			27.66			27.42		

1. Five items with 7-point Likert scale.
2. Scheffe test, p = 0.05.
3. Four items with 5-point Likert-scale.
4. Eight items with 7-point scale.
5. Six items with 7-point scale.

insignificant. Due to the limited number of participating suppliers, further break-down analysis was not attempted.

THE CAUSAL RELATION BETWEEN PERCEIVED FAIRNESS AND RELATIONSHIP QUALITY CONCEPTS

In order to explore the causal relation between fairness and relationship concepts, a number of structural equation models have been systematically compared. Based on the works of Geyskens et al. (1999), Kumar et al. (1995) and Kim and Mauborgne (1997), procedural fairness and distributive fairness were treated as independent variables and commitment as the focal dependent variable. Figure 1 shows the result. Even though the overall fitness index is not satisfactory, the goodness of fit index looks good enough for an exploratory study. It can be seen that commitment is mainly derived from trust, and trust in turn is influenced mainly by procedural fairness and a little by conflict. Procedural fairness is the main cause of conflict and trust. These findings support Geyskens et al. (1999) who find that trust is influenced more by non-economic satisfaction than by conflict. Their explanation of non-economic satisfaction, "the partner is concerned, respectable, and willing to exchange ideas," is very similar to the procedural fairness defined in this study. However, this study differs from Geyskens et al. (1999) in two points. First, conflict is believed to cause non-economic satisfaction, but this study confirms the opposite path; procedural fairness has negative influences on conflict. The second difference is that Geyskens et al. (1999) do not include the direct impact of economic satisfaction on commitment. However, as shown in Figure 1, this study confirms the causal path from distributive fairness to commitment.

To conclude the analysis of the structural relations among fairness and relationship quality concepts, procedural fairness exerts the most influence on commitment. Its impact is most dominant on trust, and trust in turn determines commitment. The impact of conflict on trust is less than that of procedural fairness. On the other hand, distributive fairness decreases conflict and can induce commitment. It does not, however, have direct influence on trust toward the other partner.

CONCLUSION

This study attempts to explore the success factors for international retailers in foreign countries from a behavioral perspective, focusing on per-

FIGURE 1. Structural Models of Fairness and Relationship Quality Constructs

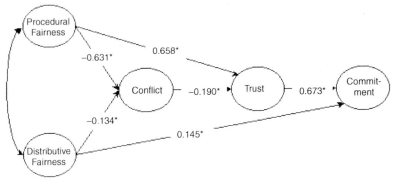

χ^2 = 1,511.97, DF = 339, P = 0.000, GFI = 0.867, NFI = 0.892, RMR = 0.103
*p = 0.000

ceived fairness and relationship quality by local suppliers. Special attention is given to procedural fairness and commitment since commitment brings forth cooperation from suppliers and leads to the competitive advantage over competitors. The result suggests that the antecedents of procedural fairness and relationship quality need to be further investigated. Possible variables include the communication skills of CEOs and buyers, buyer incentive systems, and the extent of applying the appropriate rules and systems in dealing with suppliers. A former executive of a supplier reviewed the preliminary results of this study and mentioned that Carrefour encourages the hardball playing by buyers while Wal-Mart tends to run by manuals. For example, Carrefour buyers demand as many concessions as they can while Wal-Mart buyers do not demand beyond their goals. In other words, Wal-Mart is run by system and tends to be more reliable.

Further investigation on the influence of respondent rank in companies regarding the perception of fairness would be interesting. A preliminary regression analysis with the present data shows that middle managers feel that they are being treated unfairly while the top management perceives more fairness compared to their subordinates. This is probably due to the fact that middle managers have less contact with retailers than the lower managers while at the same time are directly responsible for their work. Further study would be required to clarify this finding and it represents an interesting extension to the current study. The study examines the position at one time and so does not consider how these relationships evolve. Replication of the study would be useful to explore the dynamic nature of the concepts explored in this study.

REFERENCES

Anderson, P.E. (1982), Marketing, strategic planning and the theory of a firm, *Journal of Marketing*, 46 (spring), 15-26.

Anderson, Erin, and Barton A. Weitz (1989), Determinants of Continuity in Conventional Industrial Channel Dyads, *Marketing Science*, 8 (Fall), 310-23.

Anderson, James C. and James A. Narus (1990), A Model of Distributor Firm and Manufacturer Firm Working Relationships, *Journal of Marketing*, 54 (January), 42-58.

Ban, JeeMyung (2003), Trend Forecast of Supermarket and Super-Center, *2003 Proceeding*, Korea Distribution Association.

Celly, Kirti Sawhney and Gary L. Frazier (1996), Outcome-Based and Behavior-Based Coordination Efforts in Channel Relationships, *Journal of Marketing Research*, vol. 33 (May), 200-210.

Brown, James, Robert Lusch, and Laurie P. Smith (1991), Conflict and Satisfaction in an Industrial Channel of Distribution, *International Journal of Physical Distribution and Logistics Management*, 21 (6), 15-25.

Dawson, John (2003), Towards a model of the impacts of retail internationalisation, *The Internationalisation of Retailing in Asia*, edited by John Dawson, Masao Mukoyama, Sang Chul Choi and Roy Larke, University of Marketing and Distribution Sciences, Kobe, Japan, RoutledgeCurzon, 189-209.

Dupuis, Marc and Nathalie Prime (1996), Business distance and global retailing: a model for analysis of key success/failure factors, *International Journal of Retail & Distribution Management*, 24 (November), 30-38.

Dwyer, F. Robert, Paul H. Schurr, and Sejo Oh (1987), Developing Buyer-Seller Relationships, *Journal of Marketing*, 51 (April), 11-27.

Fock, Henry K.Y. and Ka-Shing Woo (1998), The China Market: Strategic Implications of Guanxi, *Business Strategy Review*, vol. 9 issue 3, pp. 33-43.

Geyskens, Inge, Jan-Benedict E.M. Steenkamp, and Nirmalyaya Kumar (1999), A Meta-Analysis of Satisfaction in Marketing Channel Relationships, *Journal of Marketing Research*, 36 (May), 223-238.

Grewal, Rajdeep, and Ravi Dharwadkar (2002), The Role of the Institutional Environment in Marketing Channels, *Journal of Marketing*, 66 (July), 82-97.

Kim, W.Chan, and Renee Mauborgne (2003), Fair Process: Managing in the Knowledge Economy, *Harvard Business Review*, (January), 127-136.

Korea Chamber of Commerce and Industry (2002), *Retail Industry Report 2001*. Korea Chamber of Commerce and Industry.

Kumar, Nirmalya, Lisa K. Scheer, and Han-Benedict E.M. Steenkamp (1995), The Effects of Supplier Fairness on Vulnerable Resellers, *Journal of Marketing Research*, Vol. 32 (February), 54-65.

Levy, Michael, and Barton A. Weitz (2001), *Retailing Management*, International Edition, McGraw-Hill.

Lovett, Steve, Lee C. Simmons and Raja Kali (1999), Guanxi versus The Market: Ethics and Efficiency, *Journal of International Business Studies*, 30, 2 (Second Quarter), 231-248.

Remple, John K., John G. Holmes, and Mark P. Zana (1985), Trust in Close Relationships, *Journal of Personality and Social Psychology*, 49 (1), 95-112.

Scheer, Lisa K. and Louis W. Stern (1992), The Effect of Influence Type and Performance Outcomes on Attitude Toward the Influencer, *Journal of Marketing Research*, 29 (February), 128-42.

Stern, Louis W. and Torger Reve (1980), Distribution Channels as Political Economies: A Framework for Comparative Analysis, *Journal of Marketing*, 44 (Summer), 52-64.

Some Reasons Why Foreign Retailers Have Difficulties in Succeeding in the Japanese Market

Yoshinobu Sato

SUMMARY. The paper explores the *Mystique Theory of Japanese Market* by analyzing cases of foreign-affiliated retail companies that have entered the Japanese market. As a result of the case studies, three conclusions are drawn. The first identifies three generic hurdles that foreign-affiliated retail companies face in a host country. The second conclusion is that a sufficient condition of success for the foreign-affiliated companies is the need to learn from their failures, to adapt and to change their business models in Japan. The third conclusion is concerned with a potential reason why failed foreign-affiliated companies failed to learn form their experiences in Japan. *[Article copies available for a fee from The Haworth Document Delivery Service: 1-800-HAWORTH. E-mail address: <docdelivery@haworthpress.com> Website: <http://www.HaworthPress.com> © 2004 by The Haworth Press, Inc. All rights reserved.]*

KEYWORDS. Japan, retail, success factors, internationalization, mystique theory

---

Yoshinobu Sato is Professor of Services Marketing, Faculty of Service Industries, University of Marketing and Distribution Sciences, 3-1 Gakuen Nishi-Machi, Nishi-Ku, Kobe 651-2188, Japan (E-mail: Yoshinobu_Sato@red.umds.ac.jp).

[Haworth co-indexing entry note]: "Some Reasons Why Foreign Retailers Have Difficulties in Succeeding in the Japanese Market." Sato, Yoshinobu. Co-published simultaneously in *Journal of Global Marketing* (International Business Press, an imprint of The Haworth Press, Inc.) Vol. 18, No. 1/2, 2004, pp. 21-44; and: *International Retailing Plans and Strategies in Asia* (ed: John Dawson, and Jung-Hee Lee) International Business Press, an imprint of The Haworth Press, Inc., 2004, pp. 21-44. Single or multiple copies of this article are available for a fee from The Haworth Document Delivery Service [1-800-HAWORTH, 9:00 a.m. - 5:00 p.m. (EST). E-mail address: docdelivery@haworthpress.com].

Available online at http://www.haworthpress.com/web/JGM
© 2004 by The Haworth Press, Inc. All rights reserved.
Digital Object Identifier: 10.1300/J042v18n01_03

MYSTIQUE THEORY OF JAPANESE MARKET

The misapprehensions embedded in the "theory of heterogeneity of the Japanese market," that stemmed from SII talks, have largely been discredited (Czinkota 1985; Alden 1987; Kaikati 1993; Pirog et al. 1997). The "theory" may be about to be revived, however, in response to the successive withdrawals of foreign-affiliated retail companies. Is the Japanese market truly difficult to enter for a foreign-affiliated retail company? If it is difficult, what is the reason? Are the reasons peculiar to Japan?

The purpose of this paper is to address these questions through case studies of the leading foreign-affiliated retail companies that entered the Japanese market. The first two cases are product procurement tie-ups between Wal-Mart Stores and Ito-Yokado, and J. C. Penney and DeoDeo. The paper takes the cases of The Boots Company and Sephora as a second pair of case studies. These are cases in the health and beauty sector. As a third series of case studies, Wellsave, Carrefour, and Wal-Mart Stores are considered. These are cases of food supermarkets where strong competitive responses from Japanese competitors may be expected. Finally, the case of Toys "R" Us Japan is considered as an example of success. In this paper, some of the myths about the Japanese market are clarified through case studies.

J. C. PENNEY AND WAL-MART STORES

Tie-Up of Wal-Mart Stores and Ito-Yokado

In March 1994, Ito-Yokado and Wal-Mart Stores agreed that Ito-Yokado would procure products from Wal-Mart Stores, in return for business know-how, such as single item management, etc. Ito-Yokado began selling Wal-Mart own-label products in all of their stores in December 1994. The main products were ketchup, cookies, jam, frozen vegetables, stationery, videotape, electric bulbs, towels, glass tableware, etc. Because their procurement prices were low, and they were sold at lower prices, typically 30-50% of comparable products in store, Ito-Yokado expected substantial sales.

Seven-Eleven Japan, a subsidiary of Ito-Yokado, also began to stock Wal-Mart products in January 1995. They sold at a 30-40% lower price compared to domestic national brand items. The first product was a TDK re-imported videotape (120 minutes at a price of 280 yen), and

General Electric light-bulbs (four 20 or 40W bulbs at 298 yen). The TDK videotape was stocked in all stores and the GE bulbs were stocked by over 100 shops in Chiba Prefecture. Seven-Eleven planned to continue to expand procurement from Wal-Mart Stores.

However, the products from Wal-Mart Stores did not sell well, to the disappointment of Company President Toshifumii Suzuki. The Wal-Mart ketchup was sold in 1,000ml bottles, and was disliked by Japanese consumers who prefer smaller packages. Cookies and jams were found to be too sweet for the Japanese taste. Wal-Mart's own-label products began to disappear from the shop assortments one by one. Because Wal-Mart products did not reach the ten percent of category sales initially expected, dissatisfaction of Wal-Mart Stores heightened. Although the company repeatedly requested that Ito-Yokado increase procurement of their products, Ito-Yokado refused. Moreover, Wal-Mart own-label products disappeared from the recommended products list supplied by head office to Seven-Eleven. Although Wal-Mart products had sales of around 5 billion yen at its peak, Toshifumii Suzuki said Japanese consumers preferred quality and were not interested in the low prices.

Tie-Up of J. C. Penney and DeoDeo

On 19 June 1996, Daiichi (now DeoDeo Corporation) announced a tie up with the major US department store, J. C. Penney. The Company opened a flagship store, "J. C. Penney Home Collections Head Office," inside the main Daiichi store in Hiroshima on 30 June. It was about 700 square meters, and sold various soft furnishings, including bed linen and curtains. The products were sold by Daiichi at the equivalent of US prices, averaging 30-40% lower than Japanese products. The Company aimed at 600 million yen sales in the first year. Development of stand alone stores, rather than concessions in the larger Daiichi stores, advanced on a large scale and the Company began to introduce a wider-range of J. C. Penney products, such as clothing and accessories.

Daiichi continued to diversify away from household electric appliances, for example with a link with large US stationery and office superstore, Office Depot. J. C. Penney was the leading player in the US department store industry and already gave weight to the development of clothing stores in Asia, together with Aoyama Trading, the No. 1 retailer of suits for men. President Kubo Masataka of Daiichi was reported as being impressed by the US design characteristics and was sure that J. C. Penney Home Collections would also sell in Japan.

In April 1997 DeoDeo announced that it was working with J. C. Penney to create a mail order business in Japan. DeoDeo would establish a catalogue centre and publish a Japanese version of the catalogue to enable consumers to receive orders and return products in Japan. With the catalogue, DeoDeo aimed at using the J. C. Penney products to penetrate the Japanese market, drive store development and simultaneously tackle market growth in large product fields, such as a fashion and gifts.

However, sales of the "J. C. Penney Home Collections Head Office" did not reach their target once in ten months. When DeoDeo researched the cause of the lack of sales, it emerged that there were many products that did not suit the Japanese lifestyle. For example, window sizes and ceiling heights differed between Japan and the US homes so curtain sizes were unsuitable, and also curtain hooks differed. There were also problems with bathrooms accessories. Although Americans use covers for the lid of a toilet bowl and mats for underfoot, Japanese people use both a toilet seat cover and slippers. The problems continued with bedding. Although Americans like soft pillows, Japanese people prefer the slightly hard pillows. Moreover, sizes of bed linen differed between the US and Japan.

For this reason, from May 1997, DeoDeo began to change each product to a Japanese specification. As a result of the Company renewing about 40 percent of the product assortment, sales grew to exceed target in July 1997 and beyond. However, profits were limited because the purchase and adaptation costs increased. Also substantial time and effort were needed for changing all the products to a Japanese specification.

DeoDeo announced in April 1999 that it would cancel the tie-up with J. C. Penney around June. The purpose was to concentrate management resources on sales of their core business, household electric appliances, where competition was intensifying. DeoDeo changed the name of "J. C. Penney Home Collections" of which DeoDeo had opened six shops in Japan. The company planned to continue to only procure products from J. C. Penney and stock Japanese-made curtains, bedding, etc. President Kubo Masakata stated, "We can not satisfy customers and make a profit with only the products of J. C. Penney. It will take a long time to make a profit. We will change the space occupied by the J. C. Penney's products to domestic manufacturers' products and will break even within this year"(Sato, 1999b).

THE BOOTS COMPANY AND SEPHORA

The Boots Group PLC

On 28 July 1998, Boots Group PLC, the largest health and beauty retail chain in the UK, announced that the Company had agreed to a joint venture with Mitsubishi Trading Company to develop drugstores in Japan. The name of the joint venture would be "Boots MC" and it would establish its first store around September, with its head office based in Shinjuku, Tokyo. The capital invested would be 5 billion yen, of which Mitsubishi would contribute 49% (2,450 million yen), and Boots 51% (2,550 million yen). They aimed to open a few stores in the next year and sales in the first year were expected to be 4-5 billion yen.

While the location of the first store was undecided, the shop would be opened under the name of "Boots" in the best district in Tokyo within the spring to summer 1999. It would have a broad range of products (medical supplies, cosmetics, toiletries) and stores would be equal in size to a typical Boots stores in the UK (350-600m^2). The number of products would likely be set to 13,000-14,000. The shop would stock Boots own-label products, which were best-selling premium make-up and skin care brands, such as "Number 7," "Natural Collection," "17 cosmetics," and "Botanics." The goal for annual sales per store was 1 billion yen, of which Boots own-label products were expected to comprise 30%. Moreover, the store would have a pharmacy section where prescriptions would be received and prepared.

The Company would initially open a few stores, and after judging, over one or two years, whether the concept of "Boots the Chemists" would work in the Japanese market, the Company would decide on opening stores full-scale. When established in central Tokyo, in order to create a brand image, the company intended to extend into the suburbs in the future (*Nikkan Yakugyou*, 30 July 1998).

Boots Group PLC was a major retail company, with around 1,300 stores in the UK, and group sales for the period ending March 1998 was around £4.9 billion, of which sales of their own-label accounted for a majority. The own-labels, especially "No.7," held a time-tested formula and occupied a large share of the UK market.

It seemed Boots were opening an original store with an emphasis on quality own-labels rather than on discounting national brands in Japan. Boots had been in discussions with Jusco before Mitsubishi Trading. A manager at Jusco looked back at the negotiations of 1995, saying, "They went wrong when we used the word 'discount'." In effect, negotiations with Jusco could not solve the problem of capital contribution ratio, and broke down in summer of 1996 (Yoshimura 1998).

The 5 billion yen capital of the joint venture that backed the entrance of Boots into the Japanese market surprised the industry. The foreign-affiliated company had the second largest capital, following a major drugstore company, Matsumoto Kiyoshi, with capital of 12.9 billion yen. A manager of a leading drugstore company said "Although 300 million yen will be eaten up by an initial investment if a 500m² high-class store is opened in the shopping quarter in Tokyo, this capital scale is quite large. I think the Company is considering remarkable multi-store development" (Yoshimura 1998).

On 13 July 2001 Boots and Mitsubishi announced that it would liquidate the joint drugstore venture in Japan. Four stores, developed under the name of "Boots" in Harajuku, Kichijoji, Ginza and Yokohama, were to close. Although the Company intended to sell Boots own-label cosmetics, medical supplies and health foods, as sold by Boots in the UK, the *Drugs, Cosmetics and Medical Instruments Act* made it difficult to import their own medical supplied and health foods. For this reason, the Company was unable to differentiate their stores from the existing Japanese drugstores in the medical-supplies section. The own-label cosmetics for women in their 20s-30s did not penetrate the market as they did in the UK either (*Nihon Keizai Shinbun*, 14 July 2001).

A Boots press release explained the reason for having opted for this withdrawal as being "because the foreign-operations strategy has evolved." The Company had advanced overseas development based on a UK type stand-alone store. However, since the financial performance was unsatisfactory, they gave up overseas development of stand-alone stores, instead concentrating on in-store concessions, and focusing on its own brands in department stores. The Company also said about the Japanese market, "We want to re-enter by examining various alternative entry methods." It was said that Boots' sales are steadily rising in Taiwan by opening concessions in other retail stores. Boots explained "as for their overseas expansion, it was still inexperienced. This exit plan is also one of the trial and error" (Hayashi 2001).

Sales for the year ending March 2001 of "Boots MC" were around 1,700 million yen. Net loss was 3,300 million yen. Both Boots and Mitsubishi were in conflict over their own interests in the joint-venture arrangement. Boots wanted to focus on cosmetics; however, Mitsubishi preferred to stock broad product lines, such as medical supplies and general drugstore items (*Nihon Keizai Shinbun*, 14 July 2001).

Case of Sephora

On 4 December 1998, the world's leading luxury products group in France, Moet Hennessy, Louis Vuitton (LVMH), announced that it would develop the retail chain of the high-class cosmetics "Sephora" in Japan. The first store would be opened in Tokyo around October 1999 and the Company intended to open 50 shops nationwide, with fully-owned subsidiary company Sephora EEP Japan operating in Japan.

Sephora was established in 1973. From 1993 they began to develop large cosmetics stores with a self-service selling system where customers are able to try the entire cosmetic range. Sephora began to grow rapidly after being incorporated by the LVMH group in 1997 (*Nihon Keizai Shinbun*, 27 November 1999). When Japanese cosmetic manufacturers supply retailers with luxury cosmetics, there is always the condition that the salesperson must explain the products to consumers face-to-face. So this was to be the first time that self-service would be used to sell high-class cosmetics in Japan. Moreover, in Japan high-class cosmetics manufacturers supply on the condition that the retailer makes specific selling space available for each brand, providing their own salesperson, and so on. Sephora's entry into Japan would be likely to have a major disruptive impact on the cosmetics distribution system dominated by large manufacturers. Because Sephora had already developed about 150 stores in Europe and opened 14 stores in the US, they had accumulated knowledge of the self-service selling of high-class cosmetics in overseas stores. The Company actually sold the cosmetics products of major Japanese manufacturers' cosmetics using self-service in these foreign stores. Sephora expected, "because the image of the store is high, and we can get extensive sales without eroding the high-class images of a luxury brand, we can get the understanding of domestic manufacturers" (*Nihon Keizai Shinbun*, 5 December 1998). Since the cosmetics market in Japan ranked second only to the US, Sephora decided to open its first Asian store in Japan.

Sephora opened the first Japanese store in Ginza, Tokyo on 28 November 1999. However, they were still in negotiation with manufacturers in early November about the merchandising of the high-class brands. It was thought that the Estee Lauder group which had popular brands, such as "Clinique," "Estee Lauder," "M-A-C," and "BOBBI BROWN," would postpone shipment to Sephora except for some perfumes. Moreover, a cosmetics manager in a department store in the Ginza area said, "While we try to respond to the concerns of Christian Dior of LVMH group, it seems that they will ship only perfume to

Sephora." A manager of Sephora said, "The department stores have probably put the manufacturers under considerable pressure" (*Nihon Keizai Shinbun*, 5 December 1998).

Domestic leading manufacturers also stood by their position. KOSE Corporation initially considered the shipment of more KOSE brands and specific brands sold only in department stores, but finally they supplied only "Tiffany" perfume to the first Sephora store. In the case of Kanebo, Ltd., even though President Takashi Hoashi maintained they were "fully cooperating with Sephora," the company would not supply popular brands such as "RMK RUMIKO" which was sold only in department stores. Shiseido also did not intend to supply the brand sold only in department stores.

An executive manager of a major cosmetic manufacturer said "at the time of the first negotiation, Sephora demanded that we supply at 50% of the retail price." In the case of domestic cosmetics requiring face-to-face selling by manufacturers in Japan, the shipment price from the manufacturer to their sales company was usually around 50% of a retail price. The sales company supplied to the retailer at 65 to 70% of the retail price. Vice-president Hideyuki Shiraishi of Sephora EEP Japan explained about their discount requirement, "We don't request the dispatch of salespeople from manufacturers, we cover the cost of making attractive displays, and we prepare packing materials ourselves." But an executive manager said, "There are many other stores that do not require dispatch of a cosmetics salesperson. We cannot provide special treatment only for Sephora." The negotiation involving trading conditions was not meeting Sephora's expectations (Tachiki and Hidaka 1999).

On 30 November 1999, the president of Sephora EEP Japan, Howard Meatner, visited Japan and responded to an interview with a newspaper as follows:

> Although the cosmetics market in Japan ranks second only to the US, there is no retail store which serves as a leader. Sephora, which carries out self-served sale of all cosmetics, attracts attention from consumers, and the opportunity for market development is large. As for the first store in Japan at Ginza, which opened on 28 November, as much as 9,300 people entered the store on the first day. Their response gave us some confidence in developing the Japanese market. We received criticism that the foreign-affiliated famous cosmetics brands are seldom varied, because cooperation from the manufacturers is not fully obtained. If Sephora is

well recognized, most of the manufacturers will want to provide their famous brands to us. (*Nihon Keizai Shinbun*, 9 December 1999)

On 27 November 2001, Sephora EEP Japan announced that the company would close all seven shops by the end of December. About 60 employees were discharged on 31 January 2002. There were fewer than 10 visitors to the Sephora Harajuku store on 29 November, despite a holiday. This store was the largest in Japan with three floors having in total 1,360 m² of which 950 m² was sales space. The store was the first to trial an in-store hair and beauty salon, and had a culture centre. Moreover, the store held events, such as a fragrance seminar (*Pharmaweek*, 10 December 2001). Nonetheless it failed to attract a substantial customer base.

In mid January 2002, Sephora EEP Japan set up a special site on the e-Bay Japan auction website to dispose of 600 fixtures from their stores that became redundant after their exit from Japanese market at the end of December. By doing so, the company expected to stimulate demand quickly for their specially designed used articles. Moreover, they would also sell products used for sales promotion events in Japan, which were not normally on sale (*Nihon Keizai Shinbun*, 20 December 2001).

THE CASE OF WELLSAVE, CARREFOUR, AND WAL-MART STORES

Entry and Exit of Wellsave

On 16 March 1995, Seiyu announced that they had established a new venture company to develop a discount food supermarket chain in Japan with British food company Dairy Farm International Holding (DFI) Ltd., which had the largest supermarket chain in Hong Kong. The parent company, Jardine Group, was based in Hong Kong. Unlike other major supermarket companies, Seiyu, or their group of companies, had never developed a discount store chain, so this joint venture would be their first move into the sector. The name of the new company was "DFI Seiyu," the capital was 3,500 million yen (contribution ratio: DFI 60%, Seiyu 40%) and the name given to the supermarket was "Wellsave." Dairy Farm was confident that they had the know-how to sell at lower prices.

On 5 September 1995, the first store opened as planned. On 26 October 1996, DFI Seiyu opened the its tenth domestic store at Fujimi-shi, Saitama. The previous stores had been converted from old Seiyu stores, but the Fujimi store was the first store to be developed *ab initio* from design to construction, and served as a basic model of future development. DFI Seiyu changed the Company name to Wellsave on 8 January 1997. President McDowell explained that "The Company name is unified with the store name of Wellsave, with which you were familiar at the time of celebrating the 3rd anniversary of the establishment" (Sato, 1999b).

On 5 February 1998, Seiyu announced that they would close all 14 of the Wellsave stores developed in the Kanto area, including Saitama, and Tokyo, by August that year. The cost incurred by the closures was expected to be around 40 million U.S. dollars. Why did Dairy Farm suffer a setback in Japan? The Company had three miscalculations:

- While the company could attract consumers by discounting processed foods, such as drinks and seasoning, good perishable foods must be available to gain consumer confidence in Japan. For this reason, Wellsave was obliged to adjust their stock from processed foods to perishable foods from 1996 onwards. But because the Company could not procure by itself, it was obliged to consign fresh food operations to a specialty store and was not able to manage the department well.
- Japanese consumers consider the atmosphere of stores important–for example, a feeling of cleanliness and ease of shopping. Therefore, the Japanese consumer disliked the low cost display method of Dairy Farm. The Company had to return to taking products out of their cardboard packaging boxes and arranging them on shelves. Moreover, the Company also lowered the heights of displays, to reduce the oppressive feeling that consumers felt from higher displays, and made products more easily reachable. Once these changes were implemented throughout the stores, Wellsave became no different to the ordinary Japanese supermarkets.
- The third miscalculation was that since each Japanese supermarket company reduced their prices, there was no difference in the price level of Wellsave. When the first Wellsave store opened, their prices were around 15-20% lower than other supermarkets and this was the attraction. However the price difference fell to 5-10%. Furthermore, Wellsave sold some goods at a higher price.

Because of these factors, Wellsave's sales remained flat. Although the Company remodeled their established shops, such as installing bargain corners for liquor, the result was poor. Furthermore, although they introduced their own-label goods from November 1996 (tofu, milk, ketchup, snacks, etc.) in order to improve the gross margin rate, they hardly sold. Only four shops out of fourteen had healthy monthly sales figures, and the 140 million yen monthly deficit was distributed throughout the whole company.

Dairy Farm operated 210 food supermarkets, 330 Seven-Eleven shops, and 100 drugstores in Hong Kong. The Company had 2,650 stores including those in Taiwan, China, Singapore, Britain and Australia. In spite of the successful overseas experience of the Company, they failed in Japan (Sato, 1999b).

Trial and Error of Carrefour Japan

Carrefour opened its first store in Japan, at Makuhari, Chiba, in December 2000. But sales of the first, second and third stores were less than the targeted yearly turnover. The Company announced in December 2001 that they would reduce the target number of shops in Japan by 2003 to seven stores from 13 stores. Why did Carrefour suffer in Japan?

The strengths of Carrefour were low price, by direct trading with manufacturers, and creating exciting store space. Chairman and CEO Daniel Bernard of the company has termed this the creation of "retail theatre."

However, these two strengths were not demonstrated in Japan. First, many Japanese manufacturers refused direct trading with Carrefour. Therefore, at first, Carrefour was only able to offer consumers a limited choice of food and miscellaneous goods. Moreover, Carrefour used a "whole-quantity acquisition" contract with some farmers in the purchase of vegetables and fruits in Japan. Although the whole-quantity acquisition contract had a cost merit on the procurement side, unevenness of quality, for example in class or size of fruits and vegetables, is a weak-point for Carrefour. Also, many Japanese consumers liked prepackaged fruits, and they refused to weigh the goods themselves, as required by Carrefour. Moreover, the tall displays in store were also unpopular.

Secondly, before entering into the Japanese market, the mass media reported Carrefour as a global company based in France. The Japanese consumers associate France with high-class brands. However, Carrefour was not actually carrying overseas high-class big-name brands. Carrefour sold its own-label products, but it was unpopular with the

Japanese consumer who expected discount sales of luxury brand products (Sato, 2002).

Conversion of the Store to the Japanese Type

Carrefour responded and introduced typical Japanese business practices in July 2002. At the Komyo-ike store, they conducted consumer surveys and responded to consumers' dissatisfaction to improve store management effectively. For example, they made the display cases lower because consumers claimed they felt oppressed by the clothing displays. Moreover, the selling space and the types of deli ranges were expanded three times from the time of opening. Carrefour also began to sell the high-class branded handbags that were not sold by their French stores.

The fourth store at Sayama (Saitama) opened on 16 October 2002 and introduced an organically grown vegetable counter as a special attraction for consumers. The company did not adhere to direct stocking from the manufacturers. They gave priority to product development depending on Japanese consumer needs. The introduction of lightweight shopping trolleys was evidence that they had learned about Japanese shoppers' buying habit of purchasing small volumes (*Nihon Keizai Shinbun*, 5 November 2002). Moreover, what differed from the existing three stores was that the company raised the tenant ratio for this store and invited 54 tenants, for example "COMME CA ISM" casual clothing. The store sold a wide assortment of European foods, such as wine, cheese, and bread, including wine from France. Moreover, the store sold many directly imported articles, such as clothing and general merchandise from France. In order to meet with Japanese shoppers' behavior, the store layout was changed to that of supermarkets in Japan, such as deliberately making shopping aisles narrower, and making the perishable food space larger (*Nihon Keizai Shinbun*, 17 October and 9 November 2002).

Also, Carrefour changed the personnel policy to appoint Japanese people as store managers. Although all store managers who had proceeded from head office until now were French, they changed the policy to cope with the different characteristics and business practices in every region in the Japanese market. The company appointed a Japanese store manager for the first time when the Amagasaki store (Amagasaki-shi, Hyogo) opened in October 2002. At the same time, the company began management training for the Japanese who would become candidates for management positions (*Nihon Keizai Shinbun*, 15 May 2003). In late May 2003, the company began the training system for about 15 selected store managers, focusing on 30 to 40 year olds (*Nihon Keizai Shinbun*, 2 June 2003).

Moreover, Carrefour announced in June 2003 that the company would increase the number of the French products sold in the Japanese store to 240 types during 2003, and it would expand these to 500 by 2005. In November 2002, Carrefour carried out a sales campaign at four stores in Japan, featuring products made by small and medium-sized enterprises in France. The company chose 90 products for the campaign, which would be good for sales. Almost all of the products had the local characteristic of a specific locality in France. According to the Company, these products were chosen by "the eye of Carrefour" only for the Japanese market, so that the seasoning, salt level and sweet tastes of food were not too strong. By selling these products, which were not offered in other stores, the company hoped to encourage sales in Japanese stores. The Company also scheduled a "France Discovery" campaign for November 2003, distributing 2 million 12-page fliers, and also introduced demonstration sales by French students (Hashimoto, 24 June 2003).

On 1 September 2003, Carrefour announced that in the fiscal half-year January to June, comparative store sales in Japan increased 10% compared with the corresponding period in 2002. At a press conference, Chairman Daniel Bernard explained, "This is the result of strengthening the European selection," and he said the company had "planned to introduce the same concept" into three shops which would be opened within the year (Hashimoto, 2 September 2003). The president of Carrefour Japan also said, "We respect supermarkets and consumers in Japan, and we are bowing our heads and learning from them" (Tanaka, 2004).

Entrance of the Wal-Mart Stores into the Japanese Market

Wal-Mart Stores and Seiyu announced on 14 March 2002 that Wal-Mart Stores would take over the allocation of a new share of Seiyu for a third party in May, and it would hold 6.1% of issued stocks of Seiyu. When CEO Scott of Wal-Mart Stores was asked, "What will you gain from Seiyu?", he answered,

> We want to learn about Japanese consumers, culture, and retail trade. What we learned in Britain was useful to store management in Brazil, and what we learned in Argentina contributed to product assortment in China. I heard that Japanese people's degree of expectation and demand to products are the highest in the world, especially in the area of food. If we can learn from this, it will be

useful to the business in the US. (*Nikkei Ryutsu Shinbun MJ*, 20 April 2002)

In response to the tie-up agreement, Seiyu stopped 2002's "special treatment sale" for store card members that the Company conducted in May and June every year. The Company had a plan to reduce the discount sale for the second half of the year. Moreover, Seiyu management approached management of a clothing manufacturer in mid-August and asked how that company envisaged contributing to changes in Seiyu's supply chain in order to realize EDLP (*Nikkei Ryutsu Shinbun MJ*, 19 September 2002, p. 1).

Wal-Mart Stores installed a permanent study team in July 2002, made up of eight specialists from the US, the UK and China, where the company had stores, to investigate physical distribution, merchandizing, store management, financial management, real estate and store development, strategic planning, and marketing strategy development in Japan. Staff from Seiyu and Sumitomo Trading also joined the team. Then, Wal-Mart Stores invested an additional 52 billion yen in Seiyu, and became the largest stockholder, owning 34% of the company on 27 December 2002 (*Nikkei Ryutsu Shinbun MJ*, 2 July 2002).

Conversion of Seiyu to a Wal-Mart Stores type business, however, did not go well. Although comparable store sales of Seiyu from March to August 2002 were down 1% on the corresponding period in 2001, that fell to 3% for September 2002 to January 2003. The figure fell further to 6.6% in December when Seiyu began to introduce their new long-term price-reduction campaign, "Rollback," for two months or more (*Nikkei Ryutsu Shinbun MJ*, 26 February 2003).

On 18 March 2003, Seiyu announced, at a seminar at the Super Arena in Saitama City for 600 vendors who were invited by Wal-Mart, that the company would organize a project team made up of members from the main manufacturers and wholesalers, to introduce the Wal-Mart Stores' "Retail Link" information system. The "Retail Link" would be in operation at three stores in August, and was to be tested at five stores in September 2003. Wal-Mart Stores assigned a "category captain," for every product category, who proposed selection plans for the category, including rivals' products. It seemed likely that the vendors who would become members of this project team were also likely to become the major candidates for "category captain" (*Nikkei Ryutsu Shinbun MJ*, 20 March 2003).

Seiyu announced the settlement of accounts for the fiscal year 2002 on 22 April 2003. The Company had been developing their "Rollback" campaign from December 2002. The number of "Rollback" items, including processed foods and clothing, reached 245 by the end of February 2003. The "Rollback" price reduction caused sales per customer to fall 3.9% and the increase in the customer numbers was only 1.8% due to reducing the frequency of the bargain sale. Consequently, the like-for-like sales of existing stores decreased by 2.2% (*Nihon Keizai Shinbun*, 23 April 2003).

On 1 October 2003, Seiyu distributed colored fliers advertising a "shock food special price sale." The flier focused on a few particular items to be certain to stimulate large sales. The company discounted certain fish, meat, and vegetables by 20% during mornings on a daily basis with a view to relieving the peak evening period. The period of the special price sale was October. The Company felt that the bargain sale was required until it shifted to the Wal-Mart Stores' EDLP style. Seiyu would also develop a sale, marking its 40th anniversary, from the middle of October to the end of the year, in the hope of recovering performance. Seiyu said they could "absorb the expense of the flier by the improvement of sales and the rate of gross margin" (*Nikkei Ryutsu Shinbun MJ*, 9 October 2003).

There was another problem in the strategy of Wal-Mart Stores. As explained earlier, Carrefour's fourth domestic Sayama store opened on 16 October 2002, raising the tenant ratio compared with the existing three stores to fit more with Japanese consumers' entertainment oriented shopping style. At this point Wal-Mart Stores expressed an opposite view to Carrefour.

For example, when Wal-Mart Stores inspected a total of 400 Seiyu stores after spring 2002, a member of Wal-Mart Stores asked Seiyu "If the store space is so good, why is it used by tenants and not by yourselves?" Wal-Mart, which principally occupied all selling space itself, was met with dissatisfaction by the Japanese where specialty stores occupied excellent locations in stores (*Nikkei Ryutsu Shinbun MJ*, 19 September 2002, p. 2). Then, Wal-Mart Stores stopped the standard presentation plan of Wakana, a subsidiary producing and wholesaling a daily dish, within the year. Wakana had not only opened tenant shops at Seiyu stores, it had also expanded its original roadside stores. The reason for stopping was a conflict of interest in store development policy which may also occur if the controlling power of Seiyu were to become weaker in the stock ownership (*Nikkei Ryutsu Shinbun MJ*, 14 December 2002).

On 15 January 2004, Seiyu announced that they would invite 1,500 to 1,600 people, around 25% of the regular staff, to take voluntary redundancy. This was aimed at staff who were 30 to 58 years old. If the company could not get the target number of people, they would consider providing early retirement advice. The targeted staffs were chosen individually on their job performance for the past three years and the result of a Wal-Mart ability test (*Nihon Keizai Shinbun MJ*, 16 January 2004). On 24 February, Seiyu announced that 1,613 people had applied for voluntary redundancy (*Nikkei Sangoshinbun*, 24 February 2004).

Seiyu announced that the consolidated figures for fiscal year 2003, ending 31 December 2003 resulted in a deficit of 7 billion. The deficit was over a two-year period. President Kiuchi said, "It was important to make the culture of Wal-Mart Stores permeate early" (Tanaka, 2004).

SUCCESS OF TOYS "R" US JAPAN

When Toys "R" Us expressed a willingness to enter into the Japanese market in 1988, their market share in the toy market in the United States at that time was 25%. Toys "R" Us was powerful not only in the United States, but also in several other countries Toys "R" Us chose McDonald's Japan as their partner in Japan.

The Company made demands on Japanese manufacturers for the same trade terms as in the United States and for direct dealings to ship products to the distribution center, which was to be built in Kawasaki. Furthermore, manufacturers were asked for an early large-quantity order discount, buying up products (i.e., the products shipped are not returned) discount, distribution center fee (the expenses of distribution to stores were to be partially carried by Toys "R" Us), or market development allowance.

On top of this, Toys "R" Us demanded shipment at around 40% of the manufacturer's suggested retail price. The price at which manufacturers supplied to wholesale companies was 50-55% of the manufacturer's suggested retail price at that time. Moreover, the toy distribution system typically comprised a primary wholesaler, secondary wholesaler, third wholesaler and retail store. Since each wholesaler supplied only a specific manufacturer's products, major retail companies (Daiei and Jusco, etc.) were dealing with about ten wholesale companies for their toy assortment. Moreover, in each stage of the distribution, the suggested retail price system was retained through each distribution stage. In effect, there was almost no price competition.

Naturally the manufacturers refused the demands of Toys "R" Us. Because negotiations with the manufacturers were prolonged, the opening of the first store was delayed by half a year. In the end, after Toys "R" Us compromised, the dealings with the manufacturers began. The settled trading conditions were as follows: the shipment price to Toys "R" Us by the manufacturers was equal to the price to wholesalers; the manufacturers supplied products to the distribution center, although the names of the products were passed to the wholesale companies.

After opening its first store in December 1991, Toys "R" Us expanded the store network. At Christmas 1993, Hankyu Department Stores of Osaka started a 20% discount sale of toys in order to compete with Toys "R" Us. This immediately affected all department stores in Japan. Department stores which had acknowledged the manufacturers' suggested retail price started the discount sale of toys. This move by Hankyu Department Stores spread not only to the department store industry but also to the supermarkets and specialty stores. The age of fierce price competition arrived.

Since it became difficult to obtain profits for the retail companies that rushed into price competition, they made demands on the wholesale companies for a reduction in shipment price. Moreover, although the wholesale companies were also involved in price competition, in order to gain profits they similarly demanded the reduction in shipment price to the manufacturers. The manufacturers made demands on the wholesale companies for dealings with large lots in return for price reductions. Because of this, there was considerable bankruptcy and the closure of small-scale wholesale companies. Moreover, the major wholesale companies began merger and related activity. On the other hand, the wholesale companies similarly made demands for volume orders in return for discount on the retail companies. For this reason, many small-scale retail stores had to close. Moreover, the large-scale retail companies reduced the number of wholesalers in order to expand order size. For example, most of the supermarkets reduced the number of wholesale companies to 2 or 3 from ten companies.

Consequently, concentration at the wholesale distribution stage progressed. The third and second tier wholesalers began to disappear. Moreover, selection of a company was also progressing between large primary wholesalers. For example, Bandai, a major toy manufacturer, reduced the number of wholesale companies from 350 to 50 companies. In the meantime, Toys "R" Us expanded its store network steadily. The number of Toys "R" Us stores exceeded 50 in 1996, and sales exceeded 100 billion yen, surpassing the big-name Chiyoda's sales, and becoming No. 1 in Japan. With the exception of Bandai, all manufacturers have responded to direct trade with Toys "R" Us, and it was thought that the shipment price by the manufacturers approached the line at which

Toys "R" Us demanded at the beginning. Moreover, there were also manufacturers which shipped exclusive products to Toys "R" Us. For example, Nintendo was shipping different colored Game Boys exclusively to Toys "R" Us.

As the Company increased the number of shops, Toys "R" Us was able to demonstrate buying power against the manufacturers. However, there was also a blind spot in Toys "R" Us. Their US-type business model generated a difficulty in the Japanese market. The competitive power of Toys "R" Us was based on the business model that would forecast the popular toys of the Christmas shopping season, then order in large quantities half a year in advance. In Japan, however, the life cycle of a hit toy is very short. In the case of toys tied up with a child's TV program, the life cycle is usually three months. Therefore, in Japan, when toys ordered by Toys "R" Us half a year previously arrive in large quantities, the popularity of the toys had passed. Moreover, Japanese consumers found the warehouses type stores of Toys "R" Us disorderly and the salesclerks lacking knowledge of the products. Toys "R" Us coped with such problems steadily one by one.

Furthermore, Toys "R" Us Japan entered into the baby products market formally in new business format, Babies "R" Us, in December 2002. Because Babies "R" Us supposed "Japanese consumers want to find all products required at one place," the store provided a shoe counter which was not in Babies "R" Us in the US. Moreover, all of the staff were trained in shoe fitting. Contrary to Toys "R" Us that provides only self-served shopping, Babies "R" Us is considered to be more suited to Japanese consumer needs. The Shin-Urayasu store, although open several months, still had queues of cars waiting for a parking space at weekends (Sato, 1999a).

CONCLUSION:
IS THE JAPANESE MARKET REALLY MYSTICAL?

Conclusions from the Case Studies

What is clear from these case studies of foreign-affiliated retail companies is that the companies face three hurdles in a host country. One is the realization of customer satisfaction in a host country. It is not easy to grasp that consumer needs in a host country are quite different from a home country's consumer needs in terms of economic, social and cultural environment. J. C. Penney failed in adjusting their products to the physical size of Japanese people. In the case of Wal-Mart Stores' own-label products, they failed because of the difference in consumer tastes as well as the problem of product size. These problems are in understanding the consumer needs in a host country and compiling the mix of products to satisfy their needs effectively.

The second hurdle is a problem of whether the management resources and business processes that had become strengths of the retail company in their home country are also applicable in a host country in compiling the right mix of products to satisfy customer needs in a host country. J. C. Penney tried to fit product size to Japanese specification; however, it became clear that this would involve enormous costs. That is, J. C. Penney's adaptation for the host country's customer needs prevented it from applying the strengths of the company cultivated in its home country. This is also the case for Wellsave, that entered into the Japanese market in concert with Seiyu. Improving the environment in the store according to the Japanese shopping style brought an increase in costs. Moreover, the company was obliged to depend on wholesalers in Japan, and that reduced the competitive power of Wellsave's low cost operation.

The third hurdle is the problem of whether responding to customer needs, creating a suitable retail mix and business process in a host country have competitive power in terms of their existing resources and the existing business process. For example, Boots have not demonstrated their special capabilities in the Japanese market because of the import problem with their own-label products that were popular in their home country, and also because they could not use the capability cultivated in pharmacies in the Japanese market. Sephora also faced the same difficulty. The category killer type of their business model that demonstrated great competitive advantages in the United States and Europe was unrealizable in Japan. On the contrary, Toys "R" Us is an example of a foreign-affiliated retail company that was successful in the Japanese market and has somehow managed to clear these three hurdles.

Three Hurdles to Foreign-Affiliated Retail Companies

In order for foreign-affiliated retail companies to be successful in a host country, it is necessary to develop the optimal composition of products that satisfy the customer of a host country. In this it is necessary to use business processes based on their capability and resources that makes possible sustainable competitive advantage.

This is shown in Figure 1. In this diagram, gap 1 is an aspect considered to be a problem involving conventional local adaptation. Gap 2 is considered as a problem involving standardization. An important point for success is constructing a bridge between gap 1 and gap 2 without inconsistency towards sustainable competitive advantages. That is the problem of gap 3.

Organizational Reasons Not to Learn

It is a necessary condition of success for foreign-affiliated companies to create new and/or differentiated customer value in Japan efficiently and effectively. But it is not a sufficient condition. Sometimes they need to adapt and change their original business model in Japan to create such value. It is difficult, however, for them to adapt and alter their business model. It is this factor that inhibits foreign-affiliated companies from succeeding in the Japanese market. Why do they face such difficulty in adapting and changing their business model in Japan?

Argyris and Schon (1995) and Schein (in Quick and Kets de Vries, 2000) give their reasons as to why excellent executives cannot learn.

FIGURE 1. Three Hurdles to Foreign-Affiliated Retail Company

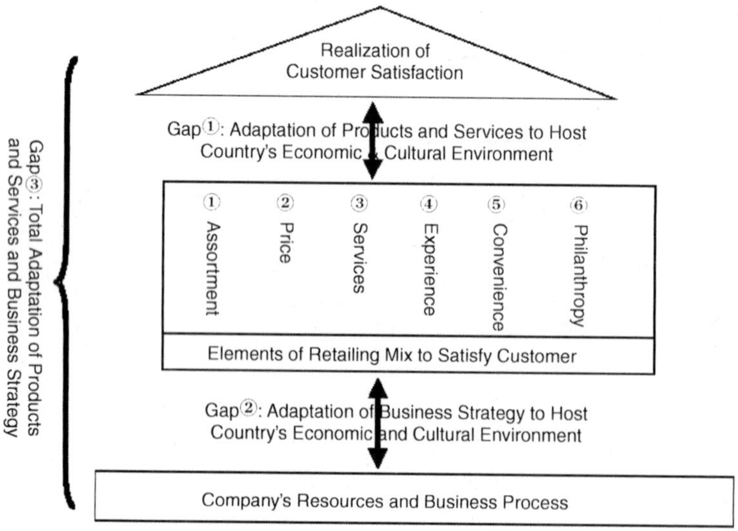

Because their explanation provides clues as to why foreign-affiliated companies fail in the Japanese market, it is useful to apply their idea to make a framework explaining the mechanism of foreign-affiliated companies' failure. At this stage, this framework is a tentative one.

Most of the foreign-affiliated companies that entered the Japanese market were successful companies in their home countries. They grew by establishing organizational routine to achieve competitive advantages, especially to achieve cost leadership position. Because of their success, they strongly believed in the superiority of their business model. As a result of both rigid organizational routine and a strong belief in the superiority of their business model, it was very difficult for them to adapt and change their business model to create new and/or differentiated customer value in a host country—even if it is necessary to do so.

A Japanese partner company usually indicates that the partner's business model has some problems in Japan. This indication creates cognitive dissonance among high-level management, especially in the headquarters in their home country. They usually attribute the reason for the emergence of these problems as peculiar at the initial stage of the business and/or inappropriate to their efforts. In an effort to improve the situation, the problems often get worse. Moreover they usually adhere to their own business model because they believe that if they change their business model to adapt to the Japanese market, the original advantages of their business model itself will dissipate. Thus they insist on adhering to the original business model more aggressively. The Japanese partner cannot help but accept their justification because they know more about the business model. But this justification causes a feeling of mistrust among top management and employees of the Japanese partner.

As a result of these justifications, the problems of foreign-affiliated companies become severe and the financial performance of the joint venture worsens. But the foreign partner does not accept the fact willingly because of their cognitive dissonance. Even if top foreign management in Japan realized the problem and were willing to change and adapt their business model, their senior management at headquarters in their home country is usually able to and/or unwilling to understand the problem. This situation creates a vicious circle, as depicted in Figure 2. The diagram explains the possible mechanism of failure of foreign-affiliated companies.

The mechanism is not only applicable to retailers, but also to manufacturers. In contrast with manufacturers, however, because retailers

FIGURE 2. Organizational Reasons Not to Learn

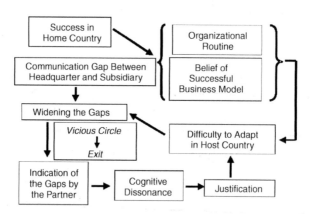

have a large amount of product to sell, their task to adapt their business model in a host country is far more difficult.

From the case studies of various foreign-affiliated retail companies that exited from the Japanese market soon after entry, it can be tentatively concluded that they failed because they exited from Japan before they could learn from their failure. The reason for their failure is indicated in Figure 2. Indeed it is learning from failure that makes foreign-affiliated companies succeed in the long run. Toys "R" Us Japan has learned by its many failures in adapting their business model in Japan. Carrefour currently is learning by its failures to adapt in Japan and so is making changes in response.

REFERENCES

Alden, Vernon R. (1987), Who says you can't crack Japanese markets? *Harvard Business Review*, January-February, pp. 52-56.

Argyris, Chris and Schon, David A. (1995), *Organizational Learning II: Theory, Method, and Practice*, 2nd Edition, Addison-Wesley Pub Co.

Argyris, Chris (1995), Action Science and Organizational Learning, *Journal of Managerial Psychology*, 10(6), pp. 20ff.

Czinkota, Michael R. (1985), Distribution in Japan: Problems and Changes, *Columbia Journal of World Business*, Fall, pp. 65-71.

Hashimoto, Miki (2003), Carrefour, Futsu-sei Shokuhin wo Kyoka: Ringo-shu nado, Nennai ni 240-shu, *Nikkei Ryutsu Shinbun MJ*, June 24, p. 11.

Hashimoto, Miki (2003), Futsu-Carrefour 1-6 Gakki, Nippon Shijyo no Uriage, Kison-ten 10% Zou: Asia ha 11% Zou, *Nikkei Ryutsu Shinbun MJ*, September 2, p. 17.

Hayashi, Rika (2001), Ei Butsu, Mitsubishi-Shoji tono Goben-Seisan, Kaigai-Senryaku Minaoshi: Tennai-Tenpo • Oroshi-Kyoka nado Suishin, *Nikkei Ryutsu Shinbun MJ*, July 17, p. 2.

Kaikati, Jack G(1993), Don't Crack the Japanese Distribution System: Just Circumvent It, *Columbia Journal of World Business*, Summer, pp. 34-45.

Nihon Keizai Shinbun (1998), Moe • Heneshi • Louis Vuitton, Kokyu-Keshohin-Ten, Nippon de Tenkai: Self-Hanbai, *Morning Edition*, December 5, p. 8.

Nihon Keizai Shinbun (1999), Futsu Keshohin Kouri Sephora, Asu Kokunai 1 Gouten: Self-Hanbai de Shoki Nerau, *Evening Edition*, November 27, p. 3.

Nihon Keizai Shinbun (1999), Sephora • EEP Shacho Meatner-shi: Tainichi-Shinshutsu ni Tegotae (Hito Talk), *Evening Edition*, December 9, p. 5.

Nihon Keizai Shinbun (2001), Ei Butsu-sya to Mitsubishi-Shoji, Drugstore Goben-Seisan: 4 Ten wo Heisa, Dokuji-Shohin Shintou Sezu, *Morning Edition*, July 14, p. 9.

Nihon Keizai Shinbun (2001), Futsu-Keshohin-Ten *Sephora* Nippon-Tettai, Tennai-Kagu nado Kyoubai, E-Baysite de, December 20, p. 17.

Nihon Keizai Shinbun (2002), Walmart, Seiyu-Honsha-nai ni Teikei-Team, *Morning Edition*, June 27, p. 13.

Nihon Keizai Shinbun (2002), Carrefour, Sayama-ten Kaigyo, Saitama-kennai Hatsu no Ryutsuu-Gaishi, Kyosou Ichidan to Gekika, *Chihou-Keizai-men*, October 17, p. 40

Nihon Keizai Shinbun (2002), Tokushu: Kyokan-Ryutsuu-Gaishi, Senryaku-Daimaku he, Nippon-Koryaku wo honkakuka, *Morning Edition*, November 5, p. 15.

Nihon Keizai Shinbun (2002), Carrefour Sayama (Saitama • Sayama-shi): Futsu-Wine nado Yunyuhin Jyujitsu (Omise-Haiken), *Evening Edition*, November 9, p. 3.

Nihon Keizai Shinbun (2003), Seiyu, Zenki-Tandoku, Keijoeki 87% Gen, Wal-Mart Kaikaku nao Jikan, Yasuuri-Koka Gentei-teki, *Morning Edition*, April 23, p. 11.

Nihon Keizai Shinbun (2003), Carrefour, Oubei-style Shusei, Nippon-jin Tencho Hajimete Touyou: Sho-Shukan wo Koryo, *Evening Edition*, May 15, p. 3.

Nihon Keizai Shinbun (2003), Carrefour, Senbatsu-sha ni Tencho-Kyoiku: Kobetsu-plan de Futokui-Kokufuku, *Morning Edition*, June 2, p. 11.

Nihon Keizai Shinbun (2004), Seiyu, Syain 25% Sakugen, Kibou 1500 Nin Boshu, *Morning Edition*, January 16, p. 1.

Nikkan Yakugyou (1998), Ei Butsu-sya, Mitsubishi-Shoji to Goben Setsuritu, NipponShinshutsu, July 30, p. 7.

Nikkei Ryutsu Shinbun MJ (2002), Mizukara wo Kae Nippon-Koryaku, Wal-Mart, Scott CEO ni Kiku: Wal-Mart no Rinen ha Fuhen, Nippon no Shohi-sha Jikkuri Manabu, April 20, p. 2.

Nikkei Ryutsu Shinbun MJ (2002), Wal-Mart, Teikei-saku, Seiyu to Honkaku-Kyogi he: Nennai ni Jigyo-Keikaku, July 2, p. 8.

Nikkei Ryutsu Shinbun MJ (2002), Wal-Mart, Sude ni Joriku, Seiyu-Kaikaku he Know-How Ishoku: Chotatsu-saki Shiborikomu, September 19, p. 1.

Nikkei Ryutsu Shinbun MJ (2002), Walmart, Seiyu he Know-How Ishoku: Wal-Mart-ryu Dounyu, Nippon no Shoukankou to Masatsu-Hisshi, September 19, p. 2.

Nikkei Ryutsu Shinbun MJ (2002), Seiyu-Henkaku, Uriba kara, Wal-Mart, Keiei-ken Shutoku: Yasuuri-Tetsugaku Tatakikamu, December 14, p. 1.

Nikkei Ryutsu Shinbun MJ (2003), Seiyu no Kabuka-Kyuraku, Wal-Mart Ryu ni Gimon no Koe: Keijo-Rieki-Gengaku wo Iyake, February 26, p. 5.

Nikkei Ryutsu Shinbun MJ (2003), Retail Rink Kon-Ka ni Shiken-Donyu, Seiyu, Torihiki-saki to Renkei-Soshiki: Hanbai-Zaiko Joho Kyoyu, March 20, p. 9.

Nikkei Ryutsu Shinbun MJ (2003), Seiyu, Tokubai-Chirashi wo Kyoka, October 9, p. 5.

Nikkei Sangyoshinbun (2004), Seiyu Group Taishoku-oubo-1613-Nin, Boshuuwaku-Toutatsu, February 24, p. 31.)

Pharmaweek (2001), Futsu • Sephora Nippon-Tettai: 12 Gatsu-sue madeni Zentenpo-Heisa he, December 10, p. 1.

Pirog, S. F., Schneider, P. A., Lam, D. K. K., (1997), Cohesiveness in Japanese distribution: A socio-cultural framework, *International Marketing Review*, 14(2), pp. 124-134.

Quick, James Campbell and Kets de Vries, Manfred F. R. (2000), The Next Frontier: Edgar Schein on Organizational Therapy/Commentary on the Edgar Schein Interview, *Academy of Management Executive*, February, 14(1), pp. 31-48.

Sato, Yoshinobu (1999a), Nihon Ryutsuu Sangyo Hatten Genkyo, Chukaminkoku Rensaten Kyokai Hen, *'98 Rensa-ten Nenkan*, pp. 16-17.

Sato, Yoshinobu (1999b), Large Foreign-affiliated Retail Companies in Japan: Their Present Position and Problem, *Collected Essays in Commemoration of Isao Nakauchi, Chief Director of the University of Marketing and Distribution Sciences*, pp. 117-143.

Sato, Yoshinobu (2002), Global Kouri-Kigyo no Seikou-Jyoken: Ryutsuu no Global Standard ni Kakawatte, *Ryutsuu Johou*, No. 391, January, pp. 8-19.

Tachiki, Nami and Hidaka, Kotoro (1999), Futsu-Kouri-Chain, Sephora Nippon ni Joriku, Keshohin-Gyokai ni Kaikoku no Ashioto: Senzairyoku aredomo, *Nikkei Ryutsuu Shinbun*, November 9, p. 1.

Tanaka, Akira (2004), Wal-Mart, Gosan-no-Housoku: Shoku, Koyou-no-Chigai, Rikai-Tarizu, *Nihon Keizai Shinbun, Morning Edition*, February 22, p. 7.

Yoshimura, Shinji (1998), Ei Butsu-sya ga Nippon de Goben, Drugstore mo Daikyousou: Shikinryoku ni Gyoukai-Sennsennkyoukyou, *Nikkei Ryutsuu Shinbun*, August 6, p. 15.

The Paradox of Competition in the World of Volatility: An Analysis of the Drivers in the Middle Market of International Fashion Retailing

Nobukazu J. Azuma

SUMMARY. This paper analyses the mechanism in which fashion is produced, marketed, and consumed from the viewpoints of the consumption and supply-side, in the midst of an increasingly complex meaning of fashion and dress in modernity. The focus of the study is a theoretical account of the paradoxical consequences of market orientation and supply chain management in the middle market of international fashion retailing in the light of the idiosyncrasy of the restraints that are innately embedded in the fashion industry. The result gleaned from this study has an implication for an alternative approach of market orientation in international fashion retailing especially in the industrial economies. *[Article copies available for a fee from The Haworth Document Delivery Service: 1-800-HAWORTH. E-mail address: <docdelivery@haworthpress.com>*

Nobukazu J. Azuma is Research Associate, Fashion Studies and Business Organisation, The School of Management and Languages, Heriot-Watt University, Riccarton, Edinburgh, Scotland and the Institute of Marketing and Distribution Sciences, UMDS Kobe, Japan (E-mail: Nobukazu_Azuma@red.umds.ac.jp).

[Haworth co-indexing entry note]: "The Paradox of Competition in the World of Volatility: An Analysis of the Drivers in the Middle Market of International Fashion Retailing." Azuma, Nobukazu J. Co-published simultaneously in *Journal of Global Marketing* (International Business Press, an imprint of The Haworth Press, Inc.) Vol. 18, No. 1/2, 2004, pp. 45-72; and: *International Retailing Plans and Strategies in Asia* (ed: John Dawson, and Jung-Hee Lee) International Business Press, an imprint of The Haworth Press, Inc., 2004, pp. 45-72. Single or multiple copies of this article are available for a fee from The Haworth Document Delivery Service [1-800-HAWORTH, 9:00 a.m. - 5:00 p.m. (EST). E-mail address: docdelivery@haworthpress.com].

KEYWORDS. International retailing, fashion, supply chain management, modernity

FASHION IN MODERNITY

Consequences to the Production and Consumption of Fashion

Fashion is always the product of the culture and the society that spawns it, embodying the concerns of the wider society in its myriad styles, regardless of whether one perceives oneself as being conscious of fashion or not. Inherently contradictory, fashion constructs a realm that is ambiguous, able to bear the weight of the varied meanings and values that flicker across the body of the wearer and the society that surrounds it. Fashion articulates a tension between conformity and differentiation, expressing the contradictory desires to fit in and stand out. Fashion is the temporal imitation of a given example and satisfies the demands for social adaptation. Simultaneously it satisfies in no less degree the need of differentiation, the tendency towards dissimilarity, the desire for constant change and contrast (Simmel, 1971; Entwistle, 2000; Finkelstein, 1991; Baudrillard, 1998; Galbraith, 1958).

The idea of fashion change is often interpreted as a phenomenon that trickles down, or emulates from the upper echelon of society to their subordinate groups. The theory contends that the process of imitation and differentiation between the superordinate and the subordinate groups in the social ladder has a progressive character and the new status markers are eventually subject to subordinate appropriation, and still newer ones must be created. It establishes a self-perpetuating cycle of change and creates an engine (Barnard, 2002) that drives fashion forward in a continual process of innovation (McCracken, 1985; Solomon and Rabolt, 2004). McCracken (1985) redefines Simmel's emulation theory by applying the concept to the adoption and symbolic exchange of fashion between genders in a business environment in which females, as subordinates, "selectively" appropriate the essence of men's business outfits in order to acquire the symbolic value that connotes masculinity and trustworthiness, which are the prerequisites at a male-dominant business front. Despite its explanatory pre-eminence in illustrating the process of fashion diffusion and symbolic exchange (McCracken, 1985), the logic behind the trickle-down theory is too oversimplified and overgeneralised to take account of the complexity, fluidity, volatility, and individuality (Veblen, 1992; Wilcox, 2001) and more profoundly the systemic commercial logic that dominates the contemporary world of fashion consumption (McCracken, 1985, 1990; Azuma et al., 2004).

Today, the group who sets the "hip" is often likely to emerge from the streets, from youth cultures rather than from the elite at the top and the mainstream of the social strata (Entwistle, 2000). In other words, fashion can and does "bubble up" the social hierarchy from the bottom up to the status of high fashion. Elite fashion often finds its sources of references in subcultures (Hebdige, 1979), ethnic costumes, and other Non-Western cultural and aesthetic elements (Kondo, 1977), which are, by definition (Polhemus and Proctor, 1978), distanced from the fashion system that identifies itself with excessi and ephemera that is historically and geographically specific to western modernity (Entwistle, 2000; Azuma et al., 2004; Lipovetsky, 1994). In fact, the nucleus of the Western fashion system substantially stands on the influence of the historical development in costumes, accessories, and materials in the so-called "non-fashionable" end of the globe, such as the Middle East, India, and China (Tsujihara, 2003; Azuma et al., 2004). Barnes and Eicher (1992) argue, in the same vein, that it is a mistake for researchers to consider fashion as a characteristic only of societies with complex technology, although fashion is generally understood as a historically and geographically specific system for the production and organisation of clothing, emerging over the course of the fourteenth century in the European courts, particularly the French court of Louis XIV, and developing with the rise of mercantile capitalism that marked the emergence and evolution of Western modernity (Bell, 1976; Finkelstein, 1991; Flugel, 1930. Laver, 1969; 1995; McDowell, 1992, Polhemus and Proctor, 1978; Rouse, 1989; Veblen, 1953; Wilson, 1985; Entwistle, 2000).

Blumer (1969) claims that potential fashionableness is determined by factors independent of the elite's control, within the cultural production system. Certain symbolic styles are chosen over others in the process of "collective selection" (Solomon and Rabolt, 2004). Modern fashion diffusion is in large part devoted to the identification of fashion leaders, instead of casually employing the trickle-down theory for a seemingly logical explanation of fashion change (King, 1963; Katz and Lazarfeld, 1955; McCracken, 1985; Azuma et al., 2004). Therefore, the study of fashion is required to cover the "dual concept" of fashion as a cultural phenomenon and as an aspect of manufacturing and marketing with the accent on production technology (Leopord, 1992; Entwistle, 2000), and a variety of cultural intermediaries (Solomon and Rabolt, 2004).

Fashion in modernity (Du Gay, 1997) affects everyone and not solely a specific section of the population. The trend surrounding fashion today is now linked with equality, self-image, and a sense of individualism within the systemic process of creation, manufacturing marketing and consumption on a global communication grid (Robinson, 1958; Wilcox, 2001; Carr and Pomoror, 1992). Whilst haute couture and high fashion still possess substantial influence over the direction of biannual trends, they way in which fashion emerges and diffuses is far from what Simmel (1971) elucidates in his emulation or class differentiation (Braham, 1997) theory. Trends and styles can spring up from any fraction of society and it quickly "trickles across" (spreads across) the entire marketplace with the aid of advanced technologies, logistical expertise, and the power of media (Azuma et al., 2004). The process is a highly commercialised one and the fashion industry being constantly geared to find "new looks" each season. The speed at which fashion spreads across the market and the concomitant effect on the interconnections among the actors in the fashion supply chain is indeed idiosyncratic to the fashion industry today (Entwistle, 2000). This, in fact, accelerates competition among fashion firms especially in the middle market, as the complexity of demands and the juxtaposed meanings/functions of fashion on the consumption side call for continuous sophistication in production and organisation of processes at each stage of the fashion supply chain, and hence the enhancement of the market orientation capability (Azuma et al., 2004) at the manufacturing/marketing end (Braham, 1997). In a quasi-institutionalised system of creation, diffusion, and obsolescence, fashion drives an endless cycle of competition, imitation, and nominal innovation in the marketplace (Tamura, 1996, 1975; Azuma et al., 2004; Baudrillard, 1998).

Fashion in Modernity from an Industrial Perspective

The fashion industry is always at the mercy of whims of styles and fickle customers who want the latest designs whilst they are still in fashion (Abernathy et al., 1999), along with the uncontrollable parameters such as weather and economic climate. It is characterised with the relentlessly changing nature of consumers, competition and technologies. Sophisticated consumers call for an adamant changeover of choices in products, brands, and even the retail trading fascias that create the space of consumption. The equation of fashion consumption with that of use value, exchange value, and symbolic value (Baudrillard, 1998) is becoming increasingly opaque (Azuma and Fernie, 2004. This, in effect, demands a social theory to bridge the gulf between the supply-side and the consumption (cultural)-side of the fashion studies (Entwistle, 2000). A global spread of corporate activities in the textiles and fashion industry has also had considerable impacts upon the way in which division of labours in the geographically spread industry is configured and hence the way that fashion is consumed at daily life level. In addition to this, continuous improvement in the core and auxiliary technologies surrounding the fashion industry has shown a tendency to level off the technological capability gaps among fashion firms and so left less room for a technology-driven differentiation, which is often deemed a nucleus of a firm's competitive advantage vis-à-vis its rivals (Tamura, 2003; Porter, 1985).

During the past decades, many of the so-called best practice fashion firms have forged their success in reshaping their supply chain and serving the consumers in an increasingly concurrent manner with the real time sales data in the marketplace and the precise forecasting based on it. Quick Response (QR) and Supply Chain Management (SCM) has emerged as a key managerial philosophy (Fernie, 1994, 1998) to realise a firm's market-oriented strategy in organisationally seeking to understand and anticipate customers' expressed and latent needs and developing superior solutions (Slater and Narver, 1999) in the form of an integrated retail marketing mix. The fashion industry is represented with a high level of competitive intensity and market turbulence with fragmented consumer needs. It consists of notoriously labour intensive multi-faceted processes with relative technological simplicity (Dickerson, 1995; Dicken, 1998). The fashion industry is susceptible not only to changing consumer tastes and socio-economic factors but also to the climate and the market fluctuation of raw material supplies in a particular season. A successful implementation of a market orientation approach is, in theory, to have a considerable impact upon improving a firm's bottom-line performance (Jaworski and Kohli, 1993; Kohli and Joworski, 1990) as well as augmenting its set of value propositions in the mind of the consumers.

However, the real problem has been how such an effectual market orientation framework is put into practice within a fashion firm's supply chain operation amidst the restraints that are specific to the fashion industry. Despite the theoretical fit between the QR/SCM concept and the market orientation approach, it is indeed an immaterialising dream for a fashion firm to achieve a sustainable competitive advantage within the limited scope of innovation that is dictated by the so-called fashion process, where general trends are preset long before the launch of a seasonal collection at various stages, for example, colour, fibre, yarn, fabric, print, silhouette, styling details, and trims (Jackson, 2001). This systemic process consequentially accelerates the competitive intensity among the fashion firms, coupled with the short-term horizon of competition (Tamura, 1996) that is innate to the phenomenon related with fashion. In a more contemporary term, styles' bubbling-up and their rapid spread further shorten the reactive time on the production side and thus narrows the scope of fashion innovation in an intrinsic sense. The prerequisite for a fashion firm to outdo its competition in such an apparently homogenised circumstance, therefore, is to create a subtle yet a communicative value to the consumers. The economies of speed (Minami, 2003), or the time-based competence (Stalk and Hout, 1990) can no longer be the single driver of a firm's competitive advantage, as time compression in the fashion supply chain has become a *de facto* standard.

In the light of the idiosyncrasies of the fashion as an integrated entity of creation (production and marketing) and consumption in the contemporary setting, this paper aims to investigate the factors that encompass fashion firms' competitive strategies in a dynamic yet institutionally constrained homogenised system, analysing the principle of competition and innovation in the middle market sartorial fashion. First, this is to highlight the theories behind the concept of market orientation with an extended perspective of marketing logistics (Christopher, 1997, 1998) and supply chain management. It is followed by a discussion on the role of imitation and innovation as part of the organisational learning process and hence the resource/capability-based (Ambrosini, 2003) competitive strategy in the fashion system. To put differently, the mechanism whereby one firm stands out from others (Collis and Montgomery, 1998) in the "world of volatility" is attempted to be explained. The concluding part proposes managerial implications and a future research agenda on the basis of the conceptual framework of this study.

THE FOCAL POINT OF MARKET ORIENTATION AND SUPPLY CHAIN MANAGEMENT

Competitive advantage is at the heart of a fashion firm's performance in a volatile business environment (Lewis and Hawkesley, 1990) that is characterised by fragmented markets with dynamic consumers, rapid technological changes and growing non-price competition (Weerawardena, 2003; Tamura, 2003) within varied spaces and meanings of consumption. Market orientation is an approach whereby a business seeks to understand and anticipate consumers' expressed and latent needs, and develop superior solutions (Day, 1994; Kohli and Jaworski, 1990; Slater and Narver, 1995; 1999) in order to remain proactive as well as responsive to the changing facet of the meanings of consumption.

Market orientation is the organisation-wide generation of market intelligence pertaining to current and future customer needs and expectations, dissemination of the intelligence across departments, and organisation-wide coordination (Tamura, 2003; Ogawa, 2000-a, 2000-b) and responsiveness to it (Kohli and Jaworski, 1990) in an efficient and effectual manner. Tamura (2003), building upon a series of conceptual frameworks of the market-oriented strategy (Day, 1994; Kohli and Jaworski, 1990; Deshpande et al., 1993; Deshpande, 1999; Jaworski and Kohli, 1993), proposes an operational model of market orientation. Figure 1 is an application of Tamura's behavioural model of market orientation to the context of the integrated fashion supply chain. This summarises the relationship between a firm's market-oriented strategy and the role of the supply chain in organisationally coordinating a series of actions in the external as well as internal processes of market orientation. The actions are:

- recognition of the market environment,
- generation of intelligence on the customer's existing needs and latent/future expectations,
- intra- and inter-organisational dissemination of the intelligence, and
- responses to satisfy the needs and feedback of the actions (Pelham, 1997; Tamura, 2001, 2003).

Much of the earlier literature on market orientation (Day, 1994; Kohli and Jaworski, 1990; Deshpande, 1999; Jaworski and Kohli, 1993) is centred around the operations within the scope of a single firm's internal organisation particularly in the manufacturing sector. Kohli and Jaworski (1990) extrapolate the role of the supply-side and demand-side moderators in addition to the environmental factors (e.g., market turbulence, competitive intensity, and technological turbulence) (Jaworski and Kohli, 1993) as the external intermediaries between a firm's market orientation practice and its bottom-line business perfor-

FIGURE 1. The Conceptual Model of the Market Orientation Approach in the Fashion Industry

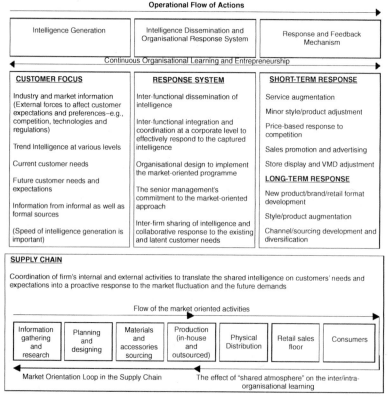

Source: Adapted from Tamura (2003-a); Levitt (1969); Kohli and Jaworski (1990); Chandra and Kumar (2000).

mance. The former stands for the nature of the competition among suppliers and the technology employed within a firm's value-adding behavioural system. The latter represents the characteristics of demands in the industry, such as the preferences and the meaning of consumption on the consumer side (see Figure 2).

Whilst their accounts on the roles of external factors insinuate the potential benefit of incorporating marketing logistics (Christopher, 1997, 1998; Christopher and Peck, 1998; Christopher and Juttner, 2000) into the concept of market orientation, it is Elg (2003) that explicitly emphasises the impacts of market orientation at an inter- as well as an

FIGURE 2. Antecedents and Consequences of Market Orientation

Top Management		Employees
Emphasis		Organisational Commitment
Risk Aversion		Esprit de Corps

Interdepartmental Dynamics	Market Orientation	Environment
Conflict		Market Turbulence
Connectedness	Intelligence Generation	Competitive Intensity
	Intelligence Dissemination	Technological Turbulence
Organisational Dynamics	Organisational Coordination	
	Responsiveness	
Formalisation		
Centralisation		
Departmentalisation		BUSINESS PERFORMANCE
Reward System		

Source: Kohli and Jaworski (1993)

intra-organisational level by defining it as a joint process by retailers, suppliers, and other supply chain members (see Figure 3). This proposition is inspired by studies by Siguaw et al. (1998, 1999) on the influence of a firm's market orientation programme over other supply chain players in the network. Placing a particular focus upon the boundary between retailers and suppliers, Elg (2003) demonstrates the latent benefit that lies in this integrated market orientation approach.

Dissemination and exchange of the data on the consumers among the members in a retail system (retailer's supply chain), in fact, are likely to encourage each player in the network to better understand and anticipate the customer needs and expectations. This also contributes to minimising the so-called Bullwhip Effect by synchronising the flow of information and inventories at various stages in the supply chain. Joint investment in sharing a common platform in delivering quick and effective market responses is to facilitate the supply chain players with opportunities to develop an interdependent (De Toni and Nassimbeni, 1995) long-term partnership. A trust that is created through a transaction-specific investment (Yahagi, 1994; Yahagi et al., 1993) is recognised as a critical factor to maintain an efficient and effectual inter-organisational partnership (Fiorito et al., 1999) in the long-term perspective.

FIGURE 3. A Framework for Analysing a Retailer's Market Orientation

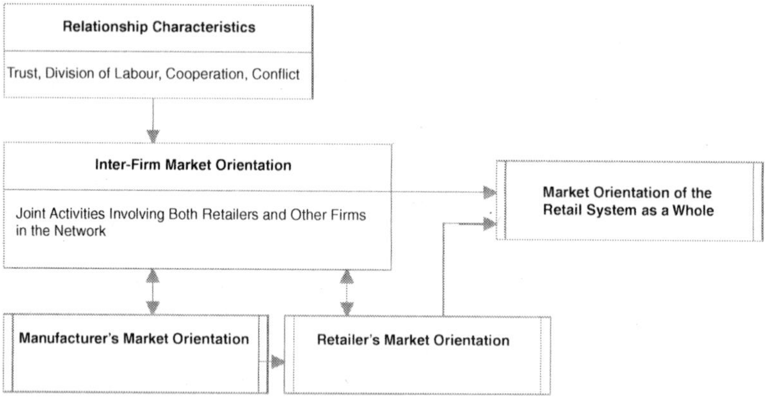

Source: Elg (2003; Siguaw (1998, 1999).

   In addition to these official settings in the supply chain relationships, Elg (2003) singles out the salience of the informal occasions where representatives of different members of distributive network may meet and exchange information and insights (Stern et al., 1996). This viewpoint shares much in common with the notion of "shared space and atmosphere" (*Ba*) that is first introduced by Itami (1999) in the context of the product development process at a Japanese automotive company. This idea has often been employed in explaining the agglomeration effects in the industrial districts in a number of studies in Japan (Yamashita, 1993, 1998, 2001; Nukata, 1998) and in Italy (Inagaki, 2003; Okamoto, 1994; Ogawa, 1998). The concept of "*Ba*" sheds light on the ambiguous effect of network members' sharing of a common platform and encoding-decoding procedure towards a particular issue, upon directing the common goals and hence collaborative behaviours and a loop of organisational learning at both intra- and inter-organisational interfaces.

   This important element adds the "missing piece" to the classic view of supply chain management that weighs more of an IT investment-driven systemic approach (Forza and Vinelli, 1996, 1997, 2000; Hunter, 1990; Riddle et al., 1999) to achieve a seamless flow of the pipeline from raw materials to retail sales floors. The traditional supply chain framework focuses on an orderly shift from a transaction-based buyer-supplier relationship to a network-based (Tamura, 2001) partnership, which is often explained by a dyadic and dynamic node of communications between the two parties (Christopher, 1997, 1998, Fernie,

1994; 1998; Azuma and Fernie, 2004). The role of "*Ba*" is deemed a moderating factor in the supply chain in a sense that it facilitates the involved parties with motivations to incessantly create a unique value in a seemingly fixed and stabilised partnership environment, that otherwise become a major inhibitor of continuous innovation. Establishing a long-term relationship with a smaller number of partners may potentially lock up the enrolled members in an institutionalised system (Piore, 1994, 2001) and there is a likelihood that a supply chain as a whole is losing the flexibility and creativity overtime in delivering an effective response to the diverse and dynamic changes in the consumption side. An intra- and inter-organisational learning loop is, thus, deemed an essential factor in the supply chain, as this deals not only with the ongoing and latent needs and expectations of the customers, but also serves as an implicit agent to monitor the competition's move and innovatively copy (Levitt, 1969, 1983; Takeishi, 2001) their operational excellence to compete in the volatile world of fashion.

The objectives of Quick Response and supply chain management in the fashion industry are simpler than is argued with the tradeoffs between the size of IT (SCM enablers) investment and the actual impact of SCM on improving the pipeline throughput and financial performance within the network (Fiorioto et al., 1999; Tamura, 2001). A supply chain, as described in Porter's (1985) value system concept, is a network of independent firms' value chains that cater for the production and marketing of particular products and services. This network of value chains target customer satisfaction and simultaneous improvement in the bottom-line performance of the pipeline as a whole, whilst the traditional value chain approach intends to increase a firm's profit margin (McGee and Johnson, 1987). The supply chain, in this vein, is a fundamental behavioural architecture in which any market-oriented firm finds itself engaged. It, therefore, is not a purpose-built package to be configured from scratch but an existing framework that needs refinement and restructuring in accordance with the degrees of a firm's market orientation. Particularly in the fashion industry where highly fragmented SME contractors commit many of the supply chain phases, the organisational aspect of supply chain management should be given more credibility than the IT investment vs. economies of scale justification.

The goals of supply chain management in the fashion industry, in short, are in delivering the wanted style at the right time in the right place (Fernie, 1994), with required variety and affordability (Giunipero et al., 2001; Lowson, 1998; Lowson et al., 1999) and more room for customisation (Pine II, 1993), thus satisfying both the existing and potential needs of the target customers (Slater and Narver, 1999). QR and SCM, in theory, play an intermediating role that induces a particular organisation to create a superior customer value/solution, and hence achieve a competitive advantage in the specific marketplace for which it caters. There exists no single universally applicable model of supply chain management. It can and does change according to the types of fashion and its "meanings" that a firm delivers and the idiosyncrasies of the consumers at which it aims.

At an operational level, the concept of QR and SCM requires a firm and its supply chain partnerships to coordinate its internal and external activities (Chandra and Kumar, 2000) in order to translate their shared intelligence on consumers' needs and expectations into a proactive response to the market fluctuation and the future demands. It aims at accurately spotting the market trend and flexibly synchronising it with the entire process in the supply chain, based upon an efficient and effectual sharing of key information, and the risks and benefits that are embedded in the long and complex pipeline of the fashion supply chain (Christopher, 1997; 1998; Christopher and Juttner, 2000).

Thus, it would be given credibility, at least at the theoretical level, to integrate the action flow in the market orientation approach into an extended concept of marketing logistics and supply chain management (Christopher, 1997, 1998; Christopher and Peck, 1998; Christopher and Juttner, 2000), since it is consistent with the intra- and inter-firm coordination mechanism of the supply chain in delivering a flexible and rapid response to the current and foreseen needs of the customer.

The Reality of Market Orientation and Supply Chain Management in the Sartorial Fashion

Despite such a strong potential for market orientation being rooted in the SCM philosophy, it is hardly possible for a fashion firm to establish a sustainable competitive advantage solely through its market orientation and supply chain effectiveness. This is due partly to an institutional mechanism in which fashion trends are set farther ahead of the beginning of each season by a variety of international bodies at various levels, such as colour directions, fibre, yarn, fabric, print and finish, silhouette, styling details, and trims (Jackson, 2001; Chimura, 2001). Although contemporary components and new blood are incessantly injected in the biannual collection on the catwalks, fashion in modernity is somewhat a more cyclical process which delicately renews and re-conceives what were once out there in different time and space. The scope of innovation is, thus, limited by its nature. More contemporary, fashion "bubbles up" from anywhere of the social strata and diffuses rapidly against the background of the technological improvement both in communication, production, and final distribution to the consumers. This, in effect, further accelerates the speed of change in the entire marketplace.

This systematic fashion process of juxtaposed style references in a technologically advanced environment considerably limits the scope of innovation and thus increases the competitive intensity in the fashion industry towards the state of competitive myopia (Tamura, 1996). No one creation in the history of modern fashion is as epoch making as the cornerstone innovations in other industries, such as James Watt's and Edison's or more recently the Internet, in terms of the impacts upon the lifestyle of the people. Despite the existence of diverse interpretations in the roles and meanings of fashion and dress in modernity, its basic functions are difficult to change, and thus are unlikely to invalidate or "de-mature" (Kuhn, 1970; Dosi, 1982; Takeishi, 2001) the existing paradigm of fashion and lifestyle (Azuma et al., 2004).

Fashion is, indeed, a unique phenomenon. It consistently transforms and fluctuates, reflecting the mood of the society and the cyclical nature of the dominant styles of the time within the cultural production system. The degree of metamorphoses, nevertheless, is to a nominal degree. Yet, it is certainly discernable in the mind of the wearer. The condition for a fashion firm to differentiate from competition, therefore, is to create a subtle yet an appealing difference to the customers in an apparently homogenised environment, where the economy of speed (Minami, 2003) can no longer deliver a sustainable competitive advantage. Compression in the three dimensions of time in marketing the fashion style, serving the customers and reacting the market change (Christopher and Peck, 1998; Hines, 2001) within a supply chain has been becoming a *de facto* standard in the fashion industry. Managing an effective portfolio of brands or retail fascias, coupled with a balanced combination of sourcing options, to flexibly respond to the quasi-cyclical process of fashion change (Robinson, 1958) within the scope of a fashion firm appears to be becoming crucial in successfully catering for the fickle consumers in the middle market (Azuma et al., 2004). This minimises the entrepreneurial risks and increases the precision of market orientation in the short time horizon.

If one assumes an entrepreneurial risk and explores to achieve a higher level of intrinsic differentiation by increasing a level of product transformation, the ideal means would be bringing the decoupling point at the material development stage back up the supply chain (Meijbroom, 1999). It nevertheless implies a significant risk to commit too much to a speculative backward integration (Bucklin, 1965; Yahagi, 2001), because a firm then has to trade off the variety of their fashion offers with the postponement benefits. It is normally up to the fabric development stage at which fashion firms can postpone their supply chain operation in reacting/proacting to the market fluctuation. This is due mainly to the lead-time constraint and the larger production lot in the upstream. In practice, little improvement has been achieved since the days of Luziano Benetton's innovation in the 1970s when he accomplished a phenomenal success in hitting upon a technique to dye greige knitted garments to the colours wanted in the marketplace (Mantle, 1999). Many of the so-called best practice fashion firms today, in fact, embark on a development and bulk sourcing of particular strategic fabrics and their versatile usages in adjusting the cuts and silhouettes to the needs and expectations of the consumers (Azuma et al., 2004).

The Japanese women's clothing sector, for example, calls for a considerable variety in designs and hence diversity in the choice of materials (Azuma and Fernie, 2004 forthcoming), some of the functions delivered by textile converters, such as (1) assortment in a smaller lot size, (2) risk avoidance, (3) finance, (4) conveyance of market information, and (5) introduction of cutting-edge materials (Tamura, 1975), are indispensable in order to execute market oriented responses to the ever-changing fragmented needs of the consumer. Thus, there still remains a question regarding this trade-off issue in the fashion supply chain.

Besides, the relationships among the supply chain members in reality tend not be motivated by common goals and objectives that are based upon an effective sharing of key information and an efficient flow of inventories in the entire supply chain. It is too often the case in the fashion industry that an extreme responsiveness of a firm's fashion supply chain is achieved through an unequal distribution of power. The players who command the creative shrewdness and the marketing function in the mid-to-down stream of the pipeline effactually impose a flexible response in the labour intensive processes on their SME subcontractors who are mostly dependent upon their order placements (Azuma, 2001; Azuma and Fernie, 2004 Forthcoming). In addition, suppliers are unwilling to disclose their inventory data to their down stream fashion firms customers in fear of the bargaining pressures from the down stream as well as the spill over of their assortment expertise to their horizontal competitors. The fashion firms on the down stream, on the other hand, tend to be reluctant to establish a long-term partnership with a smaller number of suppliers, in recognition of the risks in losing their agility and flexibility (Azuma et al., 2004). An effective sharing of *"Ba,"* in reality, is hard to be realised in a power-game relationship (Fernie, 1998; Whiteoak, 1994). Therefore, collaborative creation of a unique value "from the source" is normally hard to achieve for a fashion firm, coupled with the speculation/postponement issue (Bucklin, 1965; Alderson, 1957) explicated above. Creation of an intrinsic differentiation in the upper stream of the supply chain, in reality, is one of the most challenging tasks in the fashion industry.

Thus, the competitive environment in the fashion industry is structured in its peculiar style, and this makes it difficult for a fashion firm to differentiate from competition simply via implementing a market oriented supply chain approach. A combined programme of market orientation and supply chain management certainly provides a fashion firm and its supply chain partnerships with better visibility of its market orientation activities and helps them deliver a rapid and flexible response to the actual and latent needs in the marketplace. Nevertheless, it doesn't allow a firm to create an explicit difference from the competition and hence a sustainable competitive advantage.

It is a paradox that an inter- and intra-organisational approach to anticipate and better respond to the changing needs of the consumers for the meanings of fashion results in homogenising firms' responses to the consumers within the restrained scope of innovation in the fashion industry. A rapid and flexible response is often just a prerequisite for a fashion firm to keep abreast of the incessant fashion change and diffusion. Then, what are the real drivers of success in the middle market fashion?

THE ROLE OF IMITATION AND INNOVATION IN THE MIDDLE MARKET FASHION

The fashion industry is a quasi-institutional system in which firms' market-oriented commitment can very often result in an apparent homogenisation in the fashion retail mix beyond the boundaries of companies as well as brand labels (Azuma and Fernie, 2004). In addition to the restraint on the scope of innovation and the degree of product transformation, due to the phenomenal speed of fashion dissemination from various sources and the difficulties in bringing the decoupling point

(Meijboom, 1999) in the supply chain, there is a complex set of factors that prohibits a clear-cut fashion differentiation in the marketplace.

Whilst much of the success by a number of fashion firms increasingly derives from their time-based (Stalk and Hout, 1990; Maximov and Gottschilich, 1993) competitive capability via a flexible and responsive supply chain, their responses to the market change are predominantly oriented toward short-termism. This is partially because there exists a power-game relationship within the inter-firm network in the pipeline (Fernie, 1998; Whiteoak, 1994; Azuma, 2001; Azuma and Fernie, 2004). It prevents the creative effect of sharing *"Ba"* among the supply chain members from being realised and reduces the degree of intrinsic differentiation from the materials stage. Stronger members in the supply chain are prone to gleaning a short-term benefit rather than pursuing a long-term competitive edge. Their contracted suppliers, on the other hand, are historically highly dependable on their order placements and so have not developed their own innovative capability. A truly collaborative market-oriented supply chain in a fast-moving environment is indeed hard to achieve for a common goal and objective. Moreover, the current supply chain programmes in the fashion industry are limited to historical and current sales/inventory in the use of EPOS data. The forecasting from this data set, therefore, may well be accurate in a very short-term horizon. It nevertheless cannot foresee the more macro and long-term changes in the consumers' latent needs and expectation in their fashion purchases and hence the relationship between the body and fashion in varied time and spaces.

The influence of media around the production and consumption of fashion is another factor that inhibits a fashion firm's sustainable competitive advantage. Fashion media persistently feature the up and coming trends and styles both in graphical images and texts encoding and signifying them (Barthes, 1990), and simultaneously invalidate the trend in the "near past." Thus, what is "in" at present can possibly become an "out" even overnight with the power of the media. Business media, on the other hand, consistently search for the best practice firms in the industry and describe them as if they were universally applicable business model foreseeing the future. The result may be consumers' positive decoding of the media and hence the support of a particular fashion firm when it is "hot" in the press. Here again, a firm given a negative encoding by the media is likely to be obsolete in the marketplace, regardless of its intrinsic capability in reference to the industry's standard. The positioning of a fashion firm in the market place is, by the same token, susceptible to "what the fashion press implicate and explicate" in addition to "what the consumers expect on their own or through decoding the messages from the media" as a nucleus of the cultural production system (Solomon and Rabolt, 2004).

Finally, innovation spill-over (Porter, 1985; Takeishi, 2001) is a very conspicuous phenomenon in the fashion industry. Earlier studies identify a set of inhibitors of imitation (Levin et al., 1988; Teece, 1986; Williams, 1992; Rumelt, 1984; White, 1982; Porter, 1996; Besanko et al., 2000) as:

- legal and regulatory protection,
- superior access to the materials, resources, and customers,
- the size of the market and the economies of scale,
- company-specific intangible capabilities, and
- strategic fit.

In the fashion industry, however, these barriers are least effective to ban imitation or imitators. This is because of the nature of its multi-faceted complex supply chain configuration. First of all, tangible aspects of the fashion retail mix, such as products, services, retail formats and atmospherics, can easily be copied through observation and reverse engineering (Von Hippel, 1988), and so it is almost impossible to prevent the "*me-toos*" and the innovative imitators (Levitt, 1969,1983). In fact, many of the so-called innovative high street retailers, such as The Limited, Zara, and many of the Japanese players, embark on their capability to refer to and adapt the external fashion sources and competitors sales data in the shopping complex (e.g., shopping centres) in their own style (Minami, 2003; Levitt, 1969, 1983; Burt et al., 2003; Azuma, 2002; Fisher et al., 1999), or in other words, knock off through their short-term market oriented supply chain approaches.

Even the know-how and expertise in the backyard of the retail mix is not secure from the competitor's intelligence activities (Tamura, 2003). Sharing within the industry common suppliers, interior decorators, consulting firms, sales promotion/marketing companies, third party logistics service providers, credit card operators, and IT service providers means that a fashion firm's operational secrets are always under scrutiny by its competition. Higher occurrences of job-hopping in the fashion industry also stimulate the leakage of such enigmatic "tacit knowledge" from one firm to another. This fluid movement of human resources in the entire industry encourages the formation of unofficial human contacts, and thus a "tacit knowledge" that works within the particular environment at a specific company is translated into a "common knowledge" among a much larger group of the players in the industry. This, together with the improvement in IT and logistical practices, has, in a sense, altered the nature of the fashion process. Traditionally it was a slow process of imitation and innovation when fashion "trickles down" from the superordinate to the subordinate class (Simmel, 1904; McCracken, 1985; 1990). In the fashion system today is witnessed trends and styles of various origins quickly 'trickle across' the consumers of diverse backgrounds (King, 1963; McCracken, 1985, 1990).

Figure 4 below highlights the nature of the competition and innovation in the fashion industry, and describes the reason why the market-oriented approach in the fashion business tends to take on a short-term competitive horizon. In the light of the institutional and operational characteristics of the fashion industry and its supply chain, firms' short-termism in their market orientation may well be justified in their pursuit of spotting the focal point of creativity, consumer satisfaction, and fundamentally their bottom line performances. There exist few opportunities to leverage from the fast-mover advantage to establish a sustainable competitive advantage (Levitt, 1969; Schnaars, 1994). This, in effect, hinders the emergence of truly differentiated fashion in the middle market from the point of the materials stage of the supply chain, which often creates a "soft variable"-based (Malecki, 2000)

FIGURE 4. The Process of Fashion Homogenisation

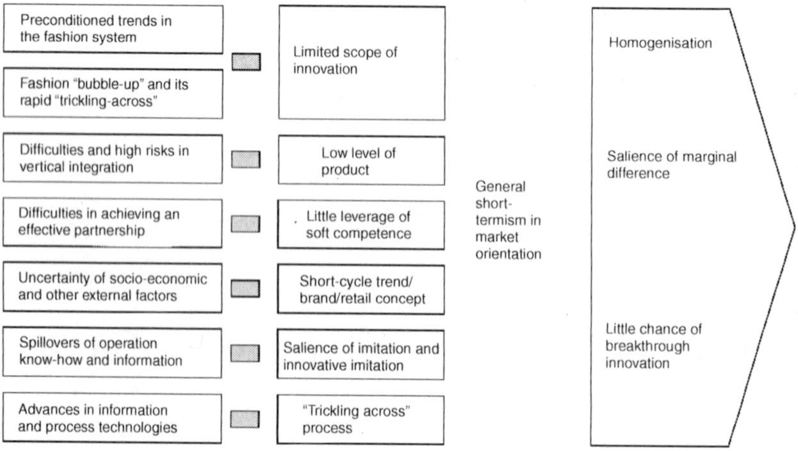

Source: Based on Schnaars (1994).

competence of the fashion industry especially in the advanced economies (Azuma, 2003).

Fashion firms' market oriented supply chain behaviours are rather sustained by an organisational learning loop of their series of market orientation activities. As Weerawardena (2003) explains, it is not solely the heterogeneous firm-specific resources (Rumelt, 1984; Montgomery and Wernerfelt, 1988; Barney, 1991), such as all assets, capabilities, organisational processes, firm attributes, information, and knowledge, that determine a firm's source of competitive advantages. Resources do not exclusively determine what the firm can do and how well it can do it (Grant, 1991; Weerawardena, 2003). It is a firm's capabilities to make better use of available resources (Penrose, 1955; Mahoney and Pandian, 1992; Weerawardena, 2003) that help a firm achieve real rents, although the corporate capability itself is counted as part of the resources.

In the specific context of the middle market of the fashion industry, this capability-based approach may fit well into the framework of firms' market orientated supply chain activities. Fashion firms are consistently faced with a situation in which the current competitive parity is innovatively imitated or leapfrogged by their entrepreneurial competition at any point in time. Whilst this is a natural phenomenon in the volatile world of the fashion industry, such a competitive intensity, coupled with the institutional factors, requires fashion firms to continuously monitor each other as well as their customers' needs/expectations and then create a subtle yet a unique "difference" that better satisfies the consumers' expectations than its rivals. This continuous loop of imitation, continuous subtle innovation, organisational learning, and resultant accumulation of new resources, and a firm's capability to utilise its internal and external resources is deemed the determinant of a fashion firm's competitive advantage in the short-term volatile competitive horizon.

This sequence of imitation and innovation among the competitors in the middle market is persistently taking place within the setting of their integrated market oriented supply chain. The one who translates the understated needs of the consumers can and does manage to create a subtle yet an effective difference in an apparently homogenised retail mix in the marketplace. In addition to this, the loop of the short-term market oriented responses to the marketplace plays a crucial role in turning the wheel of innovation in the fashion industry, although the nature of the innovation is incremental due to the industry-specific restraints. Figure 5 depicts

FIGURE 5. Organisational Learning Model in a Fashion Firm's Market Orientation

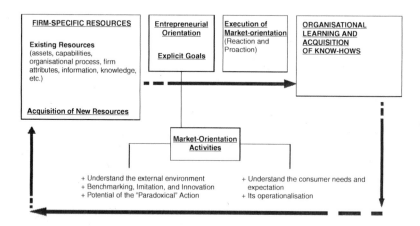

the organisational learning loop within a fashion firm's market orientation approach.

CONCLUSION AND MANAGERIAL IMPLICATIONS

This paper has explored the idiosyncrasy of imitation, innovation, and competition in the middle market fashion from an integrated view of market orientation and supply chain management. A juxtaposition of these two managerial concepts in the context of the fashion industry is found, at least in theory, to create a great potential for a fashion firm (and its supply chain members) to enhance its business performances and hence achieve a sustainable competitive advantage by effectively translating latent as well as existing customer needs and expectations into their market responses in the form of a close-knitted portfolio of retail mix offerings. The limited scope of innovation in the fashion industry, however, hinders an intrinsic fashion differentiation from taking place, and so fashion firms tend to build their market-oriented activities upon a short-term competitive horizon. Thus, firms' capability to innovatively monitor and copy their competition in the process of their market orientation activities is deemed one of the key determinants of the competitive advantage in the midst of a turbulent change in consumers' needs and expectations, and hence the meanings of fashion consumption. An implication for a firm's long-term success in such an environment is, thus, dependent on its capability in organisationally learning from their past, present, and future of their market-oriented activities in the restrained yet lucrative marketing opportunities. With continuous learning through practicising market orientation it is likely that a firm may be able to acquire the capabilities and the resources to "fashion" its strategies in effectively balancing the creativity, consumer satisfaction, and their bottom line performances in the turbulent change.

The most challenging part in a fashion firm's truly market orientation approach, therefore, lies in:

- The extent to which it can access and understand the latent needs/expectations of consumers and hence the future changes in fashion consumers' behaviours at a more macro and long-term level,
- Its capability in operationalising the gathered intelligence throughout its supply chain, and
- Its scope of entrepreneurship and learning capability to avoid competitive myopia in the apparently limited competitive horizon in the fashion industry.

In order for such a market orientation in an inherent term to be realised in the sartorial fashion in the middle market, a fashion firm and its networked organisations are required to make another step forward from the traditional short-termism in its market orientation and systemic approach towards supply chain management, which is rationalised largely by speed, technologies, efficiency, and cost reduction. As Florida maintains in his discussion on the rise of the "creative class" (Florida, 2002, 2003) whose behaviours are not motivated merely by the financial benefits but by their desire to do what they feel worthy of doing (Komiya, 2003), there has appeared a sizable population of consumers whose buying behaviours and meanings of dressing cannot be explained by a simple economic justification. This, on the one hand, suggests a necessity for a fashion firm to incorporate a rather sociological "post-EPOS" approach into its market orientation to reach a far in capturing the future consumers' needs and expectations from a more macro and long-term perspective. On the other hand, this has an implication for the nature of the supply chain management that places much focus on catering for such "creative class" expectations rather than being consistently involved in the endless ball game in the world of volatility in the middle market (Azuma, 2003).

REFERENCES

Abernathy, F.H., Dunlop, J.T., Hammond, J.H., and Weil, D. (1999) *A Stitch in Time*, Oxford University Press, N.Y.

Alderson, W. (1957) *Marketing Behaviour and Executive Action*, Richard D Irwin.

Ambrosini, V. (2003) *Tacit and Ambiguous Resources as Sources of Competitive Advantage*, Palgrave, London.

Azuma, N. (2001) The Reality of Quick Response (QR) in the Japanese Fashion Sector and the Strategy Ahead for the Domestic SME Apparel Manufacturers, *Logistics Research Network 2001 Conference Proceedings, Heriot-Watt University Edinburgh*, pp. 11-20.

Azuma, N. (2002) *Pronto Moda* Tokyo Style–Emergence of Collection-Free Street Fashion and the Tokyo-Seoul Connection, *International Journal of Retail & Distribution Management'*, 30(3), pp. 137-144.

Azuma, N. (2003) Rethinking the Centripetal Forces in Agglomeration Economies–Exploring a New Approach into the Anatomy of Agglomeration, *Institute of Marketing and Distribution Science Monograph Series*, No.41.

Azuma, N., Fernie, J., and Higashi, T. (2004) Competitive Advantages in the World of Volatility: The Paradox of Market Orientation and Supply Chain Management in the Fashion Industry, in Fernie, J, and Sparks, L. (2004) *Logistics and Retail Management 2nd Edition*, Kogan Page, London.

Azuma, N., and Fernie, J. (2004 Forthcoming) Changing Nature of Japanese Fashion: Can Quick Response Improve Supply Chain Efficiency? *European Journal of Marketing*, Special Issue on Fashion Marketing.

Barnard, M. (2002) *Fashion As Communication 2nd Edition*, Routledge, London.

Barnes, R., and Eicher, J.B. (eds.) (1992) *Dress and Gender: Making and Meaning*, Berg, Oxford.

Barney, J. (1991) Firm Resources and Sustained Competitive Advantage, *Journal of Management*, 17(1), pp. 99-120.

Barthes, R. (1990) *The Fashion System*, University of California Press, Berkley, CA.

Baudrillard, J. (1998) *The Consumer Society: Myths & Structure*, Sage Publication, London.

Bell, Q. (1976) *On Human Finery*, Hogarth Press, London.

Besanko, D., Dranove, D., and Shanley, M. (2000) *Economics of Strategy 2nd Edition*, John Wiley and Sons Ltd, N.Y.

Blumer, H. (1969) Fashion: From Class Differentiation to Collective Selection, *Sociological Quarterly*, 10, p. 275-291.

Braham, P. (1997) Fashion: Unpacking a Cultural Production, in du Gay, P. (ed.) (1997) *Production of Culture, Cultures of Production*, Sage, London.

Bucklin, L.P. (1965) Postponement, Speculation, and Structure of Distribution Channels, *Journal of Marketing Research*, 2(1).

Burt, S.L., Dawson, J., and Larke, R. (2003) Inditex–Zara: Rewriting the Rules in Apparel Retailing, Conference Proceedings, 2nd Asian Retail and Distribution Workshop, April, UMDS Kobe, Japan.

Carr, H., and Pomeror, J. (1992) *Fashion Design and Product Development*, Blackwell Scientific Publications, London.

Chandra, C., and Kumar, S. (2000) Supply Chain Management in Theory and Practice: A Passing Fad or a Fundamental Change? *Industrial Management & Data Systems*, 100(3), pp. 100-113.

Chimura, N. (2001) *Sengo Fashion Story* (Post War Fashion Story), Heibonsha, Tokyo.

Christopher, M. (1997) *Marketing Logistics*, Butterworth Heinemann, Oxford.

Christopher, M. (1998) *Logistics and Supply Chain Management 2nd Edition*, Financial Times, London.

Christopher, M. and Peck, H. (1998) Fashion Logistics in Fernie, J. and Sparks, L. (eds.) *Logistics and Retail Management*, Kogan Page, London.

Christopher, M., and Juttner, U. (2000) Achieving Supply Chain Excellence: The Role of Relationship Management, *International Journal of Logistics: Research & Application*, 3 (1), pp. 5-23.

Collis, D.J., and Montogomery, C.A. (1998) *Corporate Strategy, A Resource-Based Approach*, Irwin McGraw-Hill, MA.

Day, G. (1994) The Capabilities of Market-Driven Organization, *Journal of Marketing*, 58, pp. 37-52.

Deshpande, R., Farley, J.U., and Webster Jr., F.E. (1993) Corporate Culture, Customer Orientation, and Innovativeness in Japanese Firms: A Quadrat Analysis, *Journal of Marketing*, 57, pp. 23-37.

Deshpande, R. (ed.) (1999) *Developing a Market Orientation*, Sage Publishing, CA.

De Toni, A. and Nassimbeni, G. (1995) Supply networks: Genesis, stability and logistics implications. A comparative analysis of two districts, *International Journal of Management Science*, 23(4), pp. 403-418.

Dicken, P. (1998) *Global Shift–Transforming the World Economy 3rd Edition*, Paul Chapman Publishing Ltd., London.

Dickerson, K. (1995) *Textiles and Apparel in the Global Economy*, Prentice Hall, New Jersey.

Dosi, G. (1982) Technological Paradigms and Technological Trajectories: A Suggested Interpretation of the Determinants and Directions of Technical Change, *Research Policy*, 11(3), pp. 147-162.

du Gay (ed.) (1997) *Production of Culture/Culture of Production*, Sage Publication with Open University, London.

Elg, U. (2003) Retail market orientation: A preliminary framework, *International Journal of Retail & Distribution Management*, 31(2), pp. 107-117.

Entwistle, J. (2000) *The Fashioned Body*, Polity, Cambridge.

Fernie, J. (1994) Quick Response: An international perspective, *International Journal of Physical Distribution & Logistics Management*, 24(6), pp. 38-46.

Fernie, J. (1998) Relationships in the supply chain in Fernie, J. and Sparks, L. (eds) (1998) *Logistics and retail management*, Kogan Page, London.

Finkelstein, J. (1991) *The Fashioned Self*, Polity, Cambridge.

Fiorito, S.S., Giunipero, L.C., and Oh, J. (1999) Channel relationships and Quick Response implementation, Conference Paper, 10th International Conference on Research in the Distributive Trades, August, Stirling University.

Fisher, M.L., Raman, A., and McClelland, A.S. (1999) *Supply Chain Management at World Co., Ltd.*, World Co., Ltd., Tokyo.

Florida, R. (2002) The Rise of Creative Class, *The Washington Monthly*, May, pp. 15-25.

Florida, R. (2003) The New American Dream, *The Washington Monthly*, March, pp. 26-33.

Flugel, J.C. (1930) *The Psychology of Clothes*, Hogarth Press, London.

Forza, C., and Vinelli, A. (1996) An analytical scheme for the change of the apparel design process towards quick response, *International Journal of Clothing Science and Technology*, 8 (4), pp. 28-43.

Forza, C., and Vinelli, A. (1997) Quick Response in the textile-apparel industry and the support of information technologies, *Integrated Manufacturing Systems*, 8(3), pp. 125-136.

Galbraith, J.K. (1958) *The Affluent Society*, Penguin Books, London, (1999 new edition).

Giunipero, L.C., Fiorito, S.S., Pearcy, D.H., and Dandeo, L. (2001) The Impact of Vendor Incentives on Quick Response, *The International Review of Retail, Distribution and Consumer Research*, 11(4), pp. 359-376.

Grant, R.M. (1991) Analysing Resources and Capabilities in Grant, R.M. (ed.) (1991) *Contemporary Strategic Analysis: Concepts, Techniques and Applications*, Basil Blackwell, MA.

Hebdige, D. (1979) *Subculture: The Meaning of Style*, Routledge, London.

Hines, T. (2001) From analogue to digital supply chain: Implications for fashion marketing, in Hines, T. and Bruce, M. (eds.) (2001) *Fashion Marketing, Contemporary Issues*, Butterworth Heinemann, Oxford.

Hunter, A. (1990) *Quick Response in apparel manufacturing: A survey of the American scene*, The Textile Institute, Manchester.

Inagaki, K. (2003) *Italia no Kigyouka Network* (Entrepreneurs' Networking in Italy), Hakuto-Shobo, Tokyo.

Itami, H. (1999) *Ba no Dynamism* (*The Dynamics of Shared Space and Atmosphere*), NTT Publishing, Tokyo.

Jackson, T. (2001) The Process of Fashion Trend Development Leading to a Season, in Hines, T., and Bruce, M. (eds.) (2001) *Fashion Marketing*, Butterworth Heinemann, Oxford.

Jaworski, B, and Kohli, A. (1993) Market Orientation: Antecedents and Consequences, *Journal of Marketing*, 57, pp. 53-70.

Katz, E. and Lazarsfeld, P.F. (1955) *Personal Influence*, The Free Press, Glencoe, IL.

King, C.W. (1963) Fashion Adoption: A Rebuttal to the 'Trickle-Down' Theory in Greyser, S.A. (ed) (1963) *Toward Scientific Marketing*, American Marketing Association, Chicago.

Kohli, A., and Jaworski, B. (1990) Market Orientation: The Construct, Research Propositions, and Managerial Implications, *Journal of Marketing*, 54, pp. 1-18.

Komiya, K. (2003) Jiko Mokuteki Shiko no Kourigyosha to Shinazoroe Keisei (Self-Actualisation-Oriented Retailers and the Process of Forming Their Retail Offer), *Journal of Marketing & Distribution*, 6(1), pp. 81-94.

Kondo, D. (1977) Orientalising: Fashioning Japan in *About Face*, Routledge, London.

Kuhn, T. (1970) *The Structure of Scientific Revolutions*, University of Chicago Press, Chicago.

Laver, J. (1969) *Modesty in Dress*, Houghton Mifflin Co., Boston.

Laver, J. (1969/1995) *A Concise History of Costume*, Thames and Hudson, London.

Leopord, E. (1992) The Manufacture of the Fashion System, in Ash, J, and Wilson, E. (eds.) (1992) *Chic Thrills*, Pandora, London.

Levin, R.C., Klevorick, A.K., Nelson, R.R., and Winter, S.G. (1988) Appropriating the Returns from Industrial Research and Development, *Brooking Papers on Economic Activity*, 13(2).

Levitt, T. (1969) *The Marketing Mode*, McGraw-Hill, N.Y.

Levitt, T. (1983) *The Marketing Imagination*, Free Press, N.Y.

Lewis, B.R., and Hawkesley, A.W. (1990) Gaining a Competitive Advantage in Fashion Retailing, *International Journal of Retail & Distribution Management*, 18(4), pp. 21-32.

Lipovetsky, G. (1994) *The Empire of Fashion: Dressing Modern Democracy*, Princeton University Press, NJ.

Lowson, B. (1998) *Quick Response for small and medium-sized enterprises: A feasibility study*, The Textile Institute, Manchester.

Lowson, B., King, R., and Hunter, A. (1999) *Quick Response: Managing supply chain to meet consumer demand*, John Wiley & Sons Ltd, N.Y.

Mahoney, J.T., and Pandian, J.R. (1992) The Resource-Based View Within the Conversation of Strategic Management, *Strategic Management Journal*, 13(5), pp. 363-380.

Malecki, E. (2000) Soft Variables in Regional Science, *Review of Regional Studies*, 30(1), pp. 61-69.

Mantle, J. (1999) *Benetton*, Little Brown, UK.

Maximov, J., and Gottschlich, H. (1993) Time-Cost-Quality Leadership, *International Journal of Retail & Distribution Management*, 21(4), pp. 3-12.

McCracken, G. (1985) The Trickle-Down Theory Rehabilitated, in Solomon, M.R. (ed) (1985) *The Psychology of Fashion*, Lexington Books, Lexington.

McCracken, G. (1990) *Culture & Consumption*, Indiana University Press, Bloomington and Indianapolis.

McDowell, C. (1992) *Dressed to Kill: Sex, Power, and Clothes*, Hutchinson, London.

McGee, J, and Johnson, G. (eds.) (1987) *Retail Strategies in the UK*, John Wisely & Sons Ltd, London.

Meijboom, B. (1999) Production-to-Order and International Operations: A Case Study in the Clothing Industry, *International Journal of Operations & Production Management*, 19(5/6), pp. 602-619.

Minami, C. (2003) Fashion Business no Ronri–ZARA ni Miru Speed no Keizai (The Logic in the Fashion Business–The Impact of Economies of Speed from ZARA experiences), *Ryutsu Kenkyu*, June, pp. 31-42.

Montgomery, C.A., and Wernerfelt, J.M. (1988) Diversification, Ricardian Rents and Tobin's Q, *Rand Journal of Economics*, 19, pp. 623-632.

Nukata, H. (1998) *Sangyo Shuseki ni Okeru Bungyo no Jyunansa* (Flexible Division of Labour in Industrial Agglomerations), in Itami, H., Matushima, S., and Kitsukawa, T. (eds.) (1998) *Sangyo Shuseki no Honshitsu* (The Essence of the Industrial Agglomeration), Yuhikaku, Tokyo.

Ogawa, H. (1998) *Italia no Chusho Kigyo* (SMEs in Italy), JETRO, Tokyo.

Ogawa, S. (2000-a) *Innovation no Hassei Genri* (The Process of Innovation), Chikura Shobo, Tokyo.

Ogawa, S. (2000-b) *Demand Chain Keiei* (Demand Chain Management), Nippon Keizai Shimbunsha, Tokyo.

Okamoto, Y. (1994) *Italia no Chusho Kigyo Senryaku* (SMEs' Strategies in Italy), Mita Shuppan Kai, Tokyo.

Pelham, A.J. (1997) Market Orientation and Performance: The Moderating Effects of Product and Customer Differentiation, *Journal of Business and Industrial Marketing*, 12(5), pp. 276-296.

Penrose, E.T. (1955) *The Theory of the Growth of the Firm*, John Wiley and Sons Ltd, N.Y.

Pine II, B.J. (1993) *Mass Customisation*, Harvard Business School Press, Boston, M.A.

Piore, M.J. (1994) Corporate Reform in American Manufacturing and the Challenge to Economic Theory, in Allen, T.J. and Scott Morton, M.S. (eds.) (1994) *Information Technology and the Corporation of the 1990s: Research Studies*, Oxford University Press, Cambridge, MA.

Piore, M.J. (2001) The Emergent Role of Social Intermediaries in the New Economy, *Annals of Public and Cooperative Economics*, 72(3), pp. 339-350.

Polhemus, T., and Proctor, L. (1978) *Fashion and Anti-Fashion: An Analogy of Clothing and Adornment*, Cox and Wyman, London.

Porter, M.E. (1985) *Competitive Advantage*, Free Press, N.Y.

Porter, M.E. (1996) What is Strategy? *Harvard Business Review*, 74, pp. 61-78.

Riddle, E.J., Bradbard, D.A., Thomas, J.B., and Kincade, D.H. (1999) The role of electronic data interchange in Quick Response, *Journal of Fashion Marketing and Management*, 3(2), pp. 133-146.

Robinson, D.E. (1958) Fashion Theory and Product Design, *Harvard Business Review*, 36 (Nov, Dec), pp. 126-138.

Rouse, E. (1989) *Understanding Fashion*, BSP Professional Books, London.

Rumelt, R.P. (1984) Towards a Strategic Theory of the Firm, in Lamb, R. (ed.) (1984) *Competitive Strategic Management*, Englewood Cliffs, Prentice Hall, N.J.

Schnaars, S.P. (1994) *Managing Imitation Strategies*, Free Press, N.Y.

Siguaw, J.S., Simpson, P., and Baker, T. (1998) Effects of supplier market orientation on distributor market orientation and the channel relationship, *Journal of Marketing*, Vol. 63, pp. 99-11.

Siguaw, J.S., Simpson, P., and Baker, T. (1999) The influence of market orientation on channel relationships: a dyadic examination, in Deshpande, R. (ed) (1999) *Developing a Market Orientation*, Sage, London.

Simmel, G. (1904) Fashion, *International Quarterly*, 10, pp. 130-155.

Simmel, G. (1971) Fashion, in Levine, D. (ed.) (1971) *On Individuality and Social Forms*, University of Chicago Press, London.

Slater, S, and Narver, J. (1995) Market Orientation and the Learning Organization, *Journal of Marketing*, Vol.59, pp. 63-74.

Slater, S.F., and Narver, J.C. (1999) Research Notes and Communications: Market-Oriented Is More than Being Customer-Led, *Strategic Management Journal*, 20, pp. 1165-1168.

Solomon, M.R., and Rabolt, N.J. (2004) *Consumer Behaviour in Fashion*, Prentice Hall, New Jersey.

Stalk, G.Jr. and Hout, T.M. (1990) *Competing against time*, Free Press, N.Y.

Stern, L, El-Ansary, A, and Coughalan, A. (1996) *Marketing Channels 5th Edition*, Prentice-Hall, Englewood Cliffs, NJ.

Takeishi, A. (2001) *Innovation no Pattern* (Patterns in Innovation) in Hitotsubashi University Innovation Research Centre (2001) *Innovation Management Nyumon* (Fundamentals of Innovation Management), Nihon Keizai Shimbunsha,Tokyo.

Tamura, M. (1975) *Seni Oroshiuri-Sho no Keiei Kouritsuka no Houkou–Seni Oroshiuri-Sho no Kinou Bunseki Houkoku (The Direction towards Textiles and Apparel Wholesalers' Efficient Management–An Analysis on the Function of Textiles and Apparel Wholesale Merchants)*, Osaka Chartered Institute of Commerce, Osaka.

Tamura, M. (1996) *Marketing Ryoku* (The Power of Marketing), Chikura Shobo, Tokyo.

Tamura, M. (2001) *Ryutsu Genri* (Principles of Marketing and Distribution), Chikura Shobo, Tokyo.

Tamura, M. (2003) *Shijoushikou no Jissen Riron wo Mezashite* (Towards an Operationalisation of the Market Orientation Approach), *Institute of Marketing and Distribution Science Monograph*, No. 15.

Teece, D. (1986) Profiting from Technological Innovation: Implications for Integration, Collaboration, Licensing and Public Policy, *Research Policy*, 15, pp. 285-305.

Tsujihara, Y. (2003) *Fukushiku no Rekishi wo Tadoru Sekaichizu (Tracing the History and the Origins of Costumes and Styles)*, Kawade Shobo Shinsha, Tokyo.

Veblen, T. (1953) *The Theory of Leisure Class: An Economic Study of Institutions*, Mentor, NY.

Veblen, T. (1992) *The Theory of the Leisure Class*, Transaction Publisher, New Brunswick and London.

Von Hippel, E.A. (1988) *The Sources of Innovation*, Oxford University Press, N.Y.

Weerawardena, J. (2003) Exploring the role of market learning capability in competitive advantage, *European Journal of Marketing*, 37(3/4), pp. 407-429.

Wilcox, C. (ed.) (2001) *Radical Fashion*, V&A Publications, London.

Williams, J. (1992) How Sustainable Is Your Advantage? *California Management Review*, 34, pp. 1-23.

Wilson, E. (1985) *Adorned in Dreams: Fashion and Modernity*, Virago, London.

White, L. (1982) The Automobile Industry, in Adams, W. (ed.) (1982) *The Structure of American Industry, 6th Edition*, MacMillan, N.Y.

Whiteoak, P. (1994) The realities of quick response in the grocery sector: A supplier viewpoint, *International Journal of Physical Distribution and Logistics Management*, 29(7/8), pp. 508-519.

Yahagi, T. (1994) *Convenience Store System no Kakushin-sei* (Innovativeness of the Convenience Store System), Nihon Keizai shimbunsha, Tokyo.

Yahagi, T. Ogawa, K., and Yoshida, K. (1993) *Sei-Han Tougo Marketing* (Supplier-Retailer Integrated Marketing Approach), Hakuto Shobo, Tokyo.

Yahagi, T. (2001) *Chain Store no Seiki ha Owattanoka* (Has the Chain Store Age Ended?), *Hitotsubashi Business Review*, August, pp. 30-43.

Yamashita, Y. (1993) *Shijo ni Okeru Ba no Kino* (The Role of '*Ba*' in the Market-place), *Soshiki Kagaku*, Vol. 27, No. 1, pp. 75-87.

Yamashita, Y. (1998) *Discounter no Seisui* (The Rise and Fall of Discount Stores), in Itami, H., Kagono, T., Miyamoto, M., and Yonekura, S. (eds.)(1998) *Innovation to Gijutsu Chikuseki (Innovation and Technology Accumulation)*, Yuhikaku, Tokyo.

Yamashita, Y. (2001) Shogyo Shuseki no Dynamism (The Dynamics of Commercial Accumulation), *Hitotsubashi Business Review*, August, pp. 74-94.

New Cultures, New Strategies, New Formats and New Relationships in European Retailing: Some Implications for Asia

John Dawson

SUMMARY. During the last fifteen years there has been a substantial re-structuring of retailing in Europe. The implications of this reach beyond Europe. The restructuring involves not only competitive relationships amongst retailers but also involves new forms of relationships with suppliers. A new perspective of the role of retailing is emerging that places retailing in a global framework of international store operations, international sourcing of products, international flows of management and managerial know-how, and international awareness by consumers of the retailers who are becoming international brands. The aim of this paper is to place the re-structuring in context, to consider the nature of it and to explore how the new global framework will begin to have effects for distribution industries in Asia.

The paper comprises five parts. First, as introduction, the new role of retailing is explored. Second, there is consideration of what is changing

John Dawson is Professor of Marketing, Management School, University of Edinburgh, William Robertson Building, 50 George Square, Edinburgh, EH8 9JY, Scotland; Distinguished Professor, UMDS, Kobe; and Visiting Professor, ESADE, Barcelona (E-mail: John.Dawson@ed.ac.uk).

[Haworth co-indexing entry note]: "New Cultures, New Strategies, New Formats and New Relationships in European Retailing: Some Implications for Asia." Dawson, John. Co-published simultaneously in *Journal of Global Marketing* (International Business Press, an imprint of The Haworth Press, Inc.) Vol. 18, No. 1/2, 2004, pp. 73-97; and: *International Retailing Plans and Strategies in Asia* (ed: John Dawson, and Jung-Hee Lee) International Business Press, an imprint of The Haworth Press, Inc., 2004, pp. 73-97. Single or multiple copies of this article are available for a fee from The Haworth Document Delivery Service [1-800-HAWORTH, 9:00 a.m. - 5:00 p.m. (EST). E-mail address: docdelivery@haworthpress.com].

in the retail sector of Europe. Third, some implications of the changes are explored. The fourth part is longer and considers why the changes are taking place. Finally, in the light of the changes in Europe, a conclusion considers the underpinning nature of innovation in the changes and the question is explored as to whether this European model will become more widely applicable, particularly in East Asia. *[Article copies available for a fee from The Haworth Document Delivery Service: 1-800-HAWORTH. E-mail address: <docdelivery@haworthpress.com> Website: <http://www. HaworthPress.com> © 2004 by The Haworth Press, Inc. All rights reserved.]*

KEYWORDS. Retail strategy, international retailing, retail innovation, Europe, retail branding

THE NEW ROLES OF RETAILING

This recent re-structuring into a global context is the most recent stage of a half a century of change in European retailing that can be seen as comprising three major phases. The first phase occurred during the years after 1945 when the priority for the retail sector was the reconstruction of both the organisational and physical structures of retailing. There was a strong American influence in managerial developments, for example the introduction of self-service into the food sector and also a number of American firms, for example JC Penny, entered Europe. City and town centres were reconstructed across much of northern Europe and retailing was used as a catalyst to prime the re-construction of the urban infrastructure. Consumers were seeking more products after the several years of scarcity.

The establishment of the "common market" in Western Europe and the subsequent development into a more integrated European Union marks a second phase. The retail markets across Europe consolidated and substantial growth occurred. Marketing became accepted as a core activity of retailers with different types of retailing being designed to satisfy different consumer needs. With market segmentation, so many types of retailers explored new formats. For example, the large self-service single level superstore format, often located on the edge or out-of-town, was developed through the 1970s and early 1980s in several sectors, notably the hypermarket for general merchandise, and, superstores for food, DIY, toys, electrical goods, furniture, etc. Consumers, during this second phase, wanted different products and better quality products rather than simply more products.

The third phase, which is the period of change presently evident, is characterised by a re-structuring of retailing with new roles and functions becoming evident. The convergence of information and communication technologies, the application of new materials, and other applications of technology across the value chain are enabling retailing to take on more forceful roles within the economy (Dawson 2001). Economies of scale of organisations associated with global sourcing and international operation of stores are allowing retailers to become some of the largest firms within Europe.

A number of retail firms based in Europe are amongst the largest in the world. In terms of sales in 2002, Carrefour, Tesco, ITM Enterprises (Intermarché) and Royal Ahold are in the largest ten retailers in the world. The large firms are increasingly international in both sourcing and operations. Carrefour in 2002 had store-based operations in 31 countries and was purchasing from over 55. Tesco with stores in 11 countries is less international at an operational level but is equally international in its sourcing. There are many consequences of the large scale and international activity of retailers. Some of the consequences for Asia of the internationalisation of operations have been explored in papers in Dawson, Mukoyama, Choi and Larke (2003). One aspect that has not been widely researched is the substantial influence on patterns of consumption that a few retail managers now have. This small cadre of managers is responsible for decisions on what products will be available in the stores. This relatively small group has a major effect on consumer choice and the changes taking place in patterns of consumption. The choices available to consumers are changing and as a result the choice processes that consumers use are also changing (Marshall 1995). These changes are affecting the shopping behaviours of consumers. This is one of several potential illustrations of the more active role that retailers now have within the overall economy.

During the 1990s the role of retailing within European Economies has changed. Retailing is undergoing a period of major re-structuring that is defining a distinctive European model of retailing and distribution (Costa et al. 1997; Eurostat 2000, 2002). This European model is emerging as different from that of the USA. It is a model that is internationalist, not domestic. It is structured around an integrated demand chain, not a supply chain. And, it has innovation, not copying, at its core. This stronger position of distribution generally is reflected in macro-economic statistics, for example in 2003 it is forecast that in the UK economy the value added by distribution industries will be greater than the value added by manufacturing. The gap between these two has been closing steadily since the early 1990s when the value added contribution of manufacturing was twice that of distribution. Table 1 shows some of the relative changes between manufacturing and distribution in the UK through the 1990s. The substantial increase in labour productivity in distribution is seen with a large increase in value added with a much smaller increase in labour input. This pattern is repeated across much of Europe.

WHAT IS CHANGING?

Within the managerial processes of the retail sector there are substantial changes that are associated with the overall re-structuring that is taking place. Four are particularly apparent:

- The large firms are growing faster than the sector as a whole. Despite low growth in the European economies in recent years the large firms have been able to increase their output through entering new markets, diversifying their retail offer, acquisition and, importantly, like-for-like sales growth. Table 2 shows for the largest firms their 5 year growth. Leading companies in other more specialist sectors show comparable strong growth. For example, Zara, IKEA, Douglas, H&M, Schlecker and others have all outperformed the market to a considerable extent. The speed of growth has quickened in many of the large firms. For example through the early 1990s Carrefour was opening fewer than 20 stores per year but by 1999 was opening more than 50 per year. The result has been that by 2001 over 20% of the hypermarkets operated by Carrefour did not exist three years previously. Marionnaud provides a similar example in small perfumery stores having grown from a single store in 1984 to have over 1,200 stores across 13 countries by late 2003. Growth has been most rapid from 2000 since when shop numbers have doubled. Similarly sales growth has doubled from 502 million € in 2000 to 1,047 million € in 2003.
- Across the sector in the large and medium sized firms a strategic approach to management has been adopted more consistently. Strategies vary considerably from firm to firm but there is a wider presence of a general business strategy that is then made operational through functional strategies for marketing, merchandising, buying, branding, branding, logistics, employees, finance, etc.

- With the new role of retailing and the size of firm so the organisational structures have become more complex. The expansion of international operations, for example, has required retailers to develop a structure of country "vice-presidents" and in several cases an international Board of Directors. As international expansion has occurred so new types of ownership have been added to the organisational structure of firms, with often joint-venture arrangements and franchises being introduced into firms that previously had only company owned stores. At store level the international moves have required different organisational structures in different countries in order to respond to the different consumer cultures. It was only in 1993 that Tesco began to operate stores outside the UK in a way that required a different organisational structure to be devised. Table 3 shows the international expansion of Tesco within 10 years. This network of stores now requires a very different organisation than that needed to manage only UK stores in 1993. It is not only international operations that require a more complex organisational structure to the firm. International sourcing centres have to be accommodated in organisations. The outsourcing of many previously in-sourced functions also changes organisations. The diversification of retailers into financial and leisure services provides further organisational complexities.

- In recent years it is also evident that the nature of the value chain within the successful retailers has changed substantially. Retailers have become increasing involved in co-ordinating the relationships between retailers and suppliers. Thus value is created at a variety of places in the value chain, not simply at the point of final sale to the customer. In taking costs out of the channel of distribution there is a redistribution of the locus of value generation. An example of this is in the terms of trade that exist between retailers and suppliers such that a retailer's inventory is financed by suppliers. By providing a longer number of credit days than the inventory turn of the retailer, the retailer operates with negative working capital. Table 4 illustrates the degree of negative working capital enjoyed by three large European retailers. Table 5 illustrates for large French retailers and manufacturers the relative balance between current liabilities and current assets, in effect the working capital. From this it can be seen that for retailers the balance changed in 1994 to generate negative working capital but

manufacturing firms still have to find the working capital themselves.

These four changes illustrate the nature of the changes taking place in European retailing during this third and current phase of major re-structuring. They are clearly inter-related with the focus on strategy underpinning the rapid growth of the large firms and the change in financial relationships with suppliers. The four changes are illustrative of the totality of change and changes could be highlighted. Nonetheless the conclusion that can be drawn is that the current phase of re-structuring is meaning an increase in the complexity of the sector, a quickening in the rate of change and a more global perspective being adopted by management.

TABLE 1. Comparison of Manufacturing and Distribution Within the UK Economy

	Value added £bn			Net capital expenditure £bn			Employment million: average during year	
	1995	1998	2001	1995	1998	2001	1998	2001
Manufacturing	140	150	145	18.1	20.4	16.3	4.4	4.0
Distribution	75	107	126	9.3	12.5	12.1	4.7	4.9

Source: Office of National Statistics, Annual Business Inquiry.

TABLE 2. Sales and Operations of Selected Large European Based Grocery and General Merchandise Retailers

Retailer	Sales € mill fy 2002-3	5 year growth		Number of	
		sales	Profit	shops	countries
Carrefour	68,729	151	146	9,632	32
Metro	51,526	10	81	2,307	26
Tesco	37,358	54	56	2,291	11
Rewe	37,430	25		7,801	12
Edeka	34,200	9		10,490	6
Aldi	29,800	17		6,607	12
Auchan	27,600	31		1,133	14
Casino	22,857	62	98	8,377	13

Source: Company data.

TABLE 3. The Store Network of Tesco in 2003 and Planned Expansion for 2003-4

	End fy 2002-3 Actual		End fy 2003-4 Estimate		Net change inc. closures	
	Store number	Sales area '000 sq. ft	Store number	Sales area '000 sq. ft	Store number	Sales area '000 sq. ft
UK	1,981[1]	21,829[1]	2,023	22,870	42	1,041
Ireland	77	1,703	80	1,841	3	138
Poland	66	3,351	71	3,672	5	321
Hungary	53	2,469	58	2,836	5	367
Czech Republic	17	1,608	21	1,921	4	313
Slovakia	17	1,379	21	1,595	4	216
France	1	16	1	16	0	0
Thailand	52	4,820	58	5,368	6	548
South Korea	21	2,125	29	2,980	8	855
Malaysia	3	316	4	423	1	107
Taiwan	3	329	4	383	1	54
Total	2,291	39,944	2,370	43,905	79	3,961
Japan			81			

[1] Includes 1,202 stores with total sales area of approximately 1,830,000 sq. ft associated with the acquisition of T&S stores during the fiscal year

Source: Tesco company information

TABLE 4. Key Operating Ratios of Carrefour, Sainsbury and Tesco

	Inventory as a percentage of sales		Working capital as percentage of sales		Percentage return on capital employed	
	2002	1999	2002	1999	2002	1999
Carrefour	8.7	13.2	−9.5	−13.5	10.0	11.0
Sainsbury	5.3	5.3	−6.1	−6.1	9.6	10.8
Tesco	3.9	3.4	−8.8	−9.4	14.7	15.5
Casino	8.5	8.9	−4.2	−8.2	13.5	11.6

TABLE 5. Current Assets and Current Liabilities as Percentage of Sales for Large Firms in France

	Retailing		Manufacturing	
	Current assets	Current liabilities	Current assets	Current liabilities
2001	47.4	53.62	56.11	40.63
2000	48.93	52.61	57.1	40.83
1999	51.68	61.12	55.15	39.14
1998	50.8	55.1	54.91	37.51
1997	46.56	51.44	58.88	38.3
1996	39.4	44.13	56.69	38.01
1995	50.39	54.22	58.25	40.19
1994	52.11	55.2	56.31	38.73
1993	54.43	52.78	55.95	37.82
1992	51.48	51.22	57.28	37.88
1991	58.49	50.74	57.83	38.76
1990	56.44	52.72	58.72	39.7
1989	63.89	57.84	61.38	41.76
1988	64.07	55.11	65	45.02
1987	57.54	51.6	66.54	47.01
1986	61.4	57.55	67.82	48.57
1985	61.85	59.25	66.75	48.69
1984	63.11	59.44	67.56	50.98

Source: Bach database

THE IMPLICATIONS OF THE CHANGES

There are many implications of the changes in the role and structure of the retail sector across Europe. A major implication is an increased level of governmental intervention in retailing. The involvement of government results from several different aspects of the structural change that is underway. Four particular implications of change give rise to governmental intervention at various levels across Europe.

- *The increase in market concentration.* With the growth of already large firms and their acquisition activity, the competition agencies in individual European countries and in the European Commission have become more active in reviewing levels of market concentration (Rey and Caballero-Sanz 1996; Dobson and Waterson 1999; Clarke, Davies, Dobson and Waterson 2002). In the UK the inquiry in 2003 by the Competition Commission into the proposed acquisition of Safeway by others in the grocery sector highlighted the problems of defining the market for the purposes of measuring market concentration (Competition Commission 2003). In some cases competition authorities are now considering the competitive impacts of the acquisition of a single store by a large retailer when this is thought to have an effect of reducing potential competition at the local market level. Although there are many unresolved issues associated with measurement of market shares, particularly at local levels, nonetheless governments increasingly are involved in market interventions.

- *The decrease in the number of small and micro firms.* An aspect of long term structural change has been the decline of small firms in retailing across Europe. This loss of small firms has become more acute in recent years such that governments have been exploring ways to provide support to smaller firms through different types of policy initiative. These include limiting the local competition from large firms by restricting the establishment of new shops, providing direct financial help to the small firms to encourage investment and training, reducing the tax burdens on small firms, encouraging co-operative behaviour amongst small firms, and providing special protection to particular sub-sectors, for example pharmacists and small firms in rural areas and in the lowest income parts of cities. Governmental intervention in the market in these cases is aimed at protecting smaller firms from the full rigour of the market.

- *The change in the balance of competitive power between retailers and their suppliers.* An implication of the changes in retailing is the growth of channel power of retailers at the expense of their suppliers (Pilat 1997; Wileman and Jary 1997; OECD 1998; Competition Commission 2000; Burt and Sparks 2003). Again governments have sought to intervene in the market to regulate the behaviour of the participants in the channel. This has involved policies on the nature of the contracts between retailers and suppliers, the number of credit days allowed, the types of discount that can be used, the ability of retailers to re-sell products at below cost, etc. (London Economics 1997). Some governments, for example in Poland,

have even tried to introduce legislation to limit the amount of retailer branded goods a retailer may sell.

- *The increased international activity of retailers.* In some European
countries, most notably those in central Europe that attracted large
amounts of foreign direct investment into retailing after 1989, the
governments have been adopting policies to limit foreign ownership of retailing. The rationale for such policies is to protect local
retailers and suppliers from the business practices used by the foreign, often large, firms. Those foreign retailers that have a presence in the market, having entered early, are in effect protected
from peer-group competition and so may benefit from the policies
aimed at limiting them. In Europe outside the European Union,
governments have intervened increasingly in the market to increase the barriers to entry and influence the performance of foreign firms.

The extent of and types of intervention of governments in the retail
markets is generally increasing in Europe. The rationale for intervention
is generally to ameliorate, in some way, the consequences of the structural changes in the sector. In many cases the policies are instituted
without a clear understanding of the nature of the causes of the structural changes that generate the "undesirable" change but there is growing awareness of the complexity of the distributive trade in respect of
the vertical relationships involved (Pickering 1999).

WHY IS RETAILING CHANGING?

The reasons for the structural adjustments in this third current phase
of major change in European retailing can be presented as a process
linking changes in the environment to responses by retail managers. Retailing, as an activity linking consumers to goods and services, operates
in local markets. As such many of the managerial decisions are a response to both the local culture of the consumers and the local culture of
consumption. Within Europe these local *cultures* are subject to considerable social, economic, political and technological changes. This dynamic cultural environment requires responses from retailers that seek
success through the close matching of their operations to consumer requirements. These responses underpin the *strategies* of retailers. The
strategies are executed through the *formats and formulae*[2] that the retailer creates. In creating these formats and formulae the retailer enters

into *relationships* with other groups, for example suppliers, finance groups, consumers, etc. In the current context of activity in Europe all four of these attributes of the retail sector–*cultures, strategies, formats and formulae, and relationships*–are undergoing substantial change as they interact. It is the changes in these attributes that provide the reasons why retailing is changing in the ways that it is. In order to gain this understanding of the reasons for the changes in retailing it is useful to consider some of the important changes in each of these four attributes of retailing.

Culture

The changes in consumer culture in Europe after 1989 have been considerable. The emergence of market economies in central Europe meant the widespread privatisation of retailing. Perhaps of greater importance in terms of consumer culture, however, has been the increased demand for products and services from consumers in the former communist countries. Steady increases in consumer wealth after the initial periods of high inflation have meant that from the mid-1990s consumers have expected a more extensive range of price-quality combinations in the retailing that is available to them. In clothing for example distinct markets in street fashion, work clothes, high fashion, discount apparel, etc., have emerged very quickly to parallel the market structures that have been developed, more gradually, in West Europe (Retail Forward 2003a; b). As these countries enter fully into the European Community, from May 2004, so these cultures of consumption will develop even more rapidly. In many cases it is the retailers of the 1990s that have created the form of the cultures of consumption in the Central European countries.

Across much of Western Europe consumer cultures show apparent contradictory trends of standardisation and fragmentation. The fragmentation of demand is evident in many ways with ever smaller segments of consumers having specific patterns of demand. Consumers have translated their values into demands for goods and services such that there are many differing set of values, for example the ecologically responsive groups, vegetarian groups, designer brand groups, sport obsessed groups, etc. These are in addition to the longer established groups associated with age, educational level, income, etc. This fragmentation has been encouraged by specialist media aimed at specialist groups. The fragmentation has been extended even further with consumer demands varying on a temporal dimension–by time of day or day of the week. The consumer can no longer be considered as one person but has to be viewed as many different "people" (Ziliani 1999; Ziliani and Bellini 2004).

In apparent contradiction to this fragmentation is a Europeanisation of some aspects of consumer demand. With the wide and faster availability of information through satellite communication, the rapid diffusion of fashion, in clothes and music particularly, has generated European-wide patterns of demand. The movement of people through Europe particularly for leisure and tourism has similarly generated a diffusion of cultures, often in food items, such that consumers in Northern Europe become familiar with foods from the South and vice-versa. The availability of the international manufacturer brands, in electrical items, food and grocery, toys, etc., further stimulates this move to "sameness" or "Europeanisation."

This reinforcement of aspects of a "European" consumer culture exists alongside an increase in regional and ethnic identities that also affects consumer culture. There is in many parts of Europe a resurgence of interest in local environments and cultures particularly with the demand for local foods and local designs for fabrics and furnishings. The presence of more immigrant groups from outside Europe has also encouraged this change of consumption with these groups bringing their own cultures into Europe. These cultural groups with their own particular demands and behaviours have influenced the operation of many types of retailing.

Again as a counter-trend to these local cultures is the euro-integration of consumer infrastructures (Colla 2004). This is often facilitated by common technologies in the home or mobile "close to body" technologies (mobile phones, pocket computers, hand-held games machines, etc.). The driving force for much of this integration is a combination of the aspirations European politicians and multi-national manufacturers. Many European politicians have a vision of the future as a single and more standardised European market. Multi-national manufacturers wish to exploit economies of scale by producing goods for a large standard market.

The interplay of the opposing forces of Europeanisation and of fragmentation of consumer cultures presents European retailers with a dilemma. In strategic terms does a retailer provide specialist solutions to meet local needs and try to benefit from local economies of scope or does the retailer exploit the economies of scale that become available in addressing European-wide trends? Is it possible to develop a strategy to address both the fragmentation of demand and the Europeanisation of demand? The resolution of this dilemma has encouraged retailers to explore new approaches to strategy.

Strategy

The approach adopted to address the strategic dilemma resulting from the changes in culture is to move away from the traditional Porter approach to strategy that has an approach of either low cost or high service. Retailers have approached strategy by having a wider perspective that considers co-operation and competition both in a vertical dimension through the distribution channel and horizontally with other retailers. There is a presumption of vertical co-ordination to increase horizontal competitive ability but this basic model is subject to several detailed interpretations from firm to firm (Reynolds and Cuthbertson 2003). A much greater emphasis is placed on innovation and the generation of knowledge as the key inputs into the development of the strategy such that firms reject the idea of a 'generic' strategy and seek ones that are appropriate to their own knowledge base (Dawson 2001) and are flexible enough to accommodate the localisation-standardisation dilemma.

There are several results of this new approach. Four serve to illustrate the point:

- *Branding has become controlled by the retailer.* The stores have become brands, for example IKEA, Zara, Dia, Pimkie, Aldi and B&Q. Alongside the branding of the store the retailers have also taken control of the branding of merchandise. Individual firms have adopted different strategies to the branding of merchandise. Some use the name of the firm, some have developed different brands for different merchandise categories and other have developed different brands for different market positions (Laaksonen and Reynolds 1994). Although the implementation varies from firm to firm the rationale for the strategy is similar (Burt 2000). By controlling the brand offering inside the store it is possible to co-ordinate the merchandise brands and the store brand to make the total marketing effort more effective. Tesco, for example, has increased the share of Tesco branded merchandise in its UK stores with over 40% of grocery sales in Tesco brand and a steadily increasing amount of Tesco controlled brands in non-foods. Table 6 shows the different market positions of the Tesco brand merchandise in the UK. Within the food sector there are three market positions and two specialist markets being addressed. The third specialist market of children's healthy food is now being developed. The three market positions for Tesco branded products are being extended into non-food categories with an additional clothing brand "Cherokee" being used and the Tesco Finest brand being extended to clothing in 2003. The approach to branding has become considerably more strategic than was the case 15 years ago when retail brands were seen as low price copies of manufacturer items.

- *A wider perspective on productivity.* A more integrated view of the productivity of assets has begun to emerge in the new strategic approaches. The traditional view was of productivity being related to employees and floorspace with sales per employee and sales per square foot being the key metrics (Dawson 2000). In the new strategic approaches not only are these two traditional input measures disaggregated, for example productivity of checkout employee per hour, shelf-space productivity per cubic foot, but new assets are considered. The productivity of customers, of suppliers, of in-store services (for example in-store bakeries, clothing adjustment and coffee shops), of promotions, and of brands, are now considered and attempts made to develop a more integrated view of productivity of the firm.

- *Identification of the profit sources in the value chain.* With a more strategic approach to considerations of productivity so there has been greater awareness of the nature of the value chain in retailing. This has resulted in shifts in the balance between out-sourced and in-sourced functions. Retailers have evaluated the functions they undertake and established which generate value added to the retailer in respect of specific knowledge owned by the retailer. These they have retained as in-sourced. Thus, for example, merchandising has been concentrated inside retailers. Where value added is less in relation to the retailer's knowledge then the functions have been outsourced with contracts made with specialist groups. This is the situation with most logistics activities.

- *Consideration of new markets.* The ability to respond to the new cultures of consumption has encouraged European retailers to move into new markets in their home country and also to become more international in their operations. In their home countries there has been category diversification with food retailers moving into non-food categories. Clothing retailers have moved into new categories of home-wares. In many cases the large retailers have moved into other service retailing sectors and provide financial services, household services, etc. Movement into new international markets has been extensive in all the large and successful retailers. Table 7 shows the development of hypermarkets by four major firms. In all four cases they have moved into Central Europe and Asia and considerable more expansion is expected in these markets. It is not only large firms that have sought to expand internationally. Mintel (2003) identified 2,588 intra-European cross-border retailers operating 74,160 stores in 2002. This represents approximately two-thirds of all cross-border retail operations by European based retailers. The remaining third involves extra-European moves. The clothing sector is most active with 51% of intra-European moves being accounted for by this sector. French firms are the most active in this respect.

Formats and Formulae

The new strategies of European retailers are executed through formats and formulae. Retailers continually adjust their formulae to meet the needs of consumers and to expand the customer base. Most of the formats have been present for many years and the adjustments and innovations are introduced through formula development. In recent years the only major new format has been the Internet web page but new formats have been introduced into countries where they were previously absent. The countries of central Europe, for example, had no hypermar-

TABLE 6. Tesco's Policy for Tesco Branded Merchandise

Brand	Launch date	Market position and target	Number Skus	Extension	
				Non-foods	International
Tesco Value	1993	Discount	1,200	2001	C. Europe, Taiwan Thailand, Malaysia
Tesco	1924	Mid-market	8,000		All markets
Tesco Finest	1998	Premium	1,100	2002	Poland
Tesco Organics	1998	Organic	1,000		
Tesco Healthy Living	1985	Additive free	600	2003	
Tesco Kids	2002	Improved diets	100		
Florence and Fred	2001	Office clothing			
Cherokee	2002	Mid-price fashion clothes			

TABLE 7. International Expansion of Hypermarket Operations by Four Leading Firms

Central Europe	2001	2002	2003 [estimate]	2005 [forecast]
Auchan	19	24	34	46
Carrefour	20	25	28	33
Casino	15	15	16	16
Tesco	52	83	101	115
Asia				
Auchan	33	53	59	76
Carrefour	108	126	157	200
Casino	41	56	62	70
Tesco	50	69	85	110

Sources: Company data.

kets until the early 1990s. New formulae are more common with retailers creating formulae to target particular groups. Ahold for example has developed a new formulae supermarket, hypermarket and convenience store.

All three are in The Netherlands but influence developments elsewhere. The World of Worlds formula for a large supermarket was initiated in 1997 and five were developed over the following 4 years. The concept is for product offerings to radiate from a central space (L'Aventure) that contains a café, various delicatessen ranges, fresh juices, patisserie and prepared meals, that can be eaten in the café or taken away. Several service counters surround this central space. From this central area, sections focusing on convenience, discount and dry grocery radiate so allowing the customer to "mix and match" across different needs including discount, congruent priced and premium products. The grocery section is organised by meal type rather than by more traditional categories. The discount section was included in the first experimental store and was then dropped in later versions of the formula. There is a strong branding of Albert Heijn across the 25,000 items in the overall range. A specialist wine shop is provided within the store. A range of customer services are provided including self-scanning and demonstrations of food and meal preparation.

The second new formula is the Albert Heijn XL hypermarket. This opened in February 2002 as a conversion of an older hypermarket in

Kronenburg Centre in Arnhem. The store is 4,000 sq. m. and as with the new supermarket involves an innovative layout. The store is divided into six zones termed: escape, indulge, well-being, fresh, eat and inspire. In each zone there is a focal point, for example a fresh juice bar in the fresh zone, Internet café in the escape zone, a health and beauty adviser in the well-being zone. The aim is to allow some customers to shop quickly, for example groceries are merchandised by meal type and a meal solutions offer and other quick service counters are close to the entrance, whilst other customers can browse in the non-food areas without feeling pressured by those who wish to shop more quickly.

The third formula is "AH to go." This is a convenience store formula designed to be located at petrol filling stations, in hospitals, at railway stations and in town centres. A joint venture with Shell in 1996 had the potential for convenience stores across the 300 Shell petrol stations in the Netherlands but development was slow and the joint venture failed in 2000 with Shell wishing to develop its own Shell Select formula. This also allowed Ahold to develop a convenience store format with over 30 stores in operation by early 2003. The AH to go stores at petrol filling stations are in a new joint venture with Esso who has 350 sites across The Netherlands. Stores are between 100 and 250 sq. m. Two main ranges are provided. One is termed "Nice for now" and the second "Nice for later"

The World of Worlds supermarket formula has been influential in changes made to the standard Albert Heijn supermarket and in the concept of the XL hypermarket but it has not been widely used. The XL hypermarket appears to have been more successful and it is planned to develop up to 50 in the Dutch market by 2006. The AH to go formula is planned for rapid development with over 50 per year being planned until at least 2005.

Tesco has moved strongly in the area of formula design over the last 5 years moving from branding the items for sale to branding their store formulae. In their operations within the UK, Tesco operate several formats, all of which are strongly branded as Tesco, generating the specific formulae of:

- Tesco Extra–a hypermarket format.
- Tesco Superstore–a large dominantly food store but with some non-food items.
- Tesco Supermarket–a standard supermarket format.
- Tesco Compact–a smaller supermarket suitable for smaller communities.
- Tesco Metro–a city centre supermarket targeted at walk in customers.

- Tesco Express–a convenience store format.
- Tesco.com–an Internet format.

Tesco Express has been the most dynamic of the formats in recent years with organic development of the concept in 2000. On average there are approximately 2,500 merchandise lines, many of which are Tesco branded items. Subsequent acquisitions in 2002 and 2004 have expanded the chain to over a thousand local stores that will be converted to the Tesco Express format. Tesco Express, typically 1,500-3,000 sq. ft. of floorspace, began as a convenience store at a petrol filling station but has evolved to be convenience store with the majority of customers buying food and not petrol. Average sales in 2002 were €85,000 per week-four times higher than the sector average–with break-even profitability in the stores being achieved at approximately €45,000 per week.

The common feature of these new formats, not only in the food area but also amongst non-food, including clothing, retailers, is the concept of *"experience space."* Thus formula design has moved beyond the traditional variables associated with the marketing mix to create stores in which the customer is more involved. Customers help with the value creation exercise by being part of the formula. In this approach to the design of the formula there is process of value creation, as shown in Figure 1:

- The retailer's idea of the *formula* triggers an experience for the customer.
- The formula has *content* and differences in content trigger different experiences. This content is, in effect, the retailer's execution of the formula.
- The *involvement* of the customer with the content adds to the experience for the customer.
- This *personalisation* of the customer's experience and feelings results in the in-store decisions of the customer.
- These personal interpretations *co-create value* between customer and retailer.

The characteristic of the successful retailer is that the mutual experience of the innovation by the consumer and retailer provides a feedback loop into the retailer's formula design process (Hetzel, 2000; Lemoine 2002). This idea of "experience innovation" will be returned to later.

The involvement of the customer in this way by trying to co-create an experience and by involving the customer much more in the shopping activity has moved the design of formulae into new areas (Ritzer 1999;

FIGURE 1. The Concept of Co-Creation of Value with Formula Development (based on Prahalad and Ramaswamy, 2003)

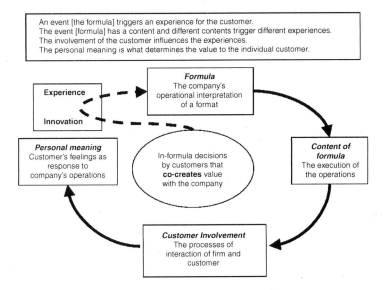

Shedroff 2001). The initial approach of 10 or more years ago was to focus on the supply chain and any innovation was in terms of traditional ideas of product. Innovation was in "product space." The customer was provided with what the retailer believed they should have. The next phase was a focus on cost control in formulae design through systems integration. More efficient supply networks were generated by innovations in "solution space." The customer was not involved but was provided with a very efficient formula in which to shop. The move into the new phase of "experience space" involves the customer in the co-creation of value and extends the design ideas to include personalisation of the experience. Figure 2 illustrates the evolution for product space to innovation space in this context.

Relationships

The final underpinning reason for success in European retailers is the development of new relationships with other groups. Whilst the changes in culture, strategy and format are important individually they interact thorough the relationships of the retailer with customers, suppliers, em-

FIGURE 2. The Concept of Experience Space Applied to Formula Design (based on Prahalad and Ramaswamy, 2003)

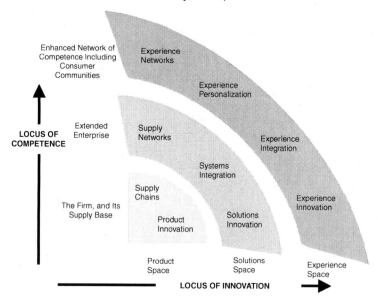

ployees and government. Some examples of these new relationships that are now actively managed by retailers are:

- Customer loyalty and reward systems (Pearson 1994; Sopanan 1996; Rayner 1996). Humby, Hunt and Phillips (2003) explain how the Tesco loyalty card changed the nature of the relationship between Tesco and its customers.
- Supplier links through global sourcing arrangements (Hughes 1999; Coopers and Lybrand 1996; GEA 1994).
- Co-operative brand development with suppliers (Nooteboom 1999).
- Team based performance related pay for employees often associated with a distinction between the knowledge workers and sales workers in the firm.
- Joint initiatives with government to increase productivity in retailing.

CONCLUSION

It has been argued in this paper that the retail sector in Europe retailing has been undergoing, since the early 1990s, a period of intense re-structuring. The reasons for this restructuring lie in the changes in the culture of consumption in Europe, in the resulting strategies of the retail firms, in the formats and formulae that have been developed and in the relationships that the retailers have generated with various other agents in the distribution channel. Implicit in these changes is the highly dynamic nature of retailing. Retailers have been attempting to compete by changing their operations. Innovation has been critical to retailer success in this regard. Retailers have moved from traditional forms of innovation to undertake "experience" innovation. Figure 3 illustrates the differences between traditional product or process based innovation and the approach through experience innovation.

   This key importance of experience innovation is in it acting as a catalyst for growth by retailers who are operating in mature economies with little increase in consumer spending. The innovation enables the growth in productivity that retailers then use as the basis for obtaining more control over activity in the channel and also undertaking marketing initiatives to provide better experiences for customers. Both routes facilitate increases in sales at a rate greater than growth in the overall economy. This growth in sales as a result of innovation is illustrated in Figure 4.

FIGURE 3. The Differences Between Traditional and Experience Based Innovation (based on Prahalad and Ramaswamy, 2003)

	Traditional Innovation	Experience Innovation
Focus of Innovation	Products and processes	Experience environments–formula and relationships
Basis of value	Products and services	Co-creation of environment with customers, retailer and suppliers
Nature of value creation	Firm creates value	Value is co-created
	Supply-chain-centric fulfillment of products and services	Experience environments for individuals to co-construct experiences in situations
	Supply push and demand pull	Individual-centric co-creation of value
Function of technology	Facilitator of features and functions	Facilitator of experiences
	Technology and systems integration	Experience integration
Function of supply chain	Supports fulfillment of products and services	Experience network supports co-construction of personalised experiences

FIGURE 4. The Links from Experience Innovation to Increased Retail Sales (Dawson 2001)

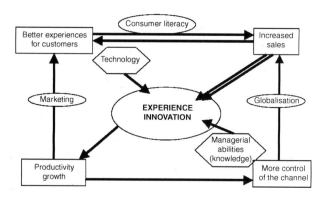

From this view of changes in Europe what implications may be drawn for future developments in Asia?

First, it is important to recognise that the European retailers who have developed these new approaches are expanding into the countries of East Asia. They are bringing with them their new approaches to strategy, formats and relationships. It is these new approaches that are designed to enable them to respond to new cultures of consumption. They have been very successful in enabling internationalisation within Europe and so they will use these new approaches to gain market share in the new markets that they enter in East Asia. The successful moves from Western to Central Europe and subsequent changes in consumer culture and retail structure resulting from foreign retailer activity illustrate the scale and scope of change that may take place as large European retailers move into Asian societies.

Second, the forms of innovation that are proving so powerful are ones that draw on the knowledge that exists inside the firm (Pontiggia and Sinatra 1997). This is not copying the activity of others but is using the knowledge that resides in the firm. This requires an organisational structure and culture for the retail firm that facilitates the harnessing of the knowledge in the firm. Competition depends on constant innovation that uses this knowledge. That the knowledge resides in the firm is important because the consequence is that different firms will have different impacts on the societies into which they move. Furthermore, the nature of the changes resulting from foreign retailer entry is controlled by the retailer and the knowledge they choose to transfer to the new market.

Third, the issues of the retailer control of brands and formats and formulae are central to the approach described and to the successful operation of the new entrant western retailers to Asia. Developments in Asia are likely to result in even greater control being exerted by retailers over brands. The nature of the relationships between entrant foreign retailers and local suppliers will be very different from the existing relationships these suppliers have with retailers. Many of the decisions traditionally taken by suppliers will be removed from the decision set of suppliers and transferred to the decision set of the foreign retailer. Although this shift in decision making will not occur immediately on entry by the foreign retailer, nonetheless the nature of the business model used by the large European retailers is such that the locus of decision making will change in favour of these foreign firms. The new roles for retailing in Europe that were discussed at the start of this paper will be transferred steadily to the Asian countries where European retailers operate.

Fourth, for Asian based firms to compete with the new entrants from Europe will require them to look beyond the traditional issues of price and service and to explore the ideas of "experience space" and "experience innovation." This will mean involving consumers much more in the shopping "experience" so that profit is co-created with relationships being of profit to the customer and to the retailer. The passive view of customers as agents for transactions, even sometimes for exploitation, will not be appropriate for retailers in the future. This will be a major change in the business model being used by the domestic retailers and changing this model will require some major changes in managerial knowledge and adaptability. Some local retailers will find this change beyond their capability and are likely to fail. Others will respond and themselves generate new innovative ways to compete that are grounded in the local knowledge they have of consumer culture. It is these adaptive and innovative local retailers who will provide the strongest competition to the foreign retail entrants.

Not all European retailers either are or will be successful in applying the new paradigms not only in Europe but also in Asia. Already we are seeing those that are able to apply them are gaining market share and profitability. Others, even large retailers, who are not able to operate under the new paradigms are failing. The same will be true in Asia. Not all Asian retailers will be able to apply these paradigms but those that do are more likely to compete successfully with the influx of foreign retailers.

NOTES

1. Tesco entered Ireland in 1978 but withdrew in 1986. The UK organisational structure was simply extended to Ireland and this is often quoted as one of the reasons for failure of the international venture. The move into France in 1993, with withdrawal in 1997, is generally regarded as the first move in the current strategy of internationalisation.

2. The formats are the generic delivery vehicles of retailers, for example, hypermarket, department store, convenience store, mail order catalogue, vending machine, etc. The formula is the branded version of the format that is created by a particular firm. Thus, a hypermarket is the format and the Tesco hypermarket, Casino hypermarket, Carrefour hypermarket, and Real hypermarket are the different formulae.

REFERENCES

Burt, S (2000) The strategic role of retail brands in British grocery retailing. *European Journal of Marketing*, 34, 875-890

Burt, S and Sparks, L (2003) Power and competition in the UK grocery market. *British Journal of Management*, 14, 237-254

Clarke, R, Davies, S, Dobson, P and Waterson, M (2002) *Buyer power and competition in European food retailing.* Edward Elgar: Cheltenham

Colla, E (2004) The outlook for European retailing. *International Review of Retail, Distribution and Consumer Research*, 14(1), in press

Competition Commission (2000) *Supermarkets: A report on the supply of groceries from multiple stores in the United Kingdom.* Stationery Office: London

Competition Commission (2003) *Safeway plc and Asda Group Limited (owned by Wal-Mart Stores Inc); Wm Morrison Supermarkets PLC; J Sainsbury plc; and Tesco plc: A report on the mergers in contemplation.* Stationery Office: London

Coopers and Lybrand (1996) *European value chain analysis study.* ECR Europe: Utrecht

Costa, C et al. (1997) *Structures and trends in the distributive trades in the European Union.* Ifo Institut: Munich

Dawson, J (2000) Employment and competitiveness. In: European Commission, *Commerce 99.* Office for Official Publications of European Communities: Luxembourg, 43-54

Dawson, J (2001) Is there a new commerce in Europe? *International Review of Retail, Distribution and Consumer Research*, 11(3), 287-299

Dawson, J, Mukoyama, M, Choi, S C and Larke, R (2003) *The internationalisation of retailing in Asia.* Routledge-Curzon: London

Dobson, P and Waterson, M (1999) Retailer power: recent developments and policy implications. *Economic Policy*, 28 (April), 135-164

Eurostat (2000) *Commerce 99–Proceedings of the Seminar on Distributive Trades in Europe.* Eurostat: Luxembourg

Eurostat (2002) *Distributive Trades in Europe 1995-1999.* Data CD Eurostat: Luxembourg

GEA (1994) *Supplier-retailer collaboration in supply chain management.* Coca-Cola Retailing Research Group-Europe: London

Hetzel, P (2000) Les approaches socio-sémiotiques du design d'environnement des lieux de distribution postmodernes. In P. Volle (ed.) *Etudes et Recherches sur la Distribution*. Economica: Paris. 145-165

Hughes, A (1999) Constructing competitive spaces: The corporate practice of British retailer-supplier relationships. *Environment and Planning*, A31, 819-839

Humby, C, Hunt, T and Phillips, T (2003) *Scoring points: How Tesco is winning customer loyalty*. Kogan Page: London

Laaksonen, H and Reynolds, J (1994) Own brands in food retailing across Europe. *Journal of Brand Management*, 2(1), 37-46

Lemoine, J F (2002) Perceptions de l'atmosphère du point de vente et rèactions comportemwntales et émotionnelles du consommateur. Paper presented at 5th Colloquium Etienne Thil: La Rochelle

London Economics (1997) Competition in Retailing. *Office of Fair Trading, Research Paper*, 13

Marshall, D W (1995) [editor] *Food choice and the consumer*. Blackie: London

Mintel (2003) Cross border retailing. *European Retail Briefing*, 44, 5-11

Nooteboom, B (1999) *Inter-Firm Alliances*. Routledge, London

OECD (1998) *Buyer power of large scale multi-product retailers*. OECD: Paris

Pearson, S (1994) How to achieve return on investment from customer loyalty–part II. *Journal of Targeting, Measurement and Analysis for Marketing*, 3, 124-133

Pickering, J F (1999) Competition policy and vertical relationships. *European Competition Law Journal*, 20(4), 225-239

Pilat, D (1997) Regulation and performance in the distribution sector. *OECD, Economics Department Working Papers*, 180

Pontiggia, A and Sinatra, A (1997) Learning for growth: The United Colors of Benetton. In: A Sinatra (editor) *Corporate transformation*. Kluwer, Dordecht

Prahalad, C K and Ramaswamy, V (2003) The new frontier of experience innovation. *MIT Sloan Management Review*, 44(4), 12-18

Rayner, S (1996) *Customer Loyalty Schemes*, Pearson, London

Retail Forward (2003a) *Apparel retailing in Western Europe*. Retail Forward, Columbus

Retail Forward (2003b) *Apparel and home-goods retailing in Central and Eastern Europe*. Retail Forward, Columbus

Rey, P and Caballero-Sanz, F (1996) The policy implications of the economic analysis of vertical restraints. *European Commission, Directorate General for Economic and Financial Affairs, Economic Papers*, 119

Reynolds, J and Cuthbertson, C (2003) *Retail strategy: A view from the bridge*. Elsevier, Amsterdam

Ritzer, G (1999) *Enchanting a disenchanted world*. Pine Forge Press: Thousand Oaks, CA

Shedroff, N (2001) *Experience design*. New Riders: Indianapolis

Sopanen, S (1996) *Customer loyalty schemes in retailing across Europe*, Oxford Institute of Retail Management, Oxford

Wileman, A and Jary, M (1997) *Retail power plays: From trading to brand leadership*. Macmillan: Basingstoke

Ziliani, C (1999) *Micromarketing*. Egea: Milan

Zilaiani, C and Bellini, S (2004) Retail micro-marketing strategies and competition. *International Review of Retail, Distribution and Consumer Research*, 14(1), 7-18

Expansion of Japanese Retailers Overseas

Roy Larke

SUMMARY. There have been a number of studies of foreign retail entry into Japan but few that consider the moves of Japanese retailers to other Asian countries. Nonetheless expansion into Asia of Japanese retailers, notably since the early 1990s, has been considerable. Many have been attracted by the large size of several national markets. Large Japanese trading houses have played a significant direct and indirect role in the international moves of Japanese retailers. China has become the major place of investment for Japanese retailers with 21 retail companies established by Japanese firms. The history of the internationalisation of Japanese retailing shows three phases of development. A first phase is characterised by department stores, a second phase is a slowing of activity in the late 1990s and a third phase of rapid expansion is presently evident. The key to the current phase is the establishment and strength of non-retail supply firms in the same East Asian region into which retailers wish to expand. *[Article copies available for a fee from The Haworth Document Delivery Service: 1-800-HAWORTH. E-mail address: <docdelivery@ haworthpress.com> Website: <http://www.HaworthPress.com> © 2004 by The Haworth Press, Inc. All rights reserved.]*

KEYWORDS. International retailers, trading houses, Japan, East Asia, facilitating factors

---

Roy Larke is Professor of Retailing, ESADE Business School, Av. Pedralbes, 60-62 E-08034 Barcelona, Spain (E-mail: roy@royzemi.com).

[Haworth co-indexing entry note]: "Expansion of Japanese Retailers Overseas." Larke, Roy. Co-published simultaneously in *Journal of Global Marketing* (International Business Press, an imprint of The Haworth Press, Inc.) Vol. 18, No. 1/2, 2004, pp. 99-120; and: *International Retailing Plans and Strategies in Asia* (ed: John Dawson, and Jung-Hee Lee) International Business Press, an imprint of The Haworth Press, Inc., 2004, pp. 99-120. Single or multiple copies of this article are available for a fee from The Haworth Document Delivery Service [1-800-HAWORTH, 9:00 a.m. - 5:00 p.m. (EST). E-mail address: docdelivery@ haworthpress.com].

INTRODUCTION

The internationalization of retailing, its reasons, processes and, to some extent, its consequences are currently popular research themes for academics with an interest in retailing. This is equally true in Japan where its popularity has been enhanced by high levels of overseas retailer penetration into the market in recent years. This has led to numerous papers in various forms considering the issue of internationalization theory as a whole (see Akehurst and Alexander, 1995; Alexander, 1990, 1997; Burt, 1995; Dawson, 1994, 2003; Salmon and Tordjman, 1989), the expansion of retailers globally (see Burt, 1991, 1993; Dawson and Henley, 1999; Dupuis and Prime, 1996; Goldman, 2001; Treadgold, 1988), and the expansion of non-Japanese retailers in the Japanese market.

There is, however, a surprising gap in the literature currently being produced in Japan. Previous studies relating to Japanese companies operating in the international market are relatively rare, although two seminal works considering historical developments are exceptional in their depth (Kawabata, 2000; Mukoyama, 1996). The others available in English are surprisingly few (Sternquist, 1997; Davies, 2000).

As the first step to correcting this omission as well as updating previous studies, the aim of this paper is to provide an overview of Japanese retail company expansion into overseas markets, and in particular into East Asia. Due to the relative lack of current academic articles that consider this movement in any detail, it takes an eclectic approach, drawing on a wide range of statistical and journalistic sources, but with reference to current theory and ideas on internationalization in general.

INTERNATIONALIZATION OF RETAILING: A JAPANESE PERSPECTIVE

Papers regarding internationalization of retailing as considered by Japanese and other Asian academics are common and increasing in number. Many of those written in Japan take a bibliographic review approach concentrating on two major themes:

1. Retail internationalization globally with some reference to Western theory (see Aoki, 1996; Kanezaki, 2003).
2. Consideration of overseas retail company entry into Japan (Aihara, 2001; Fahy and Taguchi, 2000; Ikemoto, 1999; Imoto,

1999; Larke, 2003; Mukoyama, 1997; Nemoto and Tamehiro, 2001; Sonnenborn, 2000; Takayama, 2001; Uehara, 1999).

Within both themes, the most common point of reference to date has been the current influx into East Asia of retail companies from the West. Under this approach, Japanese scholars have tended to include Japan as simply another part of East Asia, and a net recipient of entry by retailers from the West, largely overlooking the size and power of domestic retailers and the domestic retail industry. This has led to a generally critical view of retail companies originating from outside East Asia and perpetuates the view that such overseas entry is damaging to local systems. One example of this view is presented by Takayama (2001, p. 5):

> The general point of view is that Western retailers are seeking to "create distribution systems" in Asia, but in Japan, their aim is to "break the distribution system." (Original quotes)

Takayama argues that overseas entry is directly responsible for the breakdown, and therefore decline, of traditional distribution systems in Japan. This is a point of view shared by the mass media and by numerous other academic writers (see Asahi Shinbun, 2001; Nemoto and Tamehiro, 2001, p. 37). The same has been argued in other countries where non-Asian retailers have met with varying degrees of opposition, both general and political.

In several countries in the region, notably China, Thailand, Malaysia, and South Korea, non-domestic firms now have a significant share of the FMCG retail sectors and have gained this position in very short time. In China, for example, Carrefour is already the fifth largest retailer by sales, with Wal-Mart and Metro ranked sixteenth and eighteenth respectively (Shukan Toyo Keizai, 2004: 43). Despite the critical view taken by many Japanese authors of overseas entry, overseas firms do not, on the whole, have anywhere near this level of dominance in Japan. The largest independent non-Japanese retailer in 2003 by sales was Toys "R" Us, which ranked as the fifty-fifth largest retail company and had roughly 0.14% of the total retail market (Nihon Keizai Shinbun, 2003: p. 123). Of course by sub-sector, Toys "R" Us has a very large market share indeed with roughly 18% of the total market for toys (estimated from METI, 2003: p. 97), but even given this fact, there are no other sectors where a non-Japanese company has a strong market position. Even considering Wal-Mart's recent partial acquisition of Seiyu, a large, general merchandise and food retail company, it has taken control of a group of companies with a total market share of only 0.8% in 2003 (Nihon Keizai Shinbun, p. 97), and one that is one-third the size of the largest retailer by turnover, Aeon, in 2004.

Clearly, the impact of overseas companies on the Japanese retail market is hardly significant in terms of their effect on competition and sales. Concerns surrounding the negative impact of overseas companies are at least in Japan, therefore, more to do with a somewhat ethnocentric view of internationalization than to actual facts. It also means that research has tended to distinguish Japanese firms from those of other highly industrialized nations despite their current growth within the same East Asian region. This is a surprising omission as retailers from Japan are very strong indeed in East Asian markets. The importance of a manufacturing export culture in Japan has a long history and has been considered in general terms in a lot of previous literature, but the new importance of retailers and other service firms moving overseas is yet to receive very much attention. This is likely to change rapidly as the domestic economy improves and firms look to re-orientate themselves to overseas markets.

PAST STUDIES OF INTERNATIONAL ACTIVITIES OF JAPANESE RETAIL FIRMS

So far there has been few academic studies of Japanese retailers moving overseas, but two stand out. Mukoyama (1996) is an early study of the overseas activities of Japanese retailers covering great depth and many different product sectors. Using content analysis of Japanese newspapers, he builds a database of retailers that operate stores outside Japan (see Table 1). Even at this early stage, Mukoyama finds almost 300 stores operated by Japanese firms outside Japan, and, as his analysis is limited to firms operating as retailers within Japan itself, does not include investment companies and other non-retail companies that operate stores elsewhere. If the operations of major fashion manufacturers, such as Onward Kashiyama, and some investment houses, such as Nomura Securities, were also considered, the number is likely to be higher. More than 83% of the stores found in Mukoyama's study were based in Asia, and two-thirds had opened after 1990. Mukoyama's study goes on to consider global procurement activities of Japanese retailers, and concentrates particularly on the cases of Yaohan and Ryohin Keikaku (more commonly known for its Muji stores outside Japan). In both cases, the author is overwhelmingly positive, concentrating on the

TABLE 1. International Spread of Japanese Retailers, circa 1996

	Stores	% of Total	Year of Entry 1960s	1970s	1980s	1990s
Specialty Stores	135	46.2	0	3	25	107
Department Stores	81	27.7	1	14	30	36
Supermarkets	76	26.0	0	3	24	49
Total	292	100.0	1	20	79	192
Asia	**243**	**83.2**				
Hong Kong	82	28.1	1	3	25	53
Taiwan	51	17.5	0	0	6	45
China	35	12.0	0	0	2	33
Singapore	30	10.3	0	2	11	17
Thailand	18	6.2	0	0	7	11
Malaysia	17	5.8	0	0	8	9
Macao	4	1.4				
Indonesia	3	1.0				
Brunei	1	0.3				
Australia	2	0.7				
Europe	**25**	**8.6**				
UK	10	3.4				
France	8	2.7				
Spain	2	0.7				
Germany	2	0.7				
Netherlands	1	0.3				
Austria	1	0.3				
Italy	1	0.3				
North America	**24**	**8.2**				
USA	22	7.5				
Canada	1	0.3				
Costa Rica	1	0.3				
Total	292	100.0				

Based on content analysis of newspaper reports.
Source: Compiled from Mukoyama (1996: 75-81).

strengths of each company and noting the uniqueness of the Japanese approach. In the case of Muji, the company remains strong, and despite some restructuring in the late 1990s, curtailing expansion plans overseas due to less than expected demand, Yaohan proved a little too ambitious with the company entering receivership in 1997 (Kumiya, 1998). More recently, Mukoyama (2003) notes that:

> Internationalization is not the sole right of Western countries . . . Whereas Western retailers have built up their own know-how and technologies for internationalization, Asian local retailers have learnt this from being subjected to foreign competition. (p. 213)

It is clear that Japanese firms are indeed looking to expand internationally. Hypothetically, and considering the size of both the Japanese economy and the retailers that operate within it, Japanese retailers are likely to have competitive characteristics more similar to counterparts from Europe and North America than those in the rest of Asia, which is economically far less developed.

A second and more recent study by Kawabata (2000) updates and expands on Mukoyama's work, but with a more detailed empirical analysis based on interviews with retailers. Kawabata's data shows a continued expansion of Japanese retailers in the late 1990s and, as with Mukoyama's study, a concentration on Asia (see Table 2). Kawabata found that in the period following Mukoyama's study, between 1995 and 1999, 22 department stores and 130 supermarkets were opened by Japanese retailers overseas, with only one department store and one supermarket opening outside of Asia. He also found that 31 department stores were closed in the same period, half of these in Asia, along with 121 supermarkets, 103 of which closed in Asia. In contrast to Mukoyama's study, which found only 35 stores in China, Kawabata discovered 73 openings in China, including 61 new stores after 1995, and this restricted only to department stores and supermarkets. The same figures suggest a complete drop off in new stores being opened in Europe and America as would be consistent with declining business confidence in Japan itself.

Through his interview survey, Kawabata illustrated the opportunistic nature of many of these operations. He notes Kamimura's (1992) suggestion that many companies claim to have been invited to open in less developed countries and give the impression that this is their sole reason for international expansion. This he confirms in his own work. It seems a strange stance for companies to take, suggesting as it does a lack of

TABLE 2. Stores Opened and Closed by Japanese Retailers by Region, 1995-1999

	Department Stores			Supermarkets		
	Total 1995 to 1999	Stores Opened	Stores Closed	Total 1995 to 1999	Stores Opened	Stores Closed
Asia	**87**	**21**	**15**	**252**	**129**	**103**
China	7	2	2	66	59	43
Hong Kong	12	1	7	20	6	9
Taiwan	23	10		99	40	24
Singapore	19	2	2	14	4	6
Thailand	9		2	23	12	8
Malaysia	14	4	2	24	6	8
Indonesia	3	2		2	1	2
Others	0			4	1	3
Europe	**23**	**0**	**7**	**1**	**0**	**1**
UK	4		2	1		1
France	8		3			
Italy	2		1			
Germany	4					
Spain	4		1			
Austria	1					
Americas	**12**		**2**	**19**	**1**	**14**
Australia	**3**	**1**		**0**	**0**	
Other	**0**			**8**		**2**
Total	125	22	24	280	130	120

Source: Compiled from Kawabata (2000: pp. 70-75).

strategic direction and a very opportunistic approach to internationalization. This is further emphasized by the fact that department stores in particular opened stores overseas to target Japanese tourists rather than local consumers, and many experienced problems when the flow of Japanese customers declined (Kawabata, 2000: pp. 130-138).

The study also notes companies expressing surprise that local landlords and governments are unwilling to offer preferable terms in order to protect and maintain the business (pp. 119-125). The same firms are used to relatively favorable treatment by landlords and banks in Japan in order to protect existing business and their expectations of similar terms outside Japan also suggest a lack of clear international strategy. Finally, Kawabata also suggests that the same companies saw their overseas activities as single store operations with the sole aim of generating export profits. Most interviewees expressed little interest in developing and expanding markets by reinvesting profits locally. Once the original overseas retail operation was established, it was often left to operate independently with profits being repatriated to Japan.

Kawabata (2001, 2002, 2003a, 2003b, 2004) has continued his study of retail internationalization in Asia, but even here, the emphasis on the activities of Japanese firms has taken a secondary position to that of a general analysis of trends in particular countries and the activities of large Western firms. This paper seeks to take one step towards rectifying this problem in addition to introducing the topic in English rather than Japanese. As the Japanese economy once again improves, this is already driving a return to export led business growth (Shu, 2004), and one that will further encourage the expansion of retailers overseas and research and analysis thereof. This paper presents simply a starting point that will bring the activities of Japanese retailers into context vis à vis that of retailers from other highly industrialized nations in the West.

OVERSEAS RETAILER EXPANSION AND ACTIVITIES IN ASIA

The entry of international firms into retail markets in Asia has already been studied in some depth both in the West and in Asia (see Dawson et al., 2003). The background to such developments are well grounded in retail internationalization theories, particularly in relation to the growing body of work that considers the relatively new phenomenon of retail companies with global reach. A number of attempts have been made to define or even to discredit the term "global" company in reference to retailers, with most researchers still reluctant to admit that a truly global retail company exists. On the other hand, there are a clear number of super-regional corporations and the majority of the world's largest retail companies now operate at least partially outside their original home markets.

Whereas previous research has stressed that retail internationalization is by no means new and has long been an observable phenomenon

(Alexander, 1997), historically, the number of large, multi-regional companies with clear global ambitions that currently operate on several continents at one time is now at an all time high. Once again, the reasons behind these developments have been considered in some depth and present both push and pull aspects of internationalization. The first push factor is that some retail companies are reaching a scale and a scope of operations that have outgrown their original domestic markets. In almost all cases, firms that have a dominant position in their home markets and wish to maintain, or through pressure from investors are required to maintain, continued levels of growth have taken the internationalization route. This argument is so obvious and pervasive that it has become one of the theoretical "conditions" for international expansion (see Kacker, 1985; Treadgold, 1988; Alexander, 1997: pp. 124-135). Moreover, these same companies tend to be very large indeed, are mass merchandise retailers, and by name are the same ones which are most usually cited in studies of retail internationalization, i.e., Wal-Mart, Carrefour, Metro, and Tesco.

The second push factor is having a strategic business model which fits better with an international sphere of activity than solely a domestic one. With some exceptions, the companies that fit into this second group are specialists rather than mass merchandise retailers and are selling a concept that can be better exploited in multiple markets rather than in a single market, and which can be adapted to cultural conditions in many different international markets. There are more such companies in this second category, although due to their relatively smaller size of operation overall, only a very small number operate across multiple continents. Those that do, however, are clearly the most internationally widespread in terms of store coverage.

Finally, there is the simple pull factor of business opportunity and this factor in particular is important for the international expansion of retailers in Asia. As already discussed, in Asia Japan is the only large, industrialized economy. As compared to Europe, North America, South America, and the Middle East, Asia displays significant differences between countries in terms of economic development, consumer affluence, consumer sophistication, logistics and information technology infrastructure, and so on. The only other continent where one nation dominates so clearly is perhaps Africa where South Africa is ahead of the majority of its neighbors. Compared to Asia, however, much of Africa continues to lag behind in terms of economic development and it remains largely untapped by large, international retailers.

Asia, therefore, has remained an underdeveloped region in terms of retailing, but, for the past 20 years and at least partly due to the influence and activities of Japanese firms, it is now the single largest manufacturing region in the world. This has brought with it a business infrastructure that has rapidly overtaken the world's other less developed continents.

The overwhelming attraction of Asia for retailers from all over the world, however, was not just the relatively low level of local retail development or the more modern business infrastructure. It was, of course, the fact that Asia is home to the largest population of consumers of any continent. This single factor is often cited as the only main reason for international retailer expansion into the region, but the existence of consumer goods manufacturing industries, which the same retailers already employ to supply their operations across the world, the better business infrastructure, high levels of education and training in many nations, and, arguably, being a region where many countries are culturally open to capitalist trade practices, are all factors which combine to make Asia a highly attractive potential retail market.

Studies covering the total volume of international expansion of retailers in Asia are still rare. Futagami (2004), CSA (2003), and IGD (2003) are three relatively recent examples. Futagami provides a basic summary of the situation in Asia (see Table 3). Using his own index of retail globalization, Futagami looks at what he considers the largest retailers in Asia and their penetration throughout the region. The original table appeared to omit a number of major specialist retailers, which have been added. These are Body Shop, which was omitted as Futagami does not consider it a major international company in terms of sales as compared with others, and Ito-Yokado. Ito-Yokado is a less surprising omission as much of the Japanese firm's current international activities take place through its ownership of Seven-Eleven. Ito-Yokado operates Seven-Eleven directly in only Japan, China, USA, and Canada, with all other countries operating as franchises (Ito-Yokado, 2004). The recent expansion of both Seven-Eleven and the core Ito-Yokado GMS format in China are of major importance, however. In addition to these omissions, data are not available for some other firms, for example privately owned companies such as Chanel, and a number of Japanese specialist retailers that do not provide details of overseas operations. The table does illustrate the extent of international retail development in the region, and the presence of both of Japan's largest retailers, Aeon and Ito-Yokado, is as significant as that of the largest retailers from the USA, France, the UK, and Germany.

TABLE 3

	Nationality	Taiwan	China	Japan	South Korea	Thailand	Malaysia	Indonesia	Singapore	Hong Kong	Others	Total Countries
Aeon	Japan	1	6	1,050†		10	9			10		5
Ahold	Netherlands		R			49	R	24	R			2
Auchan	France	16	37			R					A	2
Body Shop	UK	52		99	54	28	40	37	31	23	35	10
Carrefour	France	28	35	8	25	17	6	10	1	R		8
Casino	France	13				37					33	3
Costco	USA	3		3	5							3
Dairy Farm	Hong Kong	A	127	R	5		19	91	353	A†	84	7
Delhaize	Belgium					34		34	R			2
IGA	USA	F	F	F	F	F		F	F		F	9
Ikea	Sweden	F	A	A*						F	F	9
Ito-Yokado	Japan	F	A	260†	F	F	F	F	F	F	F	11
Kingfisher B&Q	UK	14	8		1							3
LVNH	France	A	A	A	A	A	A	A	A	A	A	13
Makro	Netherlands	R	6		R	21	8	12			9	5
Marks & Spencer	UK				F		F	F	F	F	F	12
Metro	Germany		16	2						2		3
Office Depot	USA			19								2
Otto	Germany	A	A	A	A							4
PPR	France	A	A	A	A	A	A		A		A	8
Tesco	UK	3		106	21	52	4					5
Toys "R" Us	USA	6		134			5	3	4	6	31	11
Wal-Mart	USA		26	403	15	R		R		R		3
Total Companies		17	15	15	14	13	13	11	10	8	13	

Key:
Numbers indicate estimated number of stores.
    A: Active, but number of stores unknown.
    F: Franchise operation.
    R: Retired from market.
    *: Ikea plans to open in Japan in 2005.
    †: Home markets (Aeon and Ito-Yokado in Japan and Dairy Farm in Hong Kong, excluding convenience stores).
Sources: Adapted from Futagami (2004), Company Reports, various press releases.

On the other hand, while Ito-Yokado has connections to retail operations in eleven Asian countries including three GMS stores in China, and Aeon operates 35 stores in Asia outside Japan (Aeon, 2004), the table also makes it clear that current retail operations of Japanese retailers in Asia are on a modest scale compared to, for example, their counterparts from France or the USA. This is true only if we consider the very largest companies. If the total of Japanese retail interests are considered, Japan is clearly the leading source of international retail expansion in the region. Furthermore, this is less surprising when the network of manufacturing and wholesaling also operated by Japanese firms in Asia is also considered.

JAPANESE RETAILER EXPANSION
AND ACTIVITIES IN ASIA

The Toyo Keizai Directory of Foreign Direct Investment by Japanese companies (Toyo Keizai, 2003) attempts to list all Japanese companies with operations overseas. As Table 4 illustrates, the largest general trading houses (sogo shosha), along with a small number of other consumer goods wholesalers, have huge interests throughout Asia. The companies in question include a majority of manufacturing companies, but also a large number of trading, procurement, logistics, consulting, and other functions. Overall, the types of business operated by the trading houses cover all types of business including retailing. The same trading houses control the majority of brand licenses currently being imported into Japan, although in this case, as master licensee, the trading house facilitates production and distribution through subsidiaries and intermediaries (Shimada, 2004). Similarly, trading houses are acting as facilitators for Japanese companies, of all industrial sectors, entering markets in Asia, providing financial, logistics, and local knowledge support, and in some cases also organizing license businesses. In the case of Itochu Shoji in Korea, for example, the trading house holds a 49% stake (44.1% Itochu Shoji, 4.9% Itochu Korea) in Italian fashion brand Bulgari's retail operations.

Similarly, there are numerous cases of trading houses becoming involved more directly in retailing. Itochu owns and operates 70% of the Paul Smith operation in Hong Kong, is a major supplier to department stores, supermarkets, and convenience stores in Taiwan and Singapore, and is a major textile and apparel manufacturer throughout the region for both local sale and for import into Japan. Sumikin Bussan provides

TABLE 4

Wholesalers	Taiwan	China	South Korea	Thailand	Malaysia	Indonesia	Singapore	Hong Kong	Vietnam	Philippines	Others	Total Countries
Itochu Shoji	7	62	2	16	2	16	9	18	2	3	6	143
Sumikin Bussan		19	1	4		1	1	3	1			30
Sumitomo Shoji	8	37	1	25	12	26	15	8	7	7	7	153
Marubeni	4	42	1	11	4	11	7	9	1	8	3	101
Mitsui Bussan	4	27	2	25	8	13	14	20	2	1	5	121
Mitsubishi Shoji	6	30	2	34	6	11	5	14	5	9	5	127
Yagi Tsusho		3						1				4
	29	220	9	115	32	78	51	73	18	28	26	679

Source: Adapted from Toyo Keizai (2003: pp. 1190-1334).

procurement and logistics services to retailers in Hong Kong, Thailand, and Singapore, as does sister company Sumitomo Shoji throughout the region as well as being the main sales agent for Honda and Ford automobiles in Thailand. Mitsui Bussan and Marubeni also operate a full range of companies that can provide upstream services for Japanese and other retailers, but Mitsubishi Shoji goes one step further, operating food supermarkets itself in China (in joint venture with Daiei) and Vietnam (joint venture with Seiyu), and at least one chain of restaurants in Shanghai (joint venture with House Foods).

The extent of retail penetration in the region is also much greater than it appears from considering just the largest firms. The same Toyo Keizai directory lists 97 separate, retailer-operated companies in Asia, of which 72 are confirmed store or mail order operations (see Table 5). These are concentrated in China and Hong Kong, with 12 in Singapore—a country where Japanese retail presence is immediately and clearly visible through two major department stores and numerous specialty store chains. The numbers in the Toyo Keizai directory were collected in 2002 and analysis of more recent press releases suggest that there has been considerable growth in the past 12 months, again particularly in China. Ito-Yokado and Lawson have both been active in store expansion, and a number of specialty chains, such as Comme Ca, Narumiya, Daiso Sangyo, and others have begun to open stores across the region.

It would be inaccurate to say that Japanese retailers have any position of dominance in Asia, with the possible exception of department store retailing in Singapore and convenience store retailing in South Korea. At the same time, the data presented here show that the penetration of Japanese firms is much larger than previously recorded. At the very least, they illustrate that Japanese firms are keeping pace with internationalization of retail markets across Asia as instigated by Western entrants. Equally, it shows that it would be a mistake to consider Japanese firms as disparate from other non-local retailers entering markets in Asia. The only Japanese firms with the ambition and ability to operate overseas are the largest and most sophisticated. They are eminently capable of success in the rest of Asia and, compared to western counterparts, may even possess certain competitive advantages based on better cultural understanding as they originate from Asia themselves.

The only way to further illustrate the growth and importance of Japanese retailers within Asia without a huge international exercise in data collection and collation is to consider the cases of key markets. Historically, Singapore would be a candidate for such analysis, and Kawabata

TABLE 5

Retailers	Taiwan	China	South Korea	Thailand	Malaysia	Indonesia	Singapore	Hong Kong	Vietnam	Philipines	Others	Total Countries
Aoyama Shoji	1	1										2
Akachan Honpo		2						2				4
Aeon	1	2		2	2							7
Ito-Yokado		2										2
Isetan	1	3		1	1		1	1				8
Cabin	1	2					1					4
Seiyu		1					2	2				5
Senshukai		1		1				1				3
Takasho		2										2
Daiei		4								1		5
Daiki		2										2
Takashimaya	2			1				1				4
Tokyu Department Store				1								1
Tokyo Megane	1			1	1			1				4
Nissen		1						2				3
Nisshin Shoji					1		1					2
Parco							3					3
Hasegawa		1					2		3		1	7
Fast Retailing		2										2
Family Mart	1			1	1							3
Lawson		1										1
Best Denki					1		1	1				3
Belluna								2				2
Mycal		1						1				2
Mikimoto		1						1				2
Ministop			1							1		2
Paris Miki	1	1		1	1		1	1				6
Mitsukoshi	1							2				3
Meitetsu Pare											2	2
Ryohin Keikaku								1				1
Total companies	10	30	2	9	7	0	12	19	3	2	3	97

Source: Adapted from Toyo Keizai (2003: pp. 1334-1348).

(2000) considers the market in some depth, but in recent years a number of companies including Sogo, Daimaru, and Tokyu have exited due to problems at home. While a fascinating mix of intra-regional and rather upscale retail operations, Singapore is also a relatively small market and one that caters as much to tourists as to local consumers. As a result, the better example today is undoubtedly China. The following summary is gleaned largely from press reports.

JAPANESE ACTIVITY IN CHINA

Some economists see the potential inherent in the Chinese as the potential savior of the Japanese economy. Already China accounts for a large proportion of Japanese trade. As already noted, while China has long been a production base for Japan, it is only recently that sales within China have taken off, and with this has come a gradual build up of Japanese retailers in the country.

Table 6 lists 21 retail companies set up by Japanese firms. Due to ownership and operating restrictions, a number of Japanese firms operate several companies in the country, one in each region. This is a remaining throwback to Chinese regulations that have existed since before the country entered the World Trade Organization (WTO). A glance at the table suggests that this build up has been going on for some time, with Isetan establishing businesses in Shanghai and Tientsin as long ago as 1993, but this does not reflect the recent upsurge in retail operations. Ito-Yokado, while establishing its Changdu operation in 1998, only opened its first store in 2000. Lawson, after opening its first store in 1996, had fewer than 50 stores until 2002. Now it has close to 200 and is expanding at a rate of 100 stores a year in the Shanghai area alone.

Similarly, a number of prominent companies are absent from the table due to lack of data. Family Mart operates a single store in Shanghai, but is planning a rapid expansion in 2004, and auto-parts retailer Yellow Hat announced in April 2004 that it would be expanding its own franchise chain of stores this year with the help of Itochu Shoji.

Japanese retailers are behind in terms of store development as compared to Carrefour, Auchan, and Wal-Mart for example, and are now expanding at the same time as local firms that are developing ever more professional retail operations. A number of companies, Aeon in Shanghai, Daiei in Tientsin, and Ito-Yokado in both Changdu and Beijing, all claim that they entered China after invitations from government officials (Shukan Toyo Keizai, 2004). Similarly, while Chinese consumers

TABLE 6

Japanese Retailer	Share-holding %	Location	Retail sector	Entry date Yr.Mth	Sales ¥bn	End sales period Yr.Mth	Net Profit ¥mn	Stores	Employees
Isetan	63.0	Shanghai	Department store	1993.01	2.76	2002.12	−45.0	1	172.00
Isetan	75.0	Tientsin	Department store	1993.01	4.12	2002.12	34.0	1	447.00
Isetan	80.0	Shanghai	Department store	1997.03	5.48	2002.12	197.0	1	311.00
Ito-Yokado	51.0	Changdu	GMS	1997.11	9.00	2003.12	20.0	2	1,028.00
Ito-Yokado	36.8	Beijing	GMS	1998.04	16.00	2003.12	32.0	3	1,399.00
Aeon	65.0		SC	1995.10	75.00	-	P	5	2,144.00
Aeon	60.0	Tsingtao	SC	1996.03				2	896.00
Seiyu	42.0	Beijing	SC	1996.06	1.60	2003.12	OK	1	546.00
Daiei	95.0	Tientsin	Supermarket	1995.05	3.60	2002.12	-	12	1,000.00
Heiwado	75.0		SC	1998.11	7.60	2003.12	55.0	1	1,134.00
Lawson	49.0	Shanghai	CVS	1996.02	3.39	2003.12	L	153	149.00
Komeri	70.0	Luta	Home center	1996.03	2.23	2002.12	L	2	29.00
Itokin	100.0	Shanghai	Women's apparel	1997.07	-	-	-	1 flagship	216.00
Itokin	97.0	Tsingtao	Women's apparel	1995.12				per	
Itokin	100.0	Luta	Women's apparel	1993.10				company, 67	
								concessions,	
								66 franchise	
Itokin	95.0	Tientsin	Women's apparel	1997.00				stores	
Aigan	45.0	Beijing	Eye wear	1994.10	0.26	-	-	8	90.00
Paris Miki	100.0	Shanghai	Eye wear	1993.08	1.41	-	P	89	133.00
Paris Miki	48.0	Shanghai	Eye wear	2000.10					
Aoyama Shoji	54.0	Shanghai	Men's wear	1994.09	0.18	2002.12	L	3	369.00
Fast Retailing	71.4		Apparel retail	2002.09	0.56	2003.06	−680.0	6	-

Key: -: not available, P: Profitable, L: Loss making, OK: Undisclosed by acceptable.
Note: Net profit is after tax except for Ito-Yokado which is EBIT.
Source: Adapted from Shukan Toyo Keizai (2004: p. 57).

are not at all similar in terms of tastes and behavior as compared to Japanese, firms are happy to suggest they are used to the practices and demands of the Chinese market due to the relatively close cultural proximity of the two countries (Wada, 2004).

In the same article from which the table was derived, an article attributed to "a representative of a major trading house," Toyo Keizai lists 100 leading Japanese firms that are now fast expanding their business activities within China itself. The article also emphasizes the links between Japanese manufacturers and retailers operating within the market, and the use of Japanese consultants and logistics and transport firms when setting up in the country. Sales figures remain small, with the largest, Ito-Yokado, generating only about ¥25 billion in 2003, or about the same as one large Japanese store. Carrefour is eight times larger, with Wal-Mart and Metro already three times larger. Unlike Carrefour, which has spread stores in many locations in China, Ito-Yokado is set to concentrate on Beijing and particularly on rapid store development up to the 2008 Olympics. In addition to the first Seven-Eleven, York Benimaru, a supermarket chain and another IY Group member, will begin opening stores from 2004, giving the group a full range of small, medium, and large formats (IY Co Report 2004).

Pit falls abound, however. A number of reports note the "old fashioned" and "opaque" nature of Chinese business practices, notably the use of long payment periods and large, volume buying rebates. While this is a concern, it is ironic that these are the very same practices so bemoaned by overseas retailers and distributors entering Japan in the 1980s and early 1990s.

CONCLUSIONS

The extent of Japanese retail operations overseas has a long history and has passed through three distinct phases.

1. The first phase was one of mostly department store expansion, and, in this case in particular, was motivated by increased numbers of Japanese tourists going overseas. The preference of Japanese consumers to shop at Japanese retailers even when overseas has received only scant attention by researchers, but is proved by the initial success such retailers achieved in the 1980s and early 1990s.

2. The second phase was a brief hiatus during the worst of the Japanese economic slowdown in the second half of the 1990s. This coincides with other work, notably Dawson and Larke (2004).
3. The third and current phase is a new and rapid re-expansion, again in line with improved business confidence in Japan itself.

In each phase, Asia has been the main region of interest for the majority of Japanese retailers, and this has now become even more concentrated on China alone. Numerous press announcements came to light at the end of the financial year ending March 2004, with companies both expanding retail operations in China and others planning initial entry.

The key to the current phase, as argued in this paper, is the establishment and strength of non-retail supply firms in the same East Asian region. In addition to manufacturers which have developed a solid history within the region largely as a base to produce consumer products for the Japanese market, Japanese firms are also supported by logistics and transport companies and, most importantly, by the powerful and internationally knowledgeable hands of the trading houses.

At present, no single Japanese retailer is prominent in any of the main markets of East Asia, although the presence of department stores in Singapore should not be forgotten or discounted. Japanese firms are significant in their number, however. With various sources placing the number of separate retail companies already operating in China alone between 20 and 40, with at least 97 overseas operations established by some 30 Japanese firms across the East Asian region, retail firms are highly prominent.

Quite correctly, managers in Japan are keen to emphasize the cultural proximity of their business systems and expectations as compared to the rest of Asia. The current numbers are clearly just the beginning. Japanese retailers are set to further expand in China and the rest of East Asia.

REFERENCES

Aeon (2004) Company Report, *http://www.aeon.info*, Accessed: 12 May 2004.

Aihara, Osamu (2001) Carrefour expanding through M&A and overseas entry, *Ryutsu to Shisutemu*, 108, June: pp. 12-19. (Japanese)

Akehurst, Gary and Nicholas Alexander (1995) Developing a framework for the study of the internationalization of retailing, *Service Industries Journal*, 15(4): pp. 97-117.

Alexander, Nicholas (1990) Retailers and international markets: Motives for expansion, *International Marketing Review*, 7(4): pp. 75-85.

Alexander, Nicholas (1997) *International Retailing*, Oxford and Malden, Blackwell Publishers.

Aoki, Hitoshi (1996) Research directions in the international transfer of technology of retailers, *Sangyo Keiei*, No. 22: 197-214.

Asahi Shinbun (2001) Enemies all round: 100 days since the landing of French supermarket "Carrefour," *Asahi Shinbun*, 16 March: 13.

Burt, Steve (1991) Trends in the internationalization of grocery retailing: The European experience, *International Review of Retail, Distribution and Consumer Research*, 1(4): pp. 487-515.

Burt, Steve (1993) Temporal trends in the internationalization of British Retailing, *International Review of Retail, Distribution and Consumer Research*, 3(4): pp. 391-410.

Burt, Steve (1995) Retail internationalization: Evolution of theory and practice, in McGoldrick, P. J. and G. Davies (eds.) *International Retailing: Trends and Strategies*, London, Pitman: pp. 51-73.

CSA (Chain Store Age) (2003) Update on activities of the World's Top 10 Retailers, *Chain Store Age*, 1 December, pp. 26-35. (Japanese)

Davies, B. K. (2000) International activities of Japanese retailers, in Czinkota, M. R., and M. Kotabe (eds.) *Japanese Distribution Strategy*, London, Business Press: pp. 227-41.

Dawson, John A. (1994) The internationalization of retailing operations, *Journal of Marketing Management*, 10: pp. 267-282.

Dawson, John A. (2003) Towards a model of the impacts of retail internationalization, in Dawson, John A. et al. (eds.) *The Internationalization of Retailing in Asia*, London and New York, RoutledgeCurzon: pp. 189-209.

Dawson, John A. and John S. Henley (1999) Internationalization of hypermarket retailing in Poland: West European investment and its implications, *Journal of East-West Business*, 5(4): pp. 37-52.

Dawson, John A. and Roy Larke (2004) Japanese retailing through the 1990s: Retailer performance in a decade of slow growth, *British Journal of Management*, 15(1): pp. 73-94.

Dawson, John A., Masao Mukoyama, Sang Chul Choi, Roy Larke (eds.) (2003) *The Internationalization of Retailing in Asia*, London and New York, RoutledgeCurzon.

Dupuis, Marc and N. Prime (1996) Business distance and global retailing: a model of the analysis of key success/failure factors, *International Journal of Retail and Distribution Management*, 24(11): pp. 30-38.

Fahy, John and Fuyuki Taguchi (2000) Japan's second distribution revolution: The penetration of global retail formats, in Czinkota, M. R., and M. Kotabe (eds.) *Japanese Distribution Strategy*, London, Business Press: pp. 298-309.

Futagami (2004) Global chains enter Asia: General retailing moves to control markets, *Nikkei Marketing Journal*, 16 March, p. 15. (Japanese)

Goldman, Arieh (2001) The transfer of retail formats into developing economies: The examples of China, *Journal of Retailing*, 77(2): pp. 452-461.

IGD (2003) *Global Retailing 2004*, Lakenheath, IGD.

Ikemoto, Masayoshi (1999) The advance of overseas retailers and their impact, *Ryutsu Joho*, No. 362: pp. 4-11. (Japanese)

Imoto, Shogo (1999) The energy of overseas retailers forcing change in Japan's distribution system, *Ryutsu to Shisutemu*, No. 99: pp. 3-12. (Japanese)

Ito-Yokado (2004) *Ito-Yokado Group: Company Report 2004*, Published by Ito-Yokado.

Kacker, M. P. (1985) *Transatlantic trends in retailing: takeovers and flow of know-how*, Westport, Quorum Books.

Kamimura, Junzo (ed.) (1992) *Internationalization of the distribution industry*, Nihon Keizai Kenkyu Senta, No. 79. (Japanese)

Kanezaki, K. (2003) Internationalization of retailing: Explaining the OLI paradigm, *Kyushu Sangyo University Keiei-gaku Ronshu*, 14(2), pp. 17-30. (Japanese)

Katayama, Yoshiyuki (1998) Failure of globalization business: The case of Yaohan, Shikoku University Kiyo, 9, March: pp. 19-29. (Japanese)

Kawabata, Moto (2000) *The Overseas Expansion and Strategy of Retailers*, Tokyo, Shinhyoron. (Japanese)

Kawabata, Moto (2001) New trends in distribution in Asia: Structural change everywhere and the entry of overseas companies, *Ryutsu to Shisutemu*, 109, September: pp. 29-36. (Japanese)

Kawabata, Moto (2002) Globalization of Japanese companies and overseas expatriates, *Chiri*, 47(10): pp. 45-50, 4. (Japanese)

Kawabata, Moto (2003a) Outlook for distribution in Asia: the changing distribution in South Korea, changes in consumption style in the wave of internationalization, *Ryutsu to Shisutemu*, 117, Fall: pp. 55-62. (Japanese)

Kawabata, Moto (2003b) Retail internationalization and the reorganizing of Asia's commercial space, *Ryukoku University Keiei Ronshu*, 42(4): pp. 15-26. (Japanese)

Kawabata, Moto (2004) Survey research: Outlook for distribution in Asia: Europe, Japan, and Thailand crashes into Thai distribution, a new trend from Thailand, *Ryutsu to Shisutemu*, 118, Winter: pp. 63-70. (Japanese)

Kumiya, Hidetoshi (1998) The Yaohan Business Failure: From development to bankruptcy, from http://www.mfi.or.jp/kumiya/stock114.html: 11 May, 2004. (Japanese)

Larke, Roy (2003) International retailing in Japan, in Dawson, John A. et al. (eds.) *The Internationalization of Retailing in Asia*, London and New York, RoutledgeCurzon: pp. 6-34.

METI (2003) *Advanced Report of the Census of Commerce 2002*, Keizai Sangyo Chosakai, Tokyo. (Japanese)

Mukoyama, Masao (1996) *Towards the establishment of pure global*, Tokyo, Chikura Shobo. (Japanese)

Mukoyama, Masao (1997) Internationalizing Japanese distribution, in Tajima, Y. and H. Harada (eds.) *Introduction to Distribution Studies*, Tokyo, Nippon Keizai Shinbun: pp. 371-405.

Mukoyama, Masao (2003) Conclusion: The direction of future research on the internationalization of retailing, in Dawson, John A. et al. (eds.) *The Internationalization of Retailing in Asia*, London and New York, RoutledgeCurzon: pp. 210-213.

Nemoto, Shigeaki and Yoshihiro Tamehiro (2001) *Global retailer: Giant overseas retailers enter the Japanese market*, Tokyo, Toyo Keizai Shuppansha. (Japanese)

Nihon Keizai Shinbunsha (2003) *2004 Distribution Handbook*, Tokyo, *Nihon Keizai Shinbun.* (Japanese)

Salmon, W. J. and A. Tordjman (1989) The internationalization of retailing, *International Journal of Retailing*, 4(2): pp. 3-16.

Shimada, Katsumi (2004) The downstream strategy of general trading houses, *Seikatsu Kiten*, February: pp. 11-17. (Japanese)

Shu, En (2004) The mechanism for China's rapid economic growth to contribute to the Japanese economy, *Ekonomisto*, 11 May: 27-30. (Japanese)

Shukan Toyo Keizai (2004) Sell to the Chinese people! *Shukan Toyo Keizai*, 10 April: pp. 26-60. (Japanese)

Sonnenborn, Hans-Peter (2000) Successful market entry and performance in Japan, in Czinkota, M. R., and M. Kotabe (eds.) *Japanese Distribution Strategy*, London, Business Press: pp. 310-324.

Sternquist, Brenda (1997) Internationalization of Japanese Department Stores, *International Journal of Commerce and Management*, 7(1): pp. 57-79.

Takayama, Kunisuke (2001) The impact and reaction within the Japanese distribution industry to the overseas expansion of Western retailers, *Ryutsu to Shisutemu*, 109, June: pp. 3-11. (Japanese)

Toyo Keizai (2003) *Directory of Foreign Direct Investment by Japanese Firms*, Tokyo, Toyo Keizai Shuppan. (Japanese)

Treadgold, Alan (1988) Retailing without frontiers, *Retail and Distribution Management*, 16(6): pp. 31-37.

Uehara (1999) A personal view of the entry of overseas distribution companies, *Ryutsu Joho*, No. 362, pp. 12-17. (Japanese)

Wada, Kazuo (2004) Japanese retailers aren't making an effort: a personal call for 100 department stores a year in China, *Shukan Toyo Keizai*, 10 April: p. 56. (Japanese)

The Effects of Liberalization
in Retail Markets
on Economy and Retail Industry in Korea

Jung-Hee Lee
Sang-Chul Choi

SUMMARY. In this paper, the effects of liberalization in retail markets on the economy and retail industry in Korea are analyzed. The Korean retail market has been opened to foreign retailers since 1996. The results of the liberalization are the introduction of new types of retail business and the scale of retailers has increased. Moreover, it is said that the Korean retail market has been changed to be a more efficient market. These results of liberalization can have positive effects on the Korean economy including the retailing industry and consumers. The results in this paper, however, indicate that the effects of the liberalization on the retail industry and economy were not as positive as expected. Analysis of change in retail productivity showed that average store size and labor productivity increased, but sales per unit of space did not change. On the other hand,

Jung-Hee Lee is Professor, Department of Industrial Economics, Chung-Ang University, Republic of Korea, and Visiting Professor, Michigan State University, East Lansing, MI (E-mail: junghlee@cau.ac.kr). Sang-Chul Choi is Professor of Marketing and Distribution Systems, Faculty of Commerce, University of Marketing and Distribution Sciences, 3-1 Gakuen Nishi-Machi, Nishi-Ku, Kobe 651-2188, Japan (E-mail: choi@umds.ac.jp).

[Haworth co-indexing entry note]: "The Effects of Liberalization in Retail Markets on Economy and Retail Industry in Korea." Lee, Jung-Hee, and Sang-Chul Choi. Co-published simultaneously in *Journal of Global Marketing* (International Business Press, an imprint of The Haworth Press, Inc.) Vol. 18, No. 1/2, 2004, pp. 121-131; and: *International Retailing Plans and Strategies in Asia* (ed: John Dawson, and Jung-Hee Lee) International Business Press, an imprint of The Haworth Press, Inc., 2004, pp. 121-131. Single or multiple copies of this article are available for a fee from The Haworth Document Delivery Service [1-800-HAWORTH, 9:00 a.m. - 5:00 p.m. (EST). E-mail address: docdelivery@haworthpress.com].

Available online at http://www.haworthpress.com/web/JGM
Digital Object Identifier: 10.1300/J042v18n01_07

negative effects resulting from the liberalization have occurred especially affecting the small and medium sized retailers, and regional economies. The effects of the liberalization can be evaluated as both positive
and negative depending on the market and economic situations inside
and outside the country. Even if the effects of the liberalization have
been positive so far, future effects may be different especially due to the
influence of China's market. *[Article copies available for a fee from The
Haworth Document Delivery Service: 1-800-HAWORTH. E-mail address:
<docdelivery@haworthpress.com> Website: <http://www.HaworthPress.com>
© 2004 by The Haworth Press, Inc. All rights reserved.]*

KEYWORDS. Korea, market liberalization, retailing, space productivity, international retailing

INTRODUCTION

The Korean government has played an important role in the development of the domestic retailing industry. Large department stores
and large-scale discount stores (hereafter referred to as supercenters)
owned by the Chaebols, and small, inefficient family retailers charac-
terize Korean retailing. The recent trend has been for a decline in the
sales of department stores and an increase in the sales and role of the
supercenters.

In the 1990s, the retailing industry in Korea underwent remarkable
changes. Prior to the 1990s, the country's retailing business comprised
department stores, supermarkets, and traditional markets. Korean economic growth, the successful Seoul Olympic Game, gradual market
liberalization, and changed consumers' responses toward products
and service have brought about an increase in the variety of retailing and
a trend towards larger store sizes. A favorable response from consumers
is one of key drivers to successfully developing a new retail environment. The rapid increase in new types of retailing including supercenters,
convenience stores, TV home shopping, and Internet shopping has, in
turn, promoted the development of the retailing industry in Korea.

This paper reviews the changes in the retail industry and the government's retail policy in Korea. The main objective of this paper is to analyze the liberalization effects of the Korean retail markets on the
productivity of retail industry and consumer prices in Korea. The pros-
pects for the Korean retail industry are presented as a conclusion.

CHANGES OF KOREAN RETAIL MARKET
UNDER MARKET LIBERALIZATION

Retail Market Overview

The domestic retail market, in terms of sales, has continued to grow at an average annual growth rate of about 8% since 1999, and reached about 96 billion U.S. dollars in 2001. While the sales of traditional markets still account for about 70% of the total retail market, large-scale retailers including supercenters are quickly gaining more market share.

On the other hand, the competition among large retailers has become very intense. Since 1996 when liberalization of the retail market occurred, leading foreign retail corporations including Carrefour, Wal-Mart, Tesco, and Costco Wholesale have entered the market. These foreign retailers compete strongly with domestic retailers and competition has become more intense. In Korea, so far, all the major foreign retailers operate supercenter formats. This fast-growing retail industry is led not only by large supercenters, but also other new shopping channels such as Internet shopping malls and TV home shopping. TV home shopping is currently showing substantial growth. There are five licensed TV home shopping channels owned by domestic firms. Two of the five channels, LG Shopping and CJ Shopping, have the major share of the TV home shopping market.

Large-Scale Supercenters

In Korea, stores with more than 3,000 square meters are classified as large-scale retail stores. Supercenters are characterized by their low prices, made possible through their greater efficiency in logistics and marketing. Supercenters, whilst claiming "everyday low prices," also provide consumers with a one-stop shopping service. Their efforts are often seen as contributing to increased efficiency across the whole domestic retailing industry, and to stabilizing consumer prices resulting from retailers' greater price competition (KOTRA, 2002).

Since E-Mart, which is owned by Shinsegae, the second largest department store chain, opened as Korea's first supercenter in Seoul in 1993, the number and sales of supercenters have increased substantially. With the liberalization of the domestic retail market in 1996, leading foreign retail corporations, for example Carrefour of France and Wal-Mart of the U.S.A., entered the domestic market. As a result of the fast growth of domestic and foreign firms, there were 237 large-scale supercenters in Korea as of June 2003. Supercenters account for more than 10% of the total retail sales in Korea. The largest share of the retail market remains accounted for by traditional markets, but their share decreases steadily. Department stores used to command the second largest share of the market but supercenter sales exceeded those of department stores in 2003. Figure 1 shows the increase in number of supercenters.

Five major firms currently dominate the supercenter market: two domestic firms which are Shinsegae's E-Mart and Lotte Mart, and three foreign firms which are Carrefour, Samsung-Tesco's Home Plus, and Wal-Mart. Their share in all sales space in supercenters reached 69.1% in 2002, from 45.2% in 1996, the first year of retail market liberalization. While Shinsegae's E-Mart has remained in the No. 1 position, the competition for second place has increased with the rapid emergence of Samsung Tesco's Home Plus (Homeplus is 89% owned by Tesco and 11% by Samsung). The increase in space in supercenters operated by the 5 firms is shown in Figure 2.

EFFECTS OF LIBERALIZATION
IN RETAIL MARKET ON ECONOMY

Liberalization of Korean Retail Market Under WTO

The Korean retail market opened to foreigners in an incremental plan beginning in 1989. The goal of the market opening policy is to improve

FIGURE 1. Annual Opening of Supercenters and Total Number of Stores

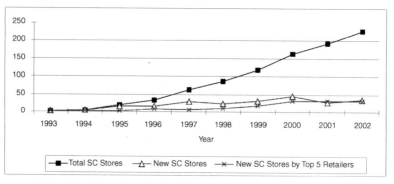

Source: Korea Chain Store Association.

FIGURE 2. Annual Additions of Space in Supercenters Share of 5 Major Firms

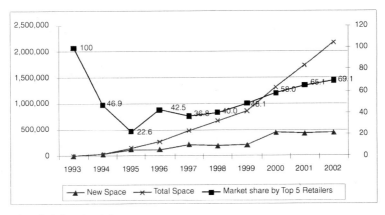

Source: Korea Chain Store Association.

the efficiency of the retailing industry. To achieve this goal the Korean government launched the retail policy in the three stages.

In the first stage, from mid-1989 to mid-1991, there was a relaxation of regulations on the establishment of foreign companies' subsidiaries and foreign direct investments. In the second stage, from mid-1991 to mid-1993, foreign retailers could open stores to a maximum size of 1,000m². But the number of stores was limited to 10 in this period. However, these regulations on the number and size of retail outlets were relaxed in the third stage of the market opening, from mid-1993 to 1995. In the third stage, foreigners were allowed to open up 20 stores with the size limit raised to 3,000m² per store.

Finally, in 1996, the Korean retail market was almost totally opened to foreign investors. Retail market liberalization has brought positive and negative impacts to the Korean economy. So far, the liberalization effects have been evaluated as generally positive by retail experts in term of increasing the efficiency of the retail industry and providing consumers with more convenience. Moreover, it is claimed that the liberalization has curbed an increasing inflation rate by increased price competition.

On the other hand, the negative effects of the liberalization include an increasing number of small and medium retailers going out of business, an increase in social problems associated with excess consumption and environmental problems including traffic congestion, noise, excess waste, etc.

Since the liberalization policy in 1996, the Korean retail market was further liberalized, by inviting more foreign investments. This policy was aimed at encouraging recovery from the Korean financial crisis in 1998. The Foreign Investment Promotion Act established in 1998 has resulted in almost no regulation on foreign investment in retail market in Korea.

Facing a new stage in the liberalization, now, all members of WTO are preparing the DDA negotiation for the additional openings of each domestic market for foreign investment. These results are expected to change the international retail market structure. Table 1 summarizes the various stages of the liberalization process.

Effects on Consumer Prices

In general, it is said that the liberalization of the retail market has contributed to a decline in consumer prices. This is regarded as the most important contribution of the liberalization to the domestic economy.

TABLE 1. The Liberalization Stages of the Korean Distribution Industry

Year	Stages	Key Policy
1989	Stage I	- Extended introduction of technology and wholesaling investment. - Extended import items for foreign subsidiaries.
1991	Stage II	- Enabled retail investments (up to maximum 10 stores: maximum 1,000 m^2 per store). - Full liberalization of the introduction of retail technology.
	Stage III	- Negative list for imports announced. - Relaxation of store limit for foreign retailers (up to maximum 20 stores: maximum 3,000m^2 per store).
1996	Full Liberalization	- Full liberalization of store limits. - Zoning regulations are deregulated.
1999	Foreign Investment Promotion Act	- Foreign Investment Promotion Act to overcome the financial crisis through encouraging foreign investment. - Relaxation of economic evaluation for investment on department stores and shopping center by foreigners. - Allowing foreigners to own land.
Present	WTO New Round (DDA)	- The new round negotiations going on for further liberalization.

Source: Korea Chamber of Commerce and Industry, *Digest of Korean Retail Market* (2001), Korea Ministry of Commerce, Industry and Energy.

According to an analysis by the Bank of Korea (BOK), the liberalization of the retail market has contributed to curbing price increases. Also, the BOK forecasts that this trend would be continued into the future. This analysis by the BOK is based on a comparison between a consumer price in 1995 and a discounted consumer price related to the discount rate of supercenters and market share of supercenters in 1999. By this analysis, the market liberalization effect was to decrease consumer prices 1.79% over 4 years from 1996 to 1999. But, this analysis simply compared a certain year before and after the liberalization.

To measure the effect of the liberalization on consumer prices, a regression analysis is used. It is assumed that the liberalization effects began in 1995 even if the Korean retail was opened in 1996, because supercenters began in 1995. In addition, the liberalization is assumed to affect consumer prices through the increasing number of supercenters and the total sizes of supercenters in operation. The regression model is as follows:

$$P_t = f(TS_t, TS_{t-1}, D_t, EXR_t, EXR_{t-1}, EXR_{t-2}, EXR_{t-3})$$

where, P_t = consumer price index in time t
TS_t = total sizes of supercenters in time t
TS_{t-1} = total sizes of supercenters in time t − 1 (one month time lag)
EXR_t = exchange rate in time t (Korean Won per 1$)
EXR_{t-1} = exchange rate in time t − 1 (Korean Won per 1$)
EXR_{t-2} = exchange rate in time t − 2 (Korean Won per 1$)
EXR_{t-3} = exchange rate in time t − 3 (Korean Won per 1$)
D_t = 1 if t after the financial crisis in Korea, otherwise 0

The monthly time series data from January 1995 to June 2002 were used for this analysis. Data for the consumer price index (base year = 2000) and exchange rate were obtained from the Statistical Data Base (KOSIS) of the Korea National Statistical Office. The total sizes of supercenters over 3,000m^2 were obtained from the Korea Chain Stores Association.

The estimated results of the regression model are summarized in Table 2. R^2 is 0.996 and adjusted R^2 is 0.996. The estimated coefficients for the total sizes of supercenters are not significant even at the 10% significance level. These results mean that increasing total sizes of supercenters have not affected consumer prices over the last 8 years from 1995 to 2002. That is, the liberalization has not affected the con-

TABLE 2. Estimated Effects on Consumer Price Index

Variables	Estimated coefficient	T	Sig.
Trend	0.27	20.26	0
Dummy (= 1 if after financial crisis in Korea, otherwise 0)	−0.939	−2.74	0.008
Total space of SC	0.000002	0.69	0.493
Exchange Rate	0.0027	2.77	0.007
Total space of SC in one month time lag	−0.00004	−1.32	0.191
Exchange Rate in one-month time lag	0.0038	2.38	0.02
Exchange Rate in two-month time lag	0.0026	1.62	0.108
Exchange Rate in three-month lag	0.0011	1.1	0.273

$R^2 = 0.996$ Adj. $R^2 = 0.996$

sumer prices. The estimated coefficient for the dummy variable representing the financial crisis in Korea is significant at the 5% significance level and shows a negative sign. This result indicates that the consumer prices after the financial crisis increased at a lower rate than before the financial crisis.

The estimated coefficients for the exchange rates in time t and $t-1$ are significant at the 5% significance level. These results indicate that a change of exchange rates cause consumer prices to increase. Also, the estimated coefficients for the time variable are significant at the 5% significance level. This result means that the consumer price index increased by an average of 0.27 points on a monthly basis.

Effects on Productivity of the Retail Industry

In order to compare productivity before and after the liberalization, this paper uses sales per store, sales per employee, and sales per space (m²). These data are based on all types of retail and wholesale and are obtained from the Statistical Data Base (KOSIS) of the Korea National Statistical Office. The annual average value from 1993 to 1995 before the liberalization is compared to the annual average from 1997 to 1999 after the liberalization. As shown earlier, consumer prices increased continuously in these periods. To avoid an inflation factor, real sales are used instead of nominal sales. The real sales are obtained from nominal sales divided by CPI.

The results (Table 3) indicate that sales per store after the liberalization increased 52% compared with before the liberalization. Sales per employee also increased 51.5%. However, sales per space (m^2) did not increase but decreased very slightly. This implies that the liberalization affected the large scale of retail stores and some aspects of productivity in retailing, but not all aspects. It is acknowledged that this analysis leaves something to be desired because profits per store, employee, and space cannot be analyzed together in this paper.

PROSPECTS OF KOREAN RETAIL MARKETS IN FUTURE

Growth of the Supercenter Market
Depending on Efficient Operation

The supercenter retail business is expected to grow steadily for several years. While discount retail stores are likely to increase, however, it appears that the domestic discount retail market is fast reaching a saturation point. Even though saturation of the supercenter market is a concern for operators, there are still opportunities for the market to grow because traditional markets still account for about 70% of the total retail market. In the future, therefore, growth of the supercenter sector depends on how efficiently stores are operated.

As pointed out earlier, however, supercenters have not exhibited a substantial change in productivity. To be more competitive in future re-

TABLE 3. Comparison of Productivity of Wholesaler and Retailers Before and After Liberalization

Sales per store in million won		Sales per employee in million won		Sales per space (m^2) in million won	
Before	After	Before	After	Before	After
262.96	399.52	100.97	152.94	4.37	4.3

Source: Korea National Statistical Office.

tail markets, therefore, supercenters need to explore more ways to increase productivity of sales space and profit management.

Chinese Market's Role in Structural Changing of Korean Retail Markets

Together with Samsung-Tesco, domestic supercentres, notably Shinsegae's E-Mart and Lotte Mart, have implemented aggressive expansion strategies. In contrast, Wal-Mart and Carrefour are slow in expanding their business mainly because they have generated relatively poor revenues compared with other competitors. Because of their abilities in global sourcing and capital resources, however, they have advantages in future competition. In the long-term, such foreign firms may play a bigger role in the Korean retail market. When foreign retailers with a global network take advantage of China as a sourcing base, they are expected to regain their power in the Korean retail market. Therefore, China will play a big role in future structural changing of the Korean retail market.

Even if the Korean retail market is already fully open, more liberalization steps will be implemented. The Korean governments regard the new round of negotiations as an opportunity for Korean retailers to make inroads into the world market. Therefore, the Korean large-scale retailers are expected to be encouraged to open their stores outside Korea. E-Mart, which previously opened a store in Shanghai, China, recently announced that it would open 10 stores more in China in the next 3 years.

CONCLUSIONS

In this paper, the effects on the Korean economy of liberalization of retail markets are analyzed. The Korean retail market has been opened to foreign retailers since 1996. Results of liberalization are that new types of retailing business have been introduced and the scale of retailers has increased. Moreover, the Korean retail market has been changed to be a more efficient market. These results of the liberalization in the retail market generate positive effects on the Korean economy and society, including the retailing industry and consumers. The effects of the liberalization, however, were not as positive as expected. The results indicate that consumer prices were not significantly affected. In addition, the analysis on a change of retail productivity due to liberalization showed that average store scale and labor productivity increased, but sales per unit of space were not changed.

The Korean retail market has a significant potential to grow further with higher productivity. To achieve better efficiency in the retail market, however, the government and the retailers have different responsibilities. When the government frames a retail policy, it should pursue market efficiency, but make efforts to cause minimal impact on small and medium sized retailers.

REFERENCES

Bank of Korea (2001), Effects of Changed Distribution Market Structure on Price, Jan.

Korea Chamber of Commerce and Industry (2001), *Digest of Korean Retail Market*, Sept.

Korea Chainstores Association, *Discount Merchandiser*, various issues.

Korea Ministry of Commerce (2001), *Industry and Energy, A Development Plan for Distribution Industry in Changing Distribution Market Environments*, Nov.

Korea National Statistical Office, *Statistical Data Base* (KOSIS), various issues.

Korea Trade Investment Promotion Agency (KOTRA) (2002), *Fast Growth of Discount Retail Stores in Korea*, Jan.

U.S. Foreign Commercial Service and U.S. Department of State (1998), *Retail Development Growth in South Korea*.

The Strategic Importance of Retail Investment in Asia and Its Implications for the Metro Group in Asia

Verena Schmekel

SUMMARY. The speed, intensity and reach of retailers' foreign expansion are rising. As more distant markets have to be chosen to stay competitive, the pressure to expand abroad is increasing. Often, changing or stretching the initial business model in order to comply with local market demand maintains the performance of the firm. This phenomenon of strategy alteration after market entry is examined, using the Metro Cash and Carry expansion into Asia as an example. First, the investment attractiveness of Asia as a region is examined. Second, there is a review of countries in Asia that are especially considered for business expansion. Finally, the question of how an overall internationalisation strategy or business concept of a company changes after market entry into Asia is explored.

KEYWORDS. Internationalisation, strategy, retail, wholesale, Asia

Verena Schmekel is affiliated with the Institute of Strategic Business Development, University of Duisberg, Essen, Germany (E-mail: schmekel1@hotmail.com).

[Haworth co-indexing entry note]: "The Strategic Importance of Retail Investment in Asia and Its Implications for the Metro Group in Asia." Schmekel, Verena. Co-published simultaneously in *Journal of Global Marketing* (International Business Press, an imprint of The Haworth Press, Inc.) Vol. 18, No. 1/2, 2004, pp. 133-150; and: *International Retailing Plans and Strategies in Asia* (ed: John Dawson, and Jung-Hee Lee) International Business Press, an imprint of The Haworth Press, Inc., 2004, pp. 133-150. Single or multiple copies of this article are available for a fee from The Haworth Document Delivery Service [1-800-HAWORTH, 9:00 a.m. - 5:00 p.m. (EST). E-mail address: docdelivery@haworthpress.com].

INTRODUCTION

When looking at the extension of the country portfolio of the largest retailers by sales, it becomes obvious that internationalisation of retail business has intensified within the last ten years. The increased speed, intensity and reach of retailers' expansion to foreign markets are facilitated by diverse factors, such as the liberalisation of trade regulations or the use of modern logistics and information technology.

Among one of the top regions currently the focus for overseas expansion by commercial groups from Europe and North America is Asia, where the number of international retailers operating successfully is still quite limited and fragmented. This is surprising, as nearly 60% of the world population resides in Asia, producing about one quarter of the world's GDP and accounting for about one-third of the total international consumer goods trade (Metro, 2003, p. 37). But Asia is a vast and heterogeneous region in respect of its population, notably density, income distribution, and culture including religion. It is similarly varied in its governmental structures. It includes highly industrialized countries, for example Japan, with a retail and wholesale trade volume of nearly 550 trillion Yen (Ministry of Public Management, 2004, p. 29) making it the second-largest consumer market in the world. Asia also includes China, one of the fastest growing consumer markets. But there are also small agriculturally oriented national economies.

To underline how complex retail internationalisation in Asia really is, this paper tries to reflect the overseas expansion of trade and retail businesses into Asia by examining the following questions:

- Why do retailers choose Asia as a region for foreign direct investment?
- What Asian countries are considered as appropriate for expanding business and for what reasons?
- How does the overall internationalisation strategy or business concept of a company change after market entry into Asian countries?

The above questions are approached by using, as an example, the German retail and wholesale company "Metro Group." Metro ranks, as measured by sales volume, number 3 in Europe and number 5 worldwide. Through the analysis of its long-term market entry strategy, the business model for its Cash & Carry formats, as well as its operations in China, India, Japan and Vietnam, the impact of the Asian market expansion on foreign retailers is illustrated.

THE REASONS FOR CHOOSING ASIA
AS A REGION FOR FOREIGN INVESTMENT

In comparison with the manufacturing sector, that has been highly international for quite some time, retailers have pursued international sales with a substantial time lag. Only in recent years have the traditionally national retail firms begun to operate on a more global basis. One can even claim that real globalisation in the commercial world has yet to come about. The following outline will examine the reasons for retailers and wholesale businesses expanding into Asia from an internal and an external perspective.

There are many internal, company specific motives for internationalisation. But looking closer, these numerous motives for overseas expansion derive from only a few sources:

* the saturation of the home market,
* growth opportunities abroad, and
* economies of scale and scope.

The most important driving force for international expansion is the saturation of the home market, combined with fierce competition within national boundaries. This is especially evident in west-central Europe, with stagnation of private consumption, a decreasing share of retail related expenditure as part of overall private consumption, diminishing sales in consumer goods retail and wholesale trade as well as continued expansion of sales area in markets with an already high density and amount of trading space.

The second factor is the presence of a successful store format and operation but no more room to expand locally, such that new markets need to be opened. This is especially true for the recent trend of European retail and trade groups investing in Asia. For example, the 30 largest food retailers, having the vast majority of their stores in Western Europe and North America, are currently focusing on Asia because growth rates in Western Europe and North America are low, the Middle East is growing fast but from a low starting point, Latin America has seen substantial growth already but with some instability, Central and Eastern Europe are approaching saturation while Africa remains unattractive to most firms. This leaves the Asia Pacific regions as the strongest destination for internationalisation with particularly great interest in China (Howard and Dragun, 2002, p. 3).

A third motive for internationalisation is a company's pursuit of quantitative growth, meaning the need to be present in as many places as possible to make use of economies of scale in order to survive global competition abroad as well as in the home market. Large retail and trade groups, for example Wal-Mart, Carrefour, Tesco and Metro, strive to operate abroad, in order to further grow on a global scale and to stay competitive in the international arena. Again, Asia provides them with a potential market into which to grow.

Sales expansion overseas is also driven by economies of scope via the amortisation of costs for research and development via the world-wide use of a company specific store format. In this sense, successful store formats are transferred to take full advantage of the learning curve and competitive edge overseas. In some cases, this leads to the prolongation of a store format life cycle, while the specific store format has already reached the declining phase in its home market. This is clearly visible with many retail and trade companies setting up business in less retail-developed countries within Asia, notably China or Vietnam where store formats like hypermarkets and Cash & Carry warehouses are still innovatory.

In addition to a company's internal motivation for expansion, there are also many external motives for international expansion into Asia, of which the most important ones are of political and economic, legislative and technological nature. These three reasons for foreign direct investent in Asia are outlined as follows.

Political and Economic

The homogenisation of political and economic conditions on an international basis are easing the expansion of retail and wholesale operations. For instance, the enlargement of the regional economic governmental organization ASEAN has dismantled protectionism in the form of direct or indirect handicaps to trade and hereby supported borderless trade and retailing to a great extent. A similar step in this direction was China's entry into the World Trade Organization (WTO), generating stronger competition among foreign retailers in China since it entered the WTO. Carrefour, Groupe Auchan and Jusco entered China several years before the country joined the WTO, to capitalize on a first phase of reduced trade barriers. Now many more are joining. According to a survey by the Chinese State Economic and Trade Commission (SETC), foreign-funded firms now account for 23% of the large-sized supermarkets (Xinhua News Agency, 2002). A similar path is expected to open up in India's economy for foreign entrants in the near future.

Legislative

Within national borders, retail and trade companies are influenced by many national laws and regulations, such as rules for construction and infrastructure of outlets, occupational health and safety rules or competition protection acts, such as laws determining store opening time frames. Different laws and regulations can be hindering but also motivating international expansion.

From a German perspective, where shops are closed on Sundays and public holidays and have limited operations hours on Saturdays (closed from 4 p.m.) and weekdays (closed from 8 p.m.), expansion to countries like China or Japan mean more sales potential in terms of time: the invested capital can be utilized more often and generate more profit through longer opening hours. Another example for efficient use of store formats abroad is the eased Large-Scale Store Retail Law in Japan that supports the opening of large scale retail formats and therefore simplifies the setup of business for foreign retail stores. Again compared to Germany, where a similar but stricter law is in place, motivation to set up business in Asian countries, where the legislative environment is sometimes easier than in the home market, is comprehensible.

Technological

Not so much a motive, but rather an accelerator for the expansion of overseas companies to Asia, are the advanced level of information technology and the easing of language barriers in recent years. Very often, the strength of a global retail and trade group is based on its intensive use of information technology, especially in respect to supply chain management, assortment planning and customer relationship management. The implementation of intelligent technologies, such as Wal-Mart's web-based Retail Link, can boost integrated, borderless internationalisation.

In conclusion, internal and external reasons for internationalisation into Asia still depend very much on the individual company strategy, the assortment as well as on the target country. Moreover, a huge global retail and trading group faces different challenges to those of a smaller specialty retailer. But in general, all retail companies are affected by the general trend of internationalisation, with Asia currently being one of the most dynamic regions.

Because Asia as a whole is not easy to grasp, it makes sense to take a closer look at individual countries belonging to a company's expansion scheme. Therefore, in the following text the Metro Group and its expansion into Asia are examined, with respect to the transfer of the Cash & Carry store format to China, Vietnam, Japan and India.

THE METRO GROUP

Overview of the Metro Group

The Metro Group is the 3rd largest trading and retailing group in Europe and the 5th largest group worldwide (*Lebensmittelzeitung*, 2002). The company's workforce accounts for 235,000 employees in 28 countries, with a sales volume of 51.5 billion Euros in 2003, of which 46% are generated outside of its German home market (*Metro*, 2003, p. 322).

The Metro Group comprises a strategic management holding company, heading the core operating businesses as well as related service companies. The so-called cross-divisional service companies provide services to all sales divisions across the group, like procurement, logistics, IT, advertising, financing and catering. Its operations are divided into four sales divisions, which consist of wholesale, food retail, non-food specialty and department stores (see Chart 1). Within these

CHART 1. Organizational Overview of the Metro Group

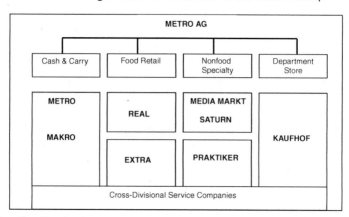

Source: Adapted from *Metro* (2003), p. 320.

four divisions six business units act independently in the market with their individual retailer brands.

One of the business units is the Cash & Carry wholesale business unit, carrying the name METRO C&C, similar to the Group's name. The name Makro is also used in some countries, but Makro is not counted as a separate business unit. In the long-run it probably will be replaced by the Metro retail brand. Metro Cash & Carry is the group's draught horse for international expansion. The concept is implemented in all of the Group's foreign markets, except Switzerland and Luxembourg. Because of its proven track record in 26 foreign markets with regional focus on Europe and Asia, the following text will elaborate on its business strategy and characteristics.

The Metro Cash & Carry Business Model and Its Characteristics

The concept behind the Metro Group Cash & Carry (Metro C&C) store format is a pure self-service wholesale business. The concept was designed and launched in Germany in 1964 by Otto Beisheim and is regarded as the driving force behind Metro Group in Germany and elsewhere. The wholesale business model of Metro C&C can be distinguished from other retail or wholesale store concepts by three main strategic factors: (1) the type of customers, (2) the single point of purchase, and (3) self-fulfilled sourcing.

1. Metro C&C offers products and services under the label of either Metro or Makro and is focussing on professional customers (retailers, restaurant owners, canteen chefs, etc.). The term "Cash & Carry" means that customers do their own order picking, pay in cash and then carry the merchandise away themselves. Consumers can reduce their inventory considerably with Metro doing the warehousing for them. Also, Metro's distribution system promises greater efficiency than traditional multi-layered supply chains in many countries.

   This makes C&C units quite flexible, first-degree purchase sources for the professional customer. In practice, at least in the home market, many professional customers shop frequently for personal consumption in addition and private customers shop along with "professionals" in order to get access to a wide assortment at wholesale prices.

   Also, additional value is created for the customer by realizing direct mailings and personal visits at the customer's place of business. Based on information from the membership cards and POS, directly mailed customers receive their promotion material (Metro Post/Makro Mail) addressed to them personally and different customer groups receive specific special promotions (e.g. brochures on drinks or fresh food).

2. Another advantage for business owners is that Cash & Carry markets can serve as a single point of purchase for products with a constantly high quality at stable prices. Metro Cash & Carry stores currently come in three formats that differ in terms of selling space, assortment size and priorities: the Classic stores, the Junior and the Eco stores. The two last mentioned have a smaller selling space and a higher share of food in the assortment.

   All the food and non-food items necessary to run the specific businesses are sold under one single roof. The claimed advantages over traditional wholesale operations are a better price/performance ratio and the quality and scope of the food and non-food assortments (stores each offer a food assortment of up to 17,000 items as well as some 30,000 items in the non-food segment). In contrast to other wholesale formats, customers do not have to meet minimum quantity requirements, get nearly all products in one location and can thus optimise their stock levels and transaction costs.

3. In contrast to most wholesale offerings, the customer is offered self-sourcing. The immediate availability of the merchandise and the adjusted business hours per week (e.g., opening early in the morning) leaves business owners room to respond quickly to their customers needs or out of stock situations in their service or retail stores. This carry-out component is one of the main strengths of the store concept as the name "Cash & Carry" already implies.

Apart from advantages for customers, the Metro Group has profited from its wholesale store format as it is based on several success factors:

- Due to the membership system, all customers can be identified and their data used for direct mailing as well as one-to-one marketing campaigns and assortment planning that can be broken down to individual customer level.
- One-stop-locations with self-service (no delivery) easy visual merchandising, similar to retail store formats.
- A high goods turnover by article allows low prices and reduces handling costs.

- Modern information systems are utilized in all areas: customer information systems, goods management systems, etc., as systems orientation is the basis for fast multiplication and internationalisation of the Cash & Carry business.
- Customer-oriented combination of global and local sourcing. In most cases over 80% of the assortment are sourced from local sources (*Metro Geschäftsbericht*, 2003, S. 39).

So far the Cash & Carry business model has proven to be successful on an international basis, with a presence in 25 countries and worldwide more than 72,000 employees working for the Cash & Carry business unit, generating positive revenue (*Metro Geschäftsbericht*, 2003, S. 38). Furthermore, it is said that plans are present to raise the share of international business in the group's total sales to more than 50% in the near future.

Analysing the overseas expansion of Metro C&C from 1968 to 2004 (see Table 1), Metro C&C's long-term market entry strategy can be divided into four phases. Phase one (1971-1986) can be characterized by Metro C&C's regional spread: the successful concept expanded to the neighbouring markets of the Netherlands, Belgium, Austria, Denmark, France and UK, across the German borders or to countries with a closely related consumer and distribution structure. Phase two (1987-1992) is determined by the more southern orientation towards countries that have no borders with Germany and therefore show slightly different consumer behaviour and distribution patterns. Phase three (from 1994) of the internationalisation plan is to export the proven Cash & Carry format to eastern European countries. This move eastwards continues with the enlargement of the European Union. The only exception in this third phase is China, clearly marking the first step towards the fourth phase and also underlying the statement of Metro Group CEO Koerber saying they had been eying East Asia for seven years now (FAZ, 2002, p. 15), around the same time as business in China was established. Phase four (from 2002) marks Metro Group's overall engagement in Asia, with the opening of C&C markets in Vietnam and Japan in 2002 as well as India in 2003. In addition, feasibility studies for other Asian countries are underway.

The table makes clearly visible where the regional focus of internationalisation lies: Metro C&C concentrates on Europe and Asia when expanding outside Germany. Since the beginning of the 1990s much has been written about threats and opportunities of investing within Europe. Similar arguments are again true for the current expansion wave to the eastbound enlargement of the EU in 2004. Therefore, a closer look

TABLE 1. Overseas Market Entry and Expansion Phases of Metro C&C

Country	Year	Brand	Stores	Expansion phase
Germany	1964	Metro	109	
Netherlands	1968	Makro	15	
Belgium	1970	Makro	6	Phase 1:
Austria	1971	Metro	11	Bordering Central
Denmark	1971	Metro	4	European countries
France	1971	Metro	78	
United Kingdom	1971	Makro	29	
Italy	1972	Metro	39	
Spain	1972	Makro	25	Phase 2:
Portugal	1990	Makro	9	Non-bordering
Turkey	1990	Metro	9	Southern European
Morocco	1991	Makro	5	countries
Greece	1992	Makro	6	
Hungary	1994	Metro	12	
Poland	1994	Makro	20	
China	1996	Metro	16	Phase 3:
Romania	1996	Metro	15	Eastern European
Czech Republic	1997	Makro	10	countries (except
Bulgaria	1999	Metro	7	China)
Slovakia	2000	Metro	4	
Croatia	2001	Metro	2	
Russia	2001	Metro	3	
Vietnam	2002	Metro	3	
Japan	2002	Metro	2	Phase 4:
India	2003	Metro	2	Asian countries

Source: Adapted from *Metro Geschäftsbericht* (2003), p. 14.

at Asia as target region for commercial investment will be taken, in this case using the Metro Group and its target markets as a vehicle.

METRO CASH & CARRY EXPANSION INTO ASIA

Asia is not only the most recent field of internationalisation, but also the most influential market for Metro Group in terms of economic value added. By 2006, sales in Asia are predicted to contribute to as much as 15% to the total wholesale sales. This seems to be quite optimistic, taking into account that the Asian share in 2002 was about 2% of overall Cash & Carry wholesales sales (FAZ, 2002, p. 15).

Within Asia, Metro is present in China, Vietnam, Japan and India. China was the first market to be entered in 1996; by 2004 there were 16 markets, to be increased to 40 by 2007. Metro Vietnam opened three stores since March 2002, with plans to invest another 150 million Euro to cover the country nationwide with eight locations in 5 years (Lebensmittelzeitung, 2002). In Japan, Metro launched a first store in 2002 and a second one in 2003. The next country in Asia for Metro to expand was India, with two stores in place since 2003 (FAZ, 2004, p. 18).

Metro Cash & Carry China

China is an attractive market due to its sheer size of 1.3 billion people. Yearly consumer spending accounts for about 2,000 Euro per person in grocery retailing and the Chinese market is estimated to generate an annual sales volume of 500 billion Euro (EHI, KPMG, 2004, p. 37 and 41). Due to a shift of the economic system from a Soviet-style centrally planned to a more liberal market-oriented economy, the Chinese market was opened to increased foreign trade and investment. The result has been a quadrupling of GDP since the political shift in 1978. Through China's access to the World Trade Organization (WTO) its ability to maintain strong growth rates and attract overseas investors has strengthened. Beijing claimed an annual growth rate of about 8% in recent years, although many observers believe the rate is rather close to 5% (CIA, 2002).

In 1995 Metro and the Chinas Jinjiang Group jointly founded Metro Jinjiang Shopping Center Co. Ltd. Jinjiang is a governmental company, concentrating on hotels, taxis and travel agencies. In addition, Jinjiang operates a chain of smaller supermarkets. Within the joint venture Metro holds 60% of shares and Jinjiang 40%. In October 1996, the Joint Venture opened the first large-scale warehousing storage and membership market in Shanghai (Metro, 2002).

Metro was the first foreign retailing company in China that got permission from the Ministry of Foreign Trade and Economic Co-operation in 2001 to set up chain stores in China's major cities. At present Metro China operates 16 stores across the country in major cities, for example Shanghai, Wuxi, Ningbo, Nanjing, Fuzhou, Qingdao and Wuhan. In total Metro employs around 5,000 staff, with national sales reaching about 600 million Euro (China Daily, 2002). The accumulated investment of Metro AG and Jinjiang Group together has so far exceeded 300 million Euros. Metro wants to speed up the opening of its chain store operations in China, while competition is growing, especially with the WTO liberalization in place by 2004.

In May 2002, Metro Cash & Carry China formed the four separate business units North, South, East and West to reflect the planned growth in management and organizational structures. Future plans have also been made to educate and qualify Chinese employees. In co-operation with the German Haniel Foundation, Metro offers a special training program for Chinese students. Within this program students who speak German are offered continuing education in business and specifically wholesale management. Part of the program is a preparation course at the East-Asian Institute in Ludwigshafen, followed by four years of studies at the University of Worms in Germany.

Metro Cash & Carry Vietnam

Although Vietnam is a poor, densely populated country, that has had to recover from the devastation of war, the loss of financial support from the former Soviet allies, and the problems of its centrally planned economy (CIA, 2002), it is very attractive for direct investment for many reasons. One explanation for its magnetism is that Vietnamese authorities are slowly implementing structural reforms to revitalize the economy and produce more competitive, export-driven industries. One manifestation of these reforms is the US-Vietnam Bilateral Trade Agreement from 2001, whereby the USA agreed to support Vietnam in reforms leading to significantly increased exports as well as direct financial investment from overseas companies. In addition, it is expected that Vietnam will eventually join the WTO.

Another reason for Vietnam being an investment opportunity for international companies like Metro Group is that Vietnam is the second most rapidly developing market in the world, second only to China (U.S.-Vietnam Business Center, 2002). This already indicates Vietnam's potential for future development, complimented by Vietnam being the only country in Southeast Asia that is a net exporter of both food and energy. The latter is especially important as it clearly shows the country's hidden wealth and future propensity to consume. Due to its considerable amount of oil reserves Vietnam is currently the fourth largest oil producer in Southeast Asia, and very likely to become the second largest oil producer after Indonesia in the region. In addition, the country has large proven reserves of natural gas that will eventually translate into guaranteed dependable affordable energy for the entire country in the future.

Other elements that encourage investment in Vietnam (instead of other Asian countries) are a large readily available work force of young energetic people with 60% of Vietnam's population of 78 million being under 40 years of age. Further considerations when selecting a country for retail business are political stability and the internal social situation.

Unlike many countries in the region, e.g., Indonesia, Vietnam is free from both religious and racial tension as it has a long history of religious tolerance and the two major groups, Buddhists and Catholics, live in relative harmony. Another positive cause of investment is the stability of the Vietnamese Dong, and the steady expansion rate of the local economy, that on the one hand mean less financial risk for the foreign investor and on the other hand an increasing amount of infrastructure, construction, distribution systems as well as the demand for consumer goods and services.

In the case of Metro Vietnam, the above view has led to an investment of 20 million Euros for a store opening in Ho-Chi-Minh City, ex-Saigon, in March 2002 (*Metro*, 2002). As of March that year, Metro C&C Vietnam issued 75,000 membership cards and signed contracts with 600 suppliers (*Vietnam News*, 2002). This first outlet in Ho-Chi-Minh-City was built within six month in the form of a junior market. On 9,000 sq.m. of sales area around 14,000 SKUs are being sold to professional customers only. The product range consists mainly of food ranges with over 90% of grocery items being sourced from local producers. Metro C&C worked for the first time with the Deutsche Investitions-und Entwicklungsgesellschaft (DEG), a German development foundation, training about 4,000 Vietnamese farmers, investing 400,000 Euros in education, and constructing nine new slaughtering factories. Plans exist for 15,000 farmers to be trained on international quality and health standards. This would be beneficial to the expansion of the initial three stores to a chain of eight markets in Vietnam with an investment sum of 150 million Euro and 2,500 new jobs (*Metro*, 2002).

Metro Cash & Carry Japan

Japan as a target market is primarily attractive to Metro because of its huge potential consumer base of 126 million Japanese within an industrialized economy plus their enormous consumer spending of nearly 50% of available income, in contrast to a mere 37% in Western Europe (*Lebensmittelzeitung*, 2002). According to Metro CEO Koerber, the company will benefit from the structural economic reforms and consumer friendly government policies.

The first Metro C&C store in Japan opened in December 2002 in Chiba, on the outskirts of Tokyo. The store covers a total area of 7,000m^2, including a sales area of 5,000 m^2 and a staff of 200 employees. Metro Group invested about 25 million Euros into their flagship store. The Metro C&C business in Japan is formed as a joint venture with trading group Marubeni Corporation holding 20%.

Although the company claims the actual store was built in only 6 months, the Metro Group researched the Japanese market for several years in advance, instead of the usual time frame of 12 months from initial market entry decision to store opening. In addition, the company already had 10,000 listed professional customers prior to opening (FAZ, 2002, p. 15). This number is not as large as it may seem, considering that the store has 160 parking spaces attached and has 12 check out points.

The assortment is made up of 14,000 items, of which 90% are food and 10% non-food articles. The emphasis is on fresh produce, accounting for 60 % of the product range and thereby reflecting the main characteristics the Japanese consumer expects from food: local origin, freshness and health effects (Jonkers and Takahashi, 2002, pp. 306-323). Some 90% of the grocery assortment is bought from Japanese suppliers.

Even though it is not common for professional customers to get all their wholesale produce from one store via self-service, Metro is not the first and only wholesaler to do so, as they often claim. The first foreign wholesaler to set up stores with a similar concept in Japan was the North American Costco Group. The main difference between the two competitors is the membership fee Costco charges from professional and private clients. Where Japanese business customers would traditionally receive their diverse product range via a number of wholesalers and mostly by delivery, Costco was the first to tap this business model of a wholesale self-service at relatively lower prices. Metro, on opening, sold to its customers at a discounted rate of 20% under average wholesale prices (FAZ, 2002, p. 15).

During the first year of business Metro C&C Japan was estimated to have sales of 50 million Euros in Chiba alone (FAZ, 2002, p. 15). Metro is planning to open another 10 markets with a longer term ambition of about 50 Metro C&C stores throughout the country.

Metro Cash & Carry in India

India has about 1 billion inhabitants and a GDP of over 240 billion Euro (FAZ 2004, p. 18). The Indian economy covers a multitude of industrialization levels: it ranges from traditional farming to modern agriculture as well as from rural craftsmanship to highly specialized modern industries, including information technology and communication support services. One of the main problems of the economy seems to be overpopulation and the wide gap between rich and poor. Whilst large numbers of the population are well-educated multi-lingual consumers, about a quarter of India's population is too poor to even afford an adequate diet. In addition, the nation is divided because of long-term political and cultural conflicts. Although exports and privatization have increased fairly slowly, government restrictions on foreign investment and imports have been liberalized. One of the foreign investors that sees a positive future in India is Metro Cash & Carry.

Metro managers analysed the market with a feasibility study in 1995, but refrained from entering the market. A second market research exercise was conducted in 1999 with the aim of getting wholesale operations approved by national authorities. It has to be mentioned that the Indian government has banned foreign investment in retailing, but allows wholesale business in the country. Metro therefore had to assure the government of restricting the consumer base not only to retailers with a tax registration number but rather all business people that had registered with some government authority. After getting the necessary permission, store opening began in 2003. The first outlet was put into operation in Bangalore in Southern India passing prices on to the consumer that lay between 30 and 45 percent under the government-set Maximum-Retail-Price (MRP) (Bist, 2003). But Metro faces problems in the Indian market.

One of them is that the product range and quality from local Indian sources does not match the group's standards (FAZ, 2004, S. 18). Often quality in India is low due to the multi-layered traditional distribution system. The product range is limited as Metro is not yet allowed to offer fresh vegetables, seeds and grains as this can only be done by designated traders. What Metro wants to offer to its customers is consistent product quality across a wide assortment at stable prices. A different but even bigger threat to its operations is the accusation of having violated wholesale license conditions, under which it is not allowed to sell to private customers. Under growing pressure Metro has implemented a minimum purchase quantity across most categories in order to demonstrate that professional customers are shopping in their stores (John, 2004). This policy was introduced as a reaction to a local government report confirming that a lot of purchases were used for private consumption and end use, e.g., a jeweller buying footwear and food items at the outlets (John, 2004).

The solution to the problems will be that the government will address the issue of foreign direct investment in retail that is currently not allowed. Such liberalization would definitely change the business environment in favor of Cash & Carry wholesale business, as well.

ASIA'S IMPACT
ON THE METRO BUSINESS UNIT STRATEGY

The country examples show that retail and wholesale business is still very much dependent on local market adaptation that results in changing the initial business concept. This can be illustrated by considering the three main strategic elements of the Cash & Carry concept that were explained earlier.

1. Professional Customers

As the example of India shows, Metro's presumed concept of sole dependence on professional customers and their volume of shopping items for professional use is misleading. In addition, by imposing minimum purchase quantities across categories, Metro defeats one of the most important purposes of its business strategy–to enable customers to buy only the quantities they require.

2. Single Point of Purchase

Becoming a single point of purchase is more or less difficult depending on country specific needs. As the Indian market showed the Cash & Carry markets are not yet offering the wide assortment one expects "under one roof," as fresh vegetables, seeds and grains cannot be listed. Assuming that time will solve this problem, there are other necessary factors to turn a store into a single point of purchase. In Japan for example, Metro had to do severe trading up of services after several months of market entry. For instance, a customer kitchen was invented to demonstrate how Japanese restaurant owners and hoteliers can make use of products sold. Also, different to the standard concept is the availability of services, for example ice at the door for free.

3. Self-Fulfilled Sourcing

Although "the carry out" element is emphasised, the Japanese stores offer their customers delivery services that are provided and charged by external partners. Again, this defeats one highlighted strategic element of the wholesale business unit, making the term "Cash & Carry" sound somewhat overrated.

While deviation from the standard concept is not noticed by the single customer in each of the countries mentioned, it clearly shows that institutional retail and wholesale business must undergo country-specific alterations, especially in countries with complex business environments as in Asia.

CONCLUSION

The paper has examined why and how overseas companies are expanding into Asia. Taking Metro Group and its wholesale business unit as an example, the different market situations that Asia comprises have been highlighted. It could be seen that a standardized Metro Cash & Carry store format in Asian markets has to be adapted. The extent of alteration depends on many factors, such as the level of industrialization in each country.

But most important, the paper has illustrated how market entry into an Asian country has an impact on the overall internationalisation strategy and business concept of a company. This implies that future research and internationalisation planning needs to further focus on country-specific adjustments to generic business models in the retail and wholesale trade.

REFERENCES

Bist, Raju (2003), German retailer not welcome in India, *Asia Times Online*, 6 November 2003.

China Daily (2002), Supplement, 30 September 2002, http://www1.chinadaily.com.cn/supplement/2002-09-30/89468.html

CIA, eds. (2002), *World Fact Book*, http://www.cia.gov/cia/publications/factbook

EHI, KPMG, eds. (2004), Status Quo und Perspektiven im deutschen Lebensmitteleinzelhandel 2004.

Frankfurter Allgemeine Zeitung (FAZ), eds. (2002), Die Metro nimmt sich den asiatischen Markt vor, No. 283, 5 December, p. 15.

Frankfurter Allgemeine Zeitung (FAZ), eds. (2004), Metros Lehrstunde in Bangalore, No. 78, 1 April 2004.

Howard, Elizabeth and Dragun, Dmitry (2002), *Retail Internationalisation: An Overview*, Templeton Research Paper.

John, Sujit (2004), The Metro dilemma, *Times News Network*, 12 March 2004.

Jonkers, Theo H. and Takahashi, Ikuo (2002), Public concerns and consumer behaviour in Japan, in Floor Brouwer and David E. Ervin (eds.), *Public Concerns, Environmental Standards and Agricultural Trade*, New York and Wallingford, p. 307-323.

Lebensmittelzeitung, eds. (2002). News and Market Facts, www.lz-net.de

Metro, eds. (2002), Company information, www.metrogroup.de, www.metro-cc.de

Metro, eds. (2003), Handelslexikon–Daten, Fakten und Adressen zum Handel in Deutschland, Europa und weltweit.

Metro Geschäftsbericht 2003, eds. (2003), Metro Group.

Ministry of Public Management, Home Affairs, Post and Telecommunications (MPM), eds. (2004), *Japan in Figures*.

U.S.-Vietnam Business Center, eds. (2002), *Foreign Direct Investment*, http://www.usvietnam.com/index.cfm?sid=19

Vietnam News, eds. (2002), German giant opens first wholesale center, http://vietnamnews.vnagency.com.vn/2002-03/30/Stories/19.htm

Xinhua News Agency (2002), Foreign Supermarkets Gain Bigger Share After WTO Entry, 25 September 2002, http://www.china.org.cn/english/government/43976.htm

How Does the Global Retailer Localize Its Format?: The Case of Toys "R" Us and Carrefour in Japan

Jungyim Baek

SUMMARY. The paper shows the decision-making and strategy in overseas expansion by global retailer's and the gradual changes after entry into foreign markets. The focus is the concept of gradual strategic change. The research on retail internationalization has pointed to an evolutionary process from domestic action to global action. However, little research has been undertaken on the change of strategy in respect of standardization-adaptation before and after entry. Examples are provided of the standardization-adaptation process in the stages of pre-entry and post-entry for Toys "R" Us and Carrefour in Japan. *[Article copies available for a fee from The Haworth Document Delivery Service: 1-800-HAWORTH. E-mail address: <docdelivery@ haworthpress.com> Website: <http://www.HaworthPress.com> © 2004 by The Haworth Press, Inc. All rights reserved.]*

KEYWORDS. Retail internationalization, standardization-adaptation, Japan, retail strategy, Carrefour, Toys "R" Us

---

Jungyim Baek is Visiting Researcher, Asian Research Institute, Osaka University of Economics and Law (Osaka, Japan), Visiting Researcher, LE CERIDICE, ESCP-EAP (Paris, France), and Doctor of Commerce, Graduate School of Business, Osaka City University, Japan (E-mail: baekjungyim@hotmail.com).

[Haworth co-indexing entry note]: "How Does the Global Retailer Localize Its Format?: The Case of Toys 'R' Us and Carrefour in Japan." Baek, Jungyim. Co-published simultaneously in *Journal of Global Marketing* (International Business Press, an imprint of The Haworth Press, Inc.) Vol. 18, No. 1/2, 2004, pp. 151-166; and: *International Retailing Plans and Strategies in Asia* (ed: John Dawson, and Jung-Hee Lee) International Business Press, an imprint of The Haworth Press, Inc., 2004, pp. 151-166. Single or multiple copies of this article are available for a fee from The Haworth Document Delivery Service [1-800-HAWORTH, 9:00 a.m. - 5:00 p.m. (EST). E-mail address: docdelivery@haworthpress.com].

Digital Object Identifier: 10.1300/J042v18n01_09

INTRODUCTION

To globalize a retail company is to attain chain store operations not only at home but also in overseas markets (Mukoyama, 1996). Irrespective of the retail formats of the firm its actions represent a search for "economies of scale" based on the principle of chain store operations. This principle is applied to both overseas and domestic markets. However, the process of chain store operation in the domestic market and that in an overseas market are considerably different. The difference comes from the "standardization-adaptation problem," that occurs when retailers move their chain store operations into overseas markets particularly when expansion possibilities are limited in the domestic market. In a domestic case, when a specific retail format is decided, economies of scale are realized by making full use of a standardization strategy. In the case of overseas markets, retailers will be faced with problems of adapting to a different market environment. Mukoyama (1996) refers to this problem using the term "global dilemma," and he indicates that in order to advance the globalization of a retail company it is necessary to explore a way to resolve this global dilemma. How is the standardization of chain store operations enabled and at the same time adapted to the characteristics of the market that has been entered? Mukoyama uses the concept "center-circumference assortment" (Mukoyama 1996) as a method of solving this contradictory standardization-adaptation problem.

Three questions are addressed in this chapter:

- Is it correct that the time-axis for adaptation may be limited only by the economic development level represented by the rise of income?
- Is it right that a problem of standardization-adaptation may be limited only to the assortment as a "reaction to environmental change"?
- Should the concept of retail format be modified in the integrated process of standardization-adaptation?

Therefore, in order to answer these three questions, it will be argued that the decision-making and actions of retail companies are gradually modified at the time of market entry as well as after entry. This paper considers the innovation of store formats and operating systems of global retailers at the time of market entry, and the change of competitive relations in the local market after entry. Toys "R" Us and Carrefour in Japan are used to examine the strategic action a global retailer takes at each stage.

LOCAL ADAPTATION PROCESS OF FOREIGN RETAILERS IN JAPAN

Toys "R" Us, is one of the more successful foreign retailers in Japan, and Carrefour is undertaking continual trial and error to find a successful pattern; both are used as case studies. Their organizational structures and the structure of their sectors are quite different from each other, although they entered the same foreign market. The marketing and distribution system and competitive situation of toy retailing is relatively less well developed than many other sectors whilst food retailing is relatively advanced.

Local Adaptation Process of Toys "R" Us

Yahagi (2001), in an analysis of the internationalization process of Japanese retailing, has pointed out two reasons to explain the difficulty facing foreign retailers in Japan. One is a group of institutional conditions, for example the liberalization of capital transactions and Large-Scale Retail Store Law that have had a decisive influence on foreign retailers at the time of entry. The second is the market difficulty on entry, for example the entry mode and "a difference between the flexibility of a standardization strategy and innovation, and the management structure." Toys "R" Us opted for entry to the toy market in Japan by using an innovative retail format drawing on their experience of development in other countries. The most important thing for foreign retailers in entering a local market is to fully understand the different environment and to develop a suitable strategy. How did Toys "R" Us understand the different environment, develop suitable strategic actions and become successful in Japan? To address this question, we will start with the examination of the toy market in Japan at the time that Toys "R" Us entered.

Deregulation and economic recession in Japan at the time of entry operated in favor of Toys "R" Us, whose strength was providing low prices. It was relatively easy for an innovative retailer like Toys "R" Us to enter the toy market in Japan, which consists of many small toy retail stores and where selling at fixed prices persists, even at department stores and general merchandise stores. Toys "R" Us, whose wide assortment of products and low prices are the source of their competitive power, needed sufficient store space in which they could demonstrate their competitive advantage. It was through the deregulation of the Large-Scale Retail Store Law, a result of the Structural Impediments Initiative, that the large stores were able to be realized.

Additionally, Toys "R" Us was able to develop several stores quickly through their joint venture with Fujita Shoten, the Japanese partner of McDonald's Co. Japan Ltd. Toys "R" Us left the management decisions to the Japanese part of the joint venture although their investment was only 20%. The rationale for this was twofold. First, they expected that the know-how of the standardization-adaptation strategy had been accumulated in other joint ventures involving Fujita Shoten with foreign retailers. Secondly, it was considered that the ability of the local company to understand the differences in the Japanese market would be an advantage. Furthermore, it was expected that the expansions of the chain store operations of Toys "R" Us would benefit from the help of a major company in the food service industry, particularly in location selection.

The overseas strategy of Toys "R" Us has three basic aspects: everyday-low-price, large assortments and full inventory. Store development, merchandising, and overseas operations were the same as those in the home market. If the environment of the foreign market seemed likely to accept a standardization strategy then it was thoroughly pursued, even if there was room for some flexible adjustment to accommodate specific issues of consumer behaviour. However, it was difficult to bring to the toy industry of Japan an American transaction system, which does not use middle men in the channel. Toys "R" Us had to find a compromise that keeps the principle of direct trade but accepts the Japanese-style transaction. Dealing through a product sales agent of Bandai provides an example. It was considered that manufacturing would move gradually to a direct trade model so a reduction in the cost of physical distribution could be obtained, while lessening the resistance of wholesalers as much as possible (http://telecom21.nikkeidb.or.jp/cb/au/papers/cgi-bin/T21_Ftbody3/papers/unihon.ht).

The change in procurement and price competitiveness enabled Toys "R" Us to open an average of ten or more stores each year. Toys "R" Us became the largest retail company in the toy sector in 1996, after only five years from the first opening (*Nihon Keizai Shimbun*, April 26, 2000). It can be concluded that Toys "R" Us succeeded in the international transfer of the retailing format of category killer to Japan.

Toys "R" Us grew rapidly with a new format and no local powerful competitors. "When we advanced to Japan, their department stores sold toys cheaply, and general merchandise stores in Japan extended the selling floor space before the Christmas season. However, at present, the toy market in Japan is shared out among all of them. Although surely there are stores which compete with each other by category, there is no store which has an assortment of goods of the large-sized stores in the 2500~3000 m² range. On this point, there is no rival" (*Innovations in Sales*, August 2000).

However, complaints from Japanese consumers' sharply increased. Japanese consumers were not satisfied with the self-service store operation. The complaints centered on the goods display system of stacking items too high and an absence of salesclerks available to help customers. It was the standardization strategy of Toys "R" Us applied to every store in the world that acted as a brake on the growth of the company. The change of the competitive environment drove Toys "R" Us to convert into the strategy adapted to the taste of Japanese consumers.

Toys "R" Us-Japan is beginning to strengthen customer service as part of an adaptive strategy. The "CS associate" system is one example of this. This system is one whereby the salesclerks encourage children to try the toys and show them how to use them (*Nikkei Marketing Journal*, November 13, 2001). This approach was adapted carefully to the needs of Japanese consumers. The improved consumer service contrasts with that at the time of entry when Toys "R" Us sought to reduce personnel expenses.

Furthermore, a new style store "concept Japan," which changes the store itself, was introduced into Toys "R" Us a year after the sales of established stores began to decrease. The physical distribution policy also began to change with the new store format. Their previous delivery system had been to use fully loaded vehicles to reduce the cost, even if it caused the delayed arrival of goods at a store. More recently they introduced a new system of "1 truck per 2 stores" that enables them to improve store level service by cooperating between the two stores to meet the consumers' demand (*Nikkei Marketing Journal*, November 13, 2001).

While Toys "R" Us in the USA is usually a suburban store of one floor, Toys "R" Us Japan has changed its preferred locations to the front of stations and tenant of large shopping centers where it is easier for consumer access. The store scale has also changed with such store location strategy. Although the standard store space in the USA is about 4000 m², the Japanese standard store space, which was 3000 m² at the time of entry, is now smaller-scale at a little more than 2000 m². Thus, judging by the various scales and various types of store openings an optimal store has not yet been established (http://telecom21nikkeidb.or. jp/cb/au/papers/cgi-bin/T21_Ftbody3/papers/unihon.ht)

However, it seems that they have undertaken a process of trial and error aiming at the development of a Japanese type of store. In order for Toys "R" Us to continue maintaining its first place in Japan in the future, they need to continue to adapt to the Japanese consumer, changing the retail format, merchandising, distribution systems, location strategies, etc. While in principle introducing "concept Japan" into all the stores opened from 2001, they are in the midst of planning the development of such a store to meet the consumer needs of Japan.

Local Adaptation Process of Carrefour

Carrefour is one of the few retail companies with an extensive experience of internationalization. However, even if their experience in overseas expansion is extensive, it takes considerable time for a retailer to complete a local type of model. The countries into which Carrefour has entered and succeeded are those where traditional marketing and distribution system still remain, and where a low price orientation is strong among consumers. On the other hand, in countries such as Britain, Germany and the USA, from which Carrefour withdrew shortly after their entry, it was hard to demonstrate their innovative variation of a standard business concept in competition with local companies. The foundation of the overseas strategy of Carrefour has been to obtain an initial advantage in a large market that is deficient in modern stores. What implications does the entry of Carrefour into Japan have in such a situation? It is considered that Carrefour intended to use all its experience and know-how accumulated from activity in other Asian countries into developing a Japanese type of hypermarket (Nishiyama, 2002). Even though Carrefour-Japan entered with such preparation, they have had difficulty developing a successful operation. They have been trying to develop a Japanese type of store by trial and error. What adaptive action has Carrefour taken in a completely different environment from the home market?

The general merchandise store industry in Japan, where entry of Carrefour was initiated in December 2000, has had slow growth for many years. The hypermarket format that Carrefour brought to Japan was a retail format already introduced by Daiei but it ended in failure (*Nihon Keizai Shimbun*, January 23, 1999). Carrefour, therefore, could not be considered as a format innovator.

The Japanese type of general merchandise store continued to have the competitive power, and was also starting overseas expansion based on its competitive power, competing with Carrefour several times in other Asian markets. Therefore, even if the Japanese stores felt the threat of Carrefour, it seems that the retail format of hypermarket brought into Japan by Carrefour did not present a serious threat to the general merchandise stores in Japan, who were used to competition with such retailers. Whilst Carrefour has stores with high ceilings, a large selling floor space and displays showing large quantities of goods, they are above all a low-price-oriented hypermarket, adopting a guaranteed minimum price. The low prices, which are their main feature, are made possible by purchasing direct from the manufacturer. So, although Carrefour required direct purchasing from manufacturers in Japan, where passing through an intermediary stage is common, this approach was refused by some major food producers. As a result, negotiation on delivery of products did not finish even on the eve of opening of the first store, and so the supply of local goods continued to make slow progress in Japan. Moreover, although some goods were sold at lower prices than that of neighboring stores immediately after opening of the store of Makuhari, the final price strategy was not clear. We can assume that there is no intense rivalry perceived by the major domestic companies. After the opening of the first Carrefour store, an employee of a domestic company said, "we have not carried out special sales promotions to compete against Carrefour." Similarly, Costco, a membership wholesale club which developed a different retail format from Carrefour, emphasized "coexistence" rather than confrontation. Costco says, "Carrefour has little impact on us; in fact they promote an effect of synergy" (*Nikkei Marketing Journal*, December 12, 2000 and *Nihon Keizai Shimbun*, December 19, 2000).

When Carrefour entered the Japanese market, using management experience in Asian countries, they believed it to be important to sell local products so as to have a close relationship with the local market. Carrefour adopted a product policy of having few imported goods, especially among processed foods. Products made by foreign brands occupied only about ten percent of all shelf space (*Nikkei Marketing Journal*, January 18, 2001), and as a result Carrefour was not able to satisfy Japanese consumers who expected a much wider selection of European products. However, about a year and a half later, Carrefour totally modified their product policy (*Nikkei Marketing Journal*, September 11, 2001). This was due to a problem in the processed food section, which could not establish direct purchasing with local producers, and also because with mostly local goods available at any store, no differentiating feature of Carrefour could be introduced. Carrefour changed to a product policy that installed special selling floor space by doubling the directly imported Carrefour branded products, and emphasizing French products (*Nikkei Marketing Journal*, June 14, 2001). Thus, Carrefour was compelled to promote a local adaptive strategy of adjusting the make-up of a store to a local market and establishing a selling technique adapted for Japanese customers (*Nikkei Marketing Journal*, May 9, 2002).

Carrefour opened a second and third store quickly, but it took about two years to open a fourth store. It is considered that store growth should be rapid after opening the first store, but Carrefour in Japan was troubled with poor performance of the three established stores, and they were obliged to examine a Japanese type of format. The fourth Carrefour store was opened after about two years of getting the first three stores on track. Table 1 shows the characteristics of the first 4 stores.

At the fourth store, a smaller sales floor space and less shelf space were used. Also in the grocery section, the selling space of meat, fresh fish, fruits and vegetables, which were separated in the previously established stores, were concentrated in one area, in a similar way to that of a Japanese style supermarket. An "organic corner" was introduced on the principle of emphasizing the freshness and the quality of fresh produce. Moreover, unlike the early store, the presence of Carrefour was more prominent and original Carrefour products were used as a merchandising focus. This change of merchandising was applied not only in the Sayama store but also in a re-merchandised Makuhari store. The goods that emphasized the image of France were given extended space in all categories (*Marketing and Management in Food Retailing*, Febru-

TABLE 1. Outline of Four Stores of Carrefour in Japan

Stores	Makuhari	Minamimachida	Komyoike	Sayama
Store Location	Chiba-city	Tokyo, Machida-city	Osaka, Izumi-city	Saitama, Sayama-city
Opening Date	December, 2000	January, 2001	February, 2001	October, 2002
Total Floorspace	29,941 m^2	8,315 m^2	20,220 m^2	19,682 m^2
Tenant Space	7,535 m^2	328 m^2	3,010 m^2	8,230 m^2
Number of Tenants	48	12	30	54

Source: Adapted from *Nikkei Marketing Journal*, October 8, 2002.

ary 2002, *Chain Store Age*, August 1, 2002 and *Chain Store Age*, November 15, 2002).

In the fourth store new products were introduced. There were many goods that had not been seen in a Japanese type of format, such as convenience goods with a French flavor. While emphasizing the French taste which Japanese customers expected, Carrefour also maintained its localization policy, for example selling special products of the region around the store.

For the three established Carrefour stores in Japan, it was attempted to directly apply the experiences from other Asian countries to Japan. This could be called a standardization strategy for an Asian market. It seems that the cause of failure of this approach was to carry into a Japanese market an Asian type of model modified according to Asian countries rather than to carry over the model of the home market. Carrefour should have aimed at the second modification, taking account of the ways the Japanese environment is different from Asian countries.

Japan differs from other Asian countries in many ways. Although the Japanese market is huge like that of China, it is an economically mature market in which a distribution system peculiar to Japan has already developed. The Japanese distribution structure of "small, excess, and many stages" is common to other Asian countries, but Japan differs very much in that large retailers exist. As a result, the impact of the hypermarket on the Japanese market was not so great, compared with other Asian countries. Differentiation from general merchandise stores, established as a Japanese type of format over 40 years, was not able to be shown. Thus, since Japanese market characteristics differ from that of other Asian countries, the adaptive capability of Carrefour built in Asia was not demonstrated in a Japanese market.

Implications from the Two Cases

Both Carrefour and Toys "R" Us show that they were trying to establish original chain store operations in Japan as is illustrated in Table 2. The retail format of category killer of Toys "R" Us made a big impact on the Japanese toy market at the time of entry, demonstrating the innovative nature of a standardization strategy. However, the strategic advantage of Toys "R" Us positioned as the standard of a large toy specialty store in Japan could not persist more than ten years. Toys "R" Us did not attain the completion of a Japanese type of model by the universal standardization strategy, so it was compelled to reexamine an adaptive strategy as competition became stronger. At present, both Toys "R" Us and

TABLE 2. Strategy Action Clarified by Stage Comparison of Toys "R" Us and Carrefour in Japan

	Toys "R" Us in Japan		Carrefour in Japan	
	The time of entry	After entry	The time of entry	After entry
Development of Format	Standardization of format concept / Innovative format in a Japanese toy market / Thoroughly low-cost oriented store management	Differential adaptation by competition with local companies / Partial modification for the Japanese type of model Reformation of a Japanese type of model	Standardization of format concept (Asian type of model)	Competitive differentiation from GMS of a Japanese format / Reformation of a Japanese type of hypermarket
Goods and Price Policy	Basic ideas of management standardized (EDLP abundant merchandise assortment, full inventory) / Goods display of piling up to a ceiling ("military style") / Unadaptation to Japanese consumers in goods	Reinforcement of PB / Goods display with the same eye as Japanese consumers	Localization-oriented merchandise assortment (supplying from local) / Original marché of selling system (selling separately)	Goods expansion emphasizing French taste (adaption of Japanese consumers' needs) / Reinforcement of packaged goods
Supply and Distribution System	Orientation to direct transaction and indirect one as compromise / Arrangement of delivery center / Delivery of large lot size and store stock / Centralised supply and distribution system	Increase of direct transaction / System of "1 truck per 2 stores" lessening opportunity loss (system of high frequency small volume delivery)	Orientation to direct transaction and indirect one as compromise / Direct delivery of goods to store	Orientation to direct transaction and indirect one as compromise
Location Policy	Securing the standard floorspace (3,000 m² and over) / Suburban store along the trunk road	Reduction of floorspace (2,000 m², 2,500 m²) / Location to front of a station and a tenant of a large shopping center	Small-sized store than home country and multiple floors	Slowdown of opening store by reformation of a Japanese type of model

Carrefour are operating a trial and error approach, such as changing the goods policy and price policy to ones more suited to the local market. In this sense, Toys "R" Us in Japan is still in the stage of building a Japanese type of model.

As for Carrefour, when they entered Japan, the format of hypermarket like that of Carrefour had already been introduced to Japan by a domestic retailer, Daiei, and the innovative nature of that format could not be demonstrated as a new concept. Carrefour had to address a strategy that could demonstrate competitive advantage, after the previous failure of the format. However, the Japanese distribution system, which is the most highly developed among Asian countries, caused the competitive relations to be different from that of other Asian markets. Carrefour introduced an adaptive strategy based on the entry experience in other Asian markets. At present, Carrefour is still unable to find a competitive strong point several years after the entry and is using a trial and error approach to develop its Japanese type of model.

GLOBAL RETAILERS' STRATEGY ACTION CLASSIFIED BY STAGE

In order to operate a chain store overseas as well as at home, retailers must undertake the international transfer process of a format. It is not until a successful local type of model is established that it is possible to expand as a chain-store overseas. In this section the concept of the strategic action classified by stage will be explored.

Standardization-Adaptation Problem

Adaptation is one of the keywords that characterizes the internationalization of a retailing company. Mukoyama (1996) states "It is generally said that the adaptation to a local market is indispensable for a retailing company" (p. 53). And "ambiguity on the concept of standardization" must be addressed as a problem of existing research. Of course, the adaptation method depends on the degree of environmental difference in a host country, the competitive power of retailers there, and so on. There is an implication for research on a standardization-adaptation problem in the above quotation of Mukoyama's. Even if the globalization of a retailing company progresses today, the fundamental view that will never change is the chain store principle.

What does globalization generally mean? The progress of the standardization of a world market permits each company to expand their business into an overseas market and to perform the management activity there. Along with the development of information media, many people in the world share common information technology, and the difference in lifestyle has narrowed. The standardization in many product fields was attained by homogenization of the consumer needs. Starting from Levitt (1983), who reviewed such phenomena in "the globalization of markets," the term "global" came to be used in the field of distribution. He insisted that the way of thinking of "multinational customization" had already retreated and so "global standardization" could only generate a homogenization of markets.

This concept of homogenization of markets is not easy to interpret if the range of standardization is expanded from the "item level" to the "merchandise assortment level" of the store. Mukoyama (1996, p. 155) pointed out the problem of the standardization in globalization of such retailing companies as follows. "Common item level, that is, the standardization in the meaning that items can be added to the merchandise assortments of every store, is not so difficult, but common merchandise assortment level, that is, the standardization in the meaning that the merchandise assortments of every store are the same, is difficult." Therefore, does Levitt's globalization of markets have the same meaning as homogenization of markets?

Mukoyama performed a study on the relation of actions at store-opening and merchandise assortment comparing the "limited merchandise assortment type of global companies with one concept" and "many product types of global companies." He argued that, while global companies overcame the heterogeneity of markets, and so adapted to the market of each country, they had to obtain goods that can provide substantial economies of scale, and so realized the standardization of goods in this manner.

How do global companies handling many types of products attempt to solve this problem? Here we require the concept of homogenization of markets. According to Mukoyama, homogenization of markets means, as the income level of each local market rises, common areas in the assortment of merchandise that do not need adaptation begin to occur, and it is possible to standardize goods in this common market. The assortment of merchandise needed at initial adaptation is a response to high heterogeneity. That is, as the heterogeneity of markets becomes lower, the area of merchandise assortment that needs to be standardized increases. The global dilemma is reduced owing to the homogenized tendency of markets and the change of "central-circumferential merchandise assortment," and the problem of standardization-adaptation can be treated as "what can be dealt independently" and respectively.

On the other hand, Kawabata (2000) considers "the problem of ambiguity of how to catch a market" to be the fundamental subject, left untouched by previous research, and in order to clarify it, he raises the concept of a "filter structure." While he accepts Mukoyama's theory of central-circumferential merchandise assortment theory as a compromise of standardization and adaptation, he points out that theoretical precision should be required to show that the rise of income strengthens the homogenized tendency of the market. From this point of view, while examining the characteristic of "the Asian middle class market" where Japanese retailers have entered, Kawabata verifies the theory of "the homogenization market," i.e., the relation of the rise in income with the characteristic of the market. According to his analysis, the characteristics of the Asian middle class market differ from those of Japan. From such recognition, the theory of a filter structure can be derived as a frame to analyze more objectively the problem of the homogeneity and of heterogeneity of markets of each country. Kawabata (2000) states, "to analyze in integration the market strategy not only emphasizing the adaptive strategy based on the difference between markets, but subsuming also the standardization (globalization) strategy by grasping inter-market structural similarities, through comparison of filter structures, which means the characteristic with which each market is equipped" (Kawabata, 2000, p. 59).

Yahagi (2003), who supports "the coexistence-position," draws two concepts of adaptation, through examination of the local adaptation process of Seven-Eleven and Toys "R" Us in the Japanese market. Although he draws two concepts of "continual adaptation" and "partial adaptation" in internationalization on the assumption that the problem of local adaptation occurs, he emphasizes that it is necessary to add another precondition. According to his idea, the precondition for retailers' internationalization is the existence of the "standard" format in each domestic market and its establishment, and the transfer of it overseas. In order to succeed in local markets where environments differ, a process in which a retailer adapts the "standard" is required, and the possibility of success for foreign retailers grows only after the compatibility of standardization with adaptation is accomplished.

Strategy Action Classified by Stages

The problem of standardization-adaptation in the early stages of entry depends on whether or not the concept of format that is introduced by a global retailer is innovative in a host country. The stage where the problem of standardization-adaptation reacts most sensitively to the competitive relations in a host country is the time when a global retailer becomes established. However, when outside environments, such as competitive relations, change, it is necessary to modify some of the strategic action taken in the early stage of entry. If a prototype suitable for the country is completed after going over the various strategies, it will be possible to expand to multiple stores by standardization. This is shown in Figure 1. The strategic actions performed at different stages is an important theme that should be strongly considered in the internationalization process of retailing companies. Figure 1 shows the balance of standardization and adaptation at the different stages of the internationalization process.

Although "adaptation," when transferring the format generated and developed in the home country to an overseas market where the environment differs, has been emphasized, it is clear from the case studies of this paper that the mechanism of "standardization" is working continuously. It is important that there are two stages, the standardization at the time of entry and the standardization as multiple stores are developed. The former, which develops stores of the same layout as at home and transfers the merchandise assortment and the management technique under the same organization, applies to the standardization strategy of an international level. In the case of the later stage standardization, a local format is obtained through trial and error and the company develops multiple stores of this model. The adaptation strategy, which is always performed considering chain store operations in a globalization process, brings about the conversion to the domestic level of the standardization strategy in a host country. Distinguishing clearly the two standardization concepts is important to understanding the nature of chain store op-

FIGURE 1. Strategy Action Clarified by Stages

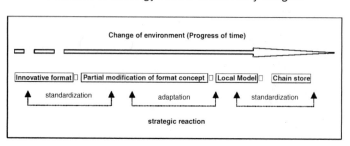

erations overseas. The strategic actions classified by stages is a long-term management strategy required by a global retailer.

CONCLUSION

Investigating the adaptation strategy of global retailers in Japan, we found that the strategic action is modified at the time of entry and after entry, and we call it "strategic action classified by stages." In showing the concept of this strategy action classified by stages, it was indicated that the standardization-adaptation problem changed at the time of entry and after entry. Toys "R" Us and Carrefour in Japan tried to carry out multi-store development, matching the particular format developed in the home country with the different environment of host country. However, Toys "R" Us, which has succeeded in the Japanese market, is in the reexamination stage to form a Japanese type of model, and Carrefour is in the initial stage of establishment in Japan.

A global retailer adopts fundamentally the standardization strategy in internationalization. A global retailer who enters a new market by copying the particular advantage cultivated in a home country aims at accomplishing a local type of model after entry. As a result of refining a local type of model, it becomes clear that the chain store principle works and multiple stores can be developed in a local market. The two cases considered in this paper are similar in that both aim at the rapid multi-store development having accomplished a local type of model. If such a chain store principle is recognized to be a standardization strategy, it will be understood that standardization has dual meaning. One is the established standardization concept of copying the pattern established at the time of entry and developing it, and the other is the standardization concept which accompanies multiple stores' development of the local type of model completed in a host country.

REFERENCES

Chain Store Age (2002), 1 August 1.
Chain Store Age (2002), 15 November 15.
Innovations in Sales (2000), August.
Kawabata, Motoo (2000) *Retailers' Overseas Expansion and Strategy*, Shinhyoron.
Levitt, T. (1983), The Globalization of Markets, *Harvard Business Review*, Vol. 61, No. 3, pp. 92-102.

Marketing and Management in Food Retailing (2002), February.

Mukoyama, Masao (1996), *Take-off on the Pure Globalization*, Chikura Shobo.

Nihon Keizai Shinbun website *http://telecom21.nikkeidb.or.jp/cb/au/papers/cgi-bin/T21_Ftbody3/papers/unihon.ht*

Nihon Keizai Shimbun (1999), 23 January.

Nihon Keizai Shimbun (2000), 26 April 26.

Nihon Keizai Shimbun (2000), 19 December.

Nikkei Marketing Journal (2000), 12 December.

Nikkei Marketing Journal (2001), 18 January.

Nikkei Marketing Journal (2001), 14 June.

Nikkei Marketing Journal (2001), 11 September.

Nikkei Marketing Journal (2001), 13 November.

Nikkei Marketing Journal (2002), 9 May.

Nikkei Marketing Journal (2002), 8 October.

Nishiyama, Kazuhiro (2002), *Truth of Wal-Mart*, Diamondsha.

Yahagi, Toshiyuki (2001), Japanese Retail Internationalization Process, *Global Retail Competition Starting from Asia*, Nihon Keizai Shimbunsha.

Yahagi, Toshiyuki (2003), Retail Internationalization, in Sekine Takashi and Oh Sejo (eds.), *New Evolution of Retailing in Japan and Korea*, Chikura Shobo, pp. 173-204.

The Linkage of Trades in Terms
of Wholesale Business Formats
in Japanese Distribution Systems

Junji Nishimura

SUMMARY. Japanese distribution and particularly wholesaling are often suggested as having complex channel structures. This can provide difficulties for international retailers who wish to develop direct links with manufacturers and agricultural producers. Wholesalers, in this system, attempt to synchronize their buying and selling functions that gives rise to different types of wholesale business format. Unlike retail formats, wholesale formats seldom have relationships with the final consumer. Results of a survey of wholesalers are presented. The results show that the buying and selling trade relationships are driven by different factors depending on the business format of the wholesaler. *[Article copies available for a fee from The Haworth Document Delivery Service: 1-800-HAWORTH. E-mail address: <docdelivery@haworthpress.com> Website: <http://www.HaworthPress.com> © 2004 by The Haworth Press, Inc. All rights reserved.]*

KEYWORDS. Wholesaler, distribution channels, trade functions, Japan, international retailing

---

Junji Nishimura is Professor of Marketing, Department of Business Administration, Konan University, 8-9-1 Okamoto Higashinad-ku, Kobe 658-8501, Japan (E-mail: junji@konan-u.ac.jp).

[Haworth co-indexing entry note]: "The Linkage of Trades in Terms of Wholesale Business Formats in Japanese Distribution Systems." Nishimura, Junji. Co-published simultaneously in *Journal of Global Marketing* (International Business Press, an imprint of The Haworth Press, Inc.) Vol. 18, No. 1/2, 2004, pp. 167-186; and: *International Retailing Plans and Strategies in Asia* (ed: John Dawson, and Jung-Hee Lee) International Business Press, an imprint of The Haworth Press, Inc., 2004, pp. 167-186. Single or multiple copies of this article are available for a fee from The Haworth Document Delivery Service [1-800-HAWORTH, 9:00 a.m. - 5:00 p.m. (EST). E-mail address: docdelivery@haworthpress.com].

167

INTRODUCTION

In recent years some global retailers, for example Toys "R" Us, Carrefour, and ZARA have entered the Japanese market. They normally do not use the Japanese wholesaling system, pointing to its complexity. The general image of complexity of the Japanese distribution system results in part from the complicated, often unclear and Japan-specific trade customs associated with Japanese wholesaling systems. The Japanese wholesale sector is normally divided into several vertical stages within the channel, for example first level wholesaler for accumulation, secondary wholesaler for sorting, and third level wholesaler for making an assortment. These vertical stages each have their own trade relationships. Sometimes these trade relationships are made within the same trading house groups and sometimes between the vertically integrated corporations. The more the stages act as discrete functions the more the uncertainty and cost associated with the channel.

This multi-stage structure is one reason why global retailers do not use Japanese wholesalers. To avoid this complexity, global retailers generally bring their own original global distribution system, trade customs and business models into the local Japanese market. They are interested in direct trade relationships with suppliers. They think that the long and multi-level channel leads to uncertainty and high cost transactions. Some studies based on transaction cost theory show that in the selection of the mode of entry to international and global markets, firms are concerned with the most efficient form of governance: the least cost solution (Brouthers et al., 2003; Shelanski and Kein, 1995; Williamson, 1991).

But foreign retailers are not always successful in the Japanese market, sometimes being obliged to change trade partners and to use Japanese wholesalers. Carrefour in Japan has changed its distribution strategy in this way since entry. It adopted the global standard strategy to enter the new market:

> Carrefour keeps the low price policy in Japan buying 55% of products from manufacturer directly and introducing private brand products more and more. (*Yomiuri* Newspaper, 21 Oct. 2000)

> . . . especially perishable foods are handled actively. Carrefour attempts to trade with the manufacturer directly in order to use a low price strategy, and invests in the Japan office of international consumer product buying group (Global Net Exchange) which uses

internet sourcing and keeps the efficient sourcing route. (*Nikkei Newspaper*, 21 Oct. 2000)

Carrefour intended to use its global strategy as in other countries; however, it had to change strategy in Japan. In developing new stores it has used Japanese local wholesalers.

> In Japan it is the orthodox distribution route to use the wholesaler. Carrefour knew but attempted to trade with manufacturers directly. For Carrefour the direct trade with the manufacturer is fundamental . . . because Carrefour could not build the physical distribution system with a major trading company; . . . finally Carrefour decided to buy the processed foods and daily necessities through wholesalers. (*Weekly Toyokeizai*, 9 Dec. 2000)

> The senior manager of the processed food division in Carrefour Japan evaluates Japanese intermediary distribution function highly and uses the strategy of keeping a wholesale route in buying national branded products. (*Japan Food Industry* Newspaper, 22 June 2001)

> Carrefour Japan now mainly buys farm products from wholesale markets. In entering the Japanese market Carrefour had wished to trade with farmers directly but now this style of trade is small. Akashi store . . . buys local farm products through local wholesale market. (*Japan Agriculture* Newspaper, 24 Jan. 2004)

Why do global retailers now use Japanese wholesalers? In this study we consider the Japanese wholesaler and wholesaling system in terms of the changes of trade relationships that are becoming apparent. There are implications for the foreign market entry strategy of global retailers, and the changes in relationships are important to our understanding of the overall dynamics of the Japanese wholesale sector.

WHOLESALING IN THE DISTRIBUTION CHANNEL

The distribution channel has a variety of structures, for example, traditional transactional distribution channel, vertically integrated channel, strategic alliance, and channel partnerships. Most channels are a sequence of trading functions. Although there are many types of distribution channels, all comprise a sequence of relationships. From this viewpoint we can establish particular linkages of trades and functions. In the typical wholesale trade stage, the one wholesaler buys from manufacturers and other wholesalers, and also sells to other wholesalers and retailers. This wholesaler basically tries to synchronize the buying and selling in terms of inventory in order to reduce trade costs and hedge risk. It is difficult for the wholesaler to fit perfectly the timing, volume and quality of products, and contract contents about trades between the buying trade partner and the selling trade partner. But, because this integration of buying stage to selling stage is the unique and wholesaling-specific role for the wholesaler, they try to use it to gain differential competitive advantage. This integration activity can be called "the linkage of trades in the wholesale trades relationship." Normally both types of trades, buying and selling, cannot be synchronized with the same timing. This linkage has time lags but it is better for wholesalers to have both trades as synonymous as possible. Presently in terms of the time lag, the selling trades to the big retailers are leading and buying trades from the major manufacturers are following (Nishimura, 2002, 2003). The ideal state for the wholesaler is to make the linkage between buying and selling smoothly and quickly, but it is obstructed by some factors. These factors, that prevent synchronization, comprise internal obstruction factors and external obstruction factors (Nishimura et al., 2004). Internal factors are organizational slack, the kind of product handled, human resources and so on. External factors are trade relationships, contract content, power balance to the trade partners, consumer preference, competition structure of manufacturing, retailing and wholesaling, institutional conditions for example trade association activity and so on.

The wholesaler tries to synchronize several aspects of trade. They may be cost saving, risk hedging, matching of assortment, business strategy, and so on. They are shared between wholesaler, retailer and manufacturer. This study is concerned with the matching of assortment and trade relationship.

CHANGE OF WHOLESALE BUSINESS FORMAT

There is little discussion about wholesale business formats. Some studies discuss the wholesale business format as a specific and unique case. In this study the dynamism and process of the changing trade relationships is one focus. A second focus is the wholesaler's concern with the change of business format. The purpose of this study therefore is to consider the dynamism of wholesale trade relationship and its relationship to the business format.

Considering the wholesale business format, it is important to recognize two points: one is common with the concept of retail business format, and the second is unique to wholesale business format. Several studies have been made of the retail business format. The retail business format relates to the retail mix and retailing innovation in management. In the retail stage of the channel, the retail format and retailing type are specific combinations of retail functions and this combination is termed the retail distribution mix. The retail distribution mix includes location, assortment, price, promotion, store atmosphere and so on. This concept can be applied to the wholesale business format. Wholesale business format is also composed of wholesale distribution mix, for example assortment, physical distribution, electrical ordering system, and so on. Retailing innovation in management includes some process innovation at the retail stage. It includes retail managerial technology (Suzuki, 1980) and handling technology of products (Ishihara, 1999). Technical innovation in the retail stage means the operational technology which can be shifted to another organization. What is in the retail stage also applies in the technical innovation of wholesale stage. Wholesalers also have produced innovations in the wholesale operation: marketing information system, physical distribution system, and so on. The wholesale distribution mix generates the wholesale business format in a similar way to the retail distribution mix.

Different from retail business format, however, is that in the wholesale stage the wholesaler trades with other wholesalers and retailers who resell products. The wholesaler mainly trades with resellers, not end users. Therefore, it is not always important for the wholesaler to adapt to end users, but it is important to build trade relationships. This aspect of business distinguishes wholesaler formats from retail business formats.

INFLUENCING FACTORS AND MECHANISMS TO CHANGE IN THE WHOLESALE BUSINESS FORMAT

The Uniqueness of the Wholesale Business Format

In considering the wholesale business format it is necessary to make a distinction between outside trade relationships and internal issues. Internal factors are the depth and width of assortment, trade areas, new product development, and so on. External factors are generally considered as social factors, technology factors, demographic factors, economic factors, and political factors. Here we focus on the trade and trade relationship, and thus the dyadic nature of trade partnerships is particularly important. In considering the wholesaler, we always have to incorporate factors of both buying relationships and selling relationships.

Secondly, changes of wholesale business format take place. The different formats may change in different ways. Voluntary chain, wholesale club, physical distributor, and highly information systematized wholesaler are distinguished with each changing in particular ways and ways that may be different from the ways that retail formats change. The critical point is who is the selling trade partner for the wholesaler. Whenever the wholesaler develops a new wholesale business format, sales are made not to end user and consumer but to retailer and other wholesaler or intermediary.

Business Format Development in Wholesaling and Retailing

The approaches to retail business format development through environmental theory, cyclic theory and conflict theory have been discussed generally (Brown, 1987). In summary, environmental theory suggests that the change in retailing is a function of developments in the environment effecting the operation of an institution and an organization. Cycle theory suggests that retail business formats change in a regular way and change is characterized by reappearance of an initial pattern. Conflict theory suggests that the conflict among institutions and organizations when a new retail format emerges generates a response that creates another new format.

Although an integrated theory and an innovation theory have been suggested, in all these theories there is a difference between retail business formats and wholesale business formats. Retail business formats emphasize the customer satisfaction and economic efficiency in buying behavior. But considering wholesale business formats customer satisfaction is less important (Shimaguchi 1984). In addition, physical distribution becomes an important aspect of the wholesale format, more so than in retail formats (Yahagi, 1994, 1997).

From the above perspectives, the wholesale trade relationships can be deduced and the wholesale business format is considered as related to the trading relationships. The development of the wholesale business format can be seen by the adaptation and correspondence with manufacturer and retailer (Table 1).

TABLE 1. Type of Wholesale Business Format

	Partial Adaptation	Whole Adaptation
Distributive Function	Wholesale type Business Format	
Assortment	Traditional Wholesaler	Retail type-specific Wholesaler

The traditional wholesaler is one type and has existed for a long time. Wholesale type business format stresses the distribution function dimension. Retail type-specific wholesaler is organized to link with a specific type retailer in assortment dimension and so has assortment-functional specialization. The retail type-specific wholesaler starts from matching the assortment and then shifts to adapting the distribution functions. The development sequence usually is from traditional wholesaler to wholesale business format type, and to retail type-specific wholesaler.

THE SURVEY OF BUYING AND SELLING TRADE IN WHOLESALING

A questionnaire survey to Japanese wholesalers was undertaken in order to analyze the nature of wholesale trade as trade partners change. This survey was sent to 3,000 wholesale companies who have a head office in Osaka and Hyogo prefectures in 2001. The number of respondents providing usable responses was 577. Table 2 shows the sector of trade of respondents and Table 3 shows their size.

Most of the responding wholesalers buy from manufacturers and overseas trade partners and sell to retailers and industrial users. A wholesale company type here is classified according to the following criteria, and is based on the weight of the main amount of trade dealings.

Direct trade wholesalers:

- buy from producers and sell to industrial users
- buy from producers and sell to purchasers in foreign countries
- buy from foreign countries and sell to industrial users
- buy from foreign countries and sell to purchasers in foreign countries
- buy from producers and sell to retailers
- buy from foreign countries and sell to retailers

Sole wholesalers:

- buy from producers and sell to wholesalers
- buy from foreign countries and sell to wholesalers

Intermediate wholesalers:

- buy from wholesalers and sell to wholesalers

Final wholesalers:

- buy from wholesalers and sell to industrial users
- buy from wholesalers and sell to purchasers in foreign countries
- buy from wholesalers and sell to retailers

On the basis of the data collected "direct trade wholesaler" as a traditional balanced type wholesaler, "sole wholesaler" as production place wholesaler, and "final wholesaler" as consuming place wholesaler are analyzed as representatives of three wholesale business format (Table 4).

THE RESULT OF FACTOR ANALYSIS

The data were analyzed in two stages. First, a factor analysis was undertaken of buying trade and selling trade and wholesalers views of each trade as related to variables measuring the different formats of direct trade wholesaler, sole wholesaler, and final wholesaler. Second, variables on the performance of wholesalers, derived from the questionnaire, were used to analyse the relationship between performance of a wholesaler and the most effective factors in the buying trade and selling trade by correlation analysis. Tables 5 and 6 show the definition of variables.

Recognition of Trade Relationship in the Wholesaler

Table 7 shows that in the buying trade three factors could be derived. The factor pattern and loadings show that the corporation related variables mostly loaded heavily on Factor 1. Factor 1 included long-term partnership, cooperation in system operation, reliability, supportability, shared management policy, and cooperation in order. This means quasi-organizing to the same organization through a continuous long-term trade relationship. Thus Factor 1 is named *Synchronization and corpo-*

TABLE 2. Sector of Wholesaling of Respondents

	Number	Percentage
General merchandise	55	9.5
Textile products	13	2.3
Apparel, apparel accessories and notions	43	7.5
Farm, livestock and fishery products	29	5
Food and beverages	50	8.7
Building materials	51	8.8
Chemical and related products	28	4.9
Minerals and metals	23	4
Recycled materials	6	1
General purpose machinery and equipment	33	5.7
Motor vehicles	5	0.9
Electrical machinery, appliances and supplies	31	5.4
Miscellaneous machinery and equipment	19	3.3
Furniture, fixtures and home furnishings	10	1.7
Drugs and toiletries	14	2.4
Miscellaneous wholesale trade	131	22.7
No answer	36	6.2
Total	577	100

TABLE 3. Sales Size of Sample Firms

	Number	Percentage
< 1 billion Yen	59	10.2
1-3 billion Yen	159	27.6
3-5 billion Yen	112	19.4
5-10 billion Yen	104	18
> 10 billion Yen	121	21
No answer	22	3.8
Total	577	100

ration of policy and organization. The variables that loaded heavily on Factor 2 are price restraint, brand power, and difficulty of switching. Factor 2 is dependent on the trade relationship rather than cooperation in R&D and it is named *Dependence.* In Factor 3 human and monetary relationships have heavy loadings. Factor 3 is named *Human and financial cooperation.*

TABLE 4. Area and Type of Wholesaler

	Osaka	Hyogo	Non-response	Total (%)
Direct trade	211	127	23	361(62.6)
Sole	55	28	3	86(14.9)
Intermediate	5	5	0	10(1.7)
Final	34	51	3	88(15.3)
Non-response	17	12	3	32(5.5)
Total	322	223	32	577(100)

TABLE 5. Variables Related to Recognition of Trade Relationship with Supplier

Variable name	Operational definition
Shared management policy	The five-point scale of "The supplier understands the management policy of your company"
Long-term partnership	The five-point scale of "The supplier recognizes your company as a long-term partner"
Reliability	The five-point scale of "The information and advice which the supplier offers are reliable"
Cooperation in order	The five-point scale of "The supplier can always meet every order"
Cooperation in system operation	The five-point scale of "The supplier cooperates in various kinds of system building between you and your partner from whom you purchase"
Supportability	The five-point scale of "The supplier offers good support when situations change"
Tie-up in capital and human resources	The five-point scale of "There is a relationship in terms of capital and human resources with your supplier"
Profit/margin compensation	The five-point scale of "The supplier gives some considerations and compensates to the appropriate margin to your company"
Difficulty of switching	The five-point scale of "Your company are obliged to maintain the present trade relationship because of the difficulty of switching the present suppliers"
Brand power	The five-point scale of "Your company needs the brand power and the assortment power of suppliers"
Price restraint	The five-point scale of "A purchase price is decided as a the price asked by the supplier"
Rivalry	The five-point measure score of "Suppliers have some strong trade relationships with your rival companies"

In the selling trade Factor 1 is the same as in the buying trade relationship. Continuous and long-term trade relationships lead the organizations to quasi-organization (Table 8). Thus Factor 1 is named *Synchronization and corporation of policy and organization*. Factor 2 includes the tie-up in capital and human resources, profit/margin compensation, coopera-

TABLE 6. Variables Measuring Recognition of Trade Relationship with Selling Partner

Variable name	Operational definition
Shared management policy	The five-point scale of "The company to whom you sell products and services understands the management policy of your company"
Long-term partnership	The five-point scale of "The company to whom you sell products and services recognizes your company as a long-term partner"
Reliability	The five-point scale of "The company to whom you sell products and services trust in the information and advice offered by your company"
Cooperation in order	The five-point scale of "Your company can always meet every order from your trade partner to whom you sell your products and services"
Cooperation in system operation	The five-point scale of "Your company cooperates in various kind of system building between you and partner company to whom you sell products and services with this partner"
Supportability	The five-point scale of "Your company changes the trade content and contract with the company to whom your company sell products according to situation changes"
Tie-up in capital and human resources	The five-point scale of "There is a relationship in terms of capital and human resources with your trade partner to whom you sell products"
Profit/margin compensation	The five-point scale of "The company to whom you sell your products gives some considerations and compensates to the appropriate margin to your company"
Difficulty of switching	The five-point scale of "Your company are obliged to maintain the present trade relationship because of the difficulty of switching the present companies to whom you sell your products"
Brand power	The five-point scale of "Your company needs to depend upon the brand power and the leading status of your trade partner to whom you sell your products"
Price restraint	The five-point scale of "Your company has the initiative about pricing against the trade partner to whom you sell your products"
Rivalry	The five-point scale of "The companies to whom you sell your products have some strong trade relationships with your rival companies"

tion in system operation, and supportability. It shows strengthening of human and monetary relationship and is named *Human and financial cooperation*. Factor 3 loads heavily on brand power, cooperation in order, and rivalry. This factor suggests as compulsory relationship and dilemma on breaking with an existing trade partner. Thus it is named *Compulsion*.

Recognition of Trade Relationship in the Direct Trade Wholesaler

Analysis was undertaken for each wholesale business format; direct trade wholesaler, sole wholesaler, and final trade wholesaler. In the case

TABLE 7. Factor Pattern and Loadings of Buying Trade

	Factor 1	Factor 2	Factor 3	Communalities
Long-term partnership	0.736			0.55
Cooperation in system operation	0.718			0.541
Reliability	0.695			0.517
Supportability	0.682			0.546
Shared management policy	0.675			0.502
Cooperation in order	0.593			0.389
Price restraint		0.846		0.735
Brand power		0.478		0.293
Difficulty of switching		0.317		0.112
Profit/margin compensation			0.623	0.565
Tie-up in capital and human resources			0.544	0.42
Rivalry			−0.404	0.178
Eigen-value	4.042	1.745	1.181	
% of Variance explained	33.685	14.544	9.853	
Cumulative %	33.685	48.229	58.067	

TABLE 8. Factor Pattern and Loadings of Selling Trade

	Factor 1	Factor 2	Factor 3	Communalities
Long-term partnership	0.748			0.655
Reliability	0.745			0.589
Shared management policy	0.618			0.519
Price restraint	0.391			0.199
Difficulty of switching	−0.348			0.189
Tie-up in capital and human resources		0.586		0.345
Profit/margin compensation		0.575		0.408
Cooperation in system operation		0.369		0.232
Supportability		0.31		0.22
Brand power			0.671	0.484
Cooperation in order			0.454	0.22
Rivalry			0.271	0.083
Eigen-value	3.182	1.48	1.256	
% of Variance explained	26.518	12.336	10.469	
Cumulative %	26.518	38.854	49.323	

of direct trade wholesaler, factor analysis of buying trade showed the same result as wholesaler as a whole. Factor 1 is derived as *Synchronization and corporation of policy and organization*, Factor 2 as *Dependence*, and Factor 3 as *Human and financial cooperation* (Table 9). In the selling trade Factor 1 is *Synchronization and corporation of policy and organization* as well, but Factor 2 is named *Compulsion* being different from wholesalers as a whole. Factor 3 is *Human and financial cooperation*. Comparing with wholesalers as a whole in buying trade, the direct trade wholesaler had the same recognition of trading variables. However in the selling trade the compulsion factor had a heavier loading and Factor 2 became the *Compulsion* factor. The direct trade wholesaler felt an obligation to have a trade relationship with partner in selling trade (Table 10).

Recognition of Trade Relationship in Sole Wholesaler

Analysis of the sole wholesaler in the buying trade shows Factor 1 loads on supportability, shared management policy, long-term partnership, co-operation in system operation, reliability, and profit/margin compensation (Table 11). This is interpreted as synchronization as a whole and a continuous long-term trade relationship. Thus it is named

TABLE 9. Factor Pattern and Loadings of Buying Trade for Direct Trade Wholesaler

	Factor 1	Factor 2	Factor 3	Communalities
Cooperation in system operation	0.723			0.556
Reliability	0.718			0.557
Long-term partnership	0.717			0.534
Shared management policy	0.682			0.515
Supportability	0.618			0.51
Cooperation in order	0.588			0.399
Price restraint		0.796		0.656
Brand power		0.494		0.307
Difficulty of switching		0.315		0.11
Profit/margin compensation			0.75	0.674
Tie-up in capital and human resources			0.447	0.318
Rivalry			−0.344	0.141
Eigen-value	3.943	1.78	1.166	
% of Variance explained	32.855	14.831	9.717	
Cumulative %	32.855	47.686	57.404	

TABLE 10. Factor Pattern and Loadings of Selling Trade for Direct Trade Wholesaler

	Factor 1	Factor 2	Factor 3	Communalities
Long-term partnership	0.797			0.649
Reliability	0.76			0.59
Shared management policy	0.658			0.497
Price restraint	0.473			0.24
Cooperation in system operation	0.364			0.24
Supportability	0.336			0.138
Difficulty of switching	−0.318			0.222
Brand power		0.64		0.441
Cooperation in order		0.551		0.314
Rivalry		0.32		0.113
Tie-up in capital and human resources			0.621	0.396
Profit/margin compensation			0.494	0.409
Eigen-value	3.231	1.558	1.301	
% of Variance explained	26.921	12.987	10.838	
Cumulative %	26.921	39.908	50.746	

Synchronization as a whole. Factor 2 highlights dependent and subordinate relationships, that is, the sole wholesaler is controlled by supplier and it is named *Controlled.* Factor 3 is named *Integration* and Factor 4 is named *Dependence.* Factor 3 indicates a relationship in which an organization shares its fate with others, and Factor 4 is literally the relationship dependency to the supplier. Although buying trade phase is similar to the pattern with wholesalers as a whole, selling trade was different (Table 12). Factor 1 is named *Hardware commitment* and is the fixing of trade in terms of hardware. Factor 2 is based on the reliability which is assured by trade partner and is termed *Reliability.* Factor 3 is *Synchronization and corporation of policy and organization* and Factor 4 is *Dependence.* In the selling trade of sole wholesaler *Reliability* factor is placed second and it seems to precede fixing of the trade relationship with linkage to the hardware in the trade.

Recognition of Trade Relationship in Final Wholesaler

In the buying trade of the final wholesaler type, derived factors are similar to those of the buying trade of wholesalers as a whole (Table

TABLE 11. Factor Pattern and Loadings of Buying Trade for Sole Wholesaler

	Factor 1	Factor 2	Factor 3	Factor 4	Communalities
Supportability	0.801				0.583
Shared management policy	0.757				0.597
Long-term partnership	0.747				0.627
Cooperation in system operation	0.723				0.566
Reliability	0.681				0.512
Profit/margin compensation	0.531				0.55
Price restraint		0.813			0.453
Brand power		0.671			0.421
Rivalry			−0.716		0.256
Tie-up in capital and human resources			0.448		0.375
Cooperation in order				0.64	0.401
Difficulty of switching				0.504	0.238
Eigen-value	4.208	1.863	1.263	1.126	
% of Variance explained	35.065	15.524	10.522	9.381	
Cumulative %	35.065	50.589	61.111	70.491	

TABLE 12. Factor Pattern and Loadings of Selling Trade for Sole Wholesaler

	Factor 1	Factor 2	Factor 3	Factor 4	Communalities
Cooperation in system operation	0.716				0.406
Supportability	0.704				0.438
Tie-up in capital and human resources	0.471				0.29
Reliability		0.842			0.494
Profit/margin compensation		0.529			0.392
Cooperation in order		0.372			0.143
Shared management policy			0.637		0.463
Long-term partnership			0.583		0.551
Rivalry			0.262		0.108
Brand power				−0.487	0.28
Difficulty of switching				−0.433	0.135
Price restraint				0.341	0.25
Eigen-value	3.242	1.51	1.332	1.144	
% of Variance explained	27.017	12.581	11.097	9.533	
Cumulative %	27.017	39.598	50.695	60.228	

13). Factor 1 is named *Synchronization as a whole*, Factor 2 is *Dependence*, Factor 3 is *Human and financial cooperation*. This composition of factors is the same as the buying trade of the wholesaler as a whole. Selling trade relationships of the final wholesaler generate 4 factors: Factor 1 is *Controlled*, Factor 2 is *Dependence*, Factor 3 is *Stability*, and Factor 4 is *Uncertainty*. The *Controlled* factor indicates subordination to suppliers as a whole, *Stability* means obtaining the stable trade relationship, and *Uncertainty* highlights the risk for the trade partner of switching the partnership to a rival company even though investing to hardware. Final wholesalers are in uncertain, higher risk conditions of subordinate trade relationships without synchronization.

Correlation Analysis Involving the Performance of Wholesaler

Correlation analysis between the performance of the wholesaler and the major factor of buying and selling trade was undertaken for each wholesale business format: direct trade wholesaler, sole wholesaler, and final wholesaler. The major factors that represent the recognition to buying trade and selling trade relationships of wholesalers are shown below. For buying trade, in the case of direct trade wholesaler *Synchronization and corporation of policy and organization,* in the case of sole

TABLE 13. Factor Pattern and Loadings of Buying Trade for Final Wholesaler

	Factor 1	Factor 2	Factor 3	Communalities
Supportability	0.779			0.641
Cooperation in order	0.729			0.589
Cooperation in system operation	0.726			0.545
Long-term partnership	0.708			0.617
Profit/margin compensation	0.707			0.679
Shared management policy	0.672			0.537
Reliability	0.624			0.52
Price restraint		0.86		0.539
Difficulty of switching		0.502		0.356
Brand power		0.457		0.346
Rivalry		0.334		0.187
Tie-up in capital and human resources			0.875	0.479
Eigen-value	4.484	1.848	1.049	
% of Variance explained	37.367	15.4	8.739	
Cumulative %	37.367	52.767	61.506	

TABLE 14. Factor Pattern and Loadings of Selling Trade for Final Wholesaler

	Factor 1	Factor 2	Factor 3	Factor 4	Communalities
Long-term partnership	0.79				0.636
Shared management policy	0.735				0.659
Profit/margin compensation	0.667				0.365
Reliability	0.617				0.566
Price restraint	0.47				0.246
Tie-up in capital and human resources	0.38				0.153
Brand power		0.619			0.264
Cooperation in order		0.552			0.25
Difficulty of switching			0.756		0.267
Supportability			0.479		0.199
Rivalry				0.456	0.129
Cooperation in system operation				0.453	0.22
Eigen-value	3.319	1.685	1.407	1.06	
% of Variance explained	27.66	14.042	11.725	8.836	
Cumulative %	27.66	41.702	53.428	62.264	

wholesaler is *Synchronization as a whole*, and in the case of final wholesaler it is *Synchronization as a whole*. For selling trade, in the case of the direct trade wholesaler it is *Synchronization and corporation of policy and organization*, in the case of sole wholesaler it is *Hardware Commitment*, and in the case of final wholesaler it is *Controlled*.

Tables 15-17 are the results of correlation analysis. Each table has three variables; two variables of the factor scores of main three factors in the buying trade, and same ones in the selling trade, and one variable of the ordinary profit of wholesalers compared with 5 years ago.

First, for direct trade wholesaler, the factor *Synchronization and corporation of policy and organization* has a significant positive relation to the ordinary profit in the selling trade (Table 15). That is the direct trade wholesaler lays the stress on the selling trade and intends to organize this.

Second, for the sole wholesalers, the factor *Synchronization as a whole* has the significant positive relation to the ordinary profit in the buying trade. In the selling trade, the factor *Hardware commitment* has the significant positive relation to the ordinary profit (Table 16). For the sole wholesaler buying trade has the priority over selling trade and the more the sole wholesaler commits to the hardware relationship with the trade partner to whom the sole wholesaler sells, the more the sole wholesaler generates the profit.

Finally, for the final stage wholesaler the major factors in both the buying trade and the selling trade do not have significant relations to the performance of wholesaler. But the factor in the buying trade, *Synchronization as a whole*, and the factor in the selling trade, *Controlled*, have significant positive correlation with each other. The closer the wholesaler is to retailer, the more the wholesaler is affected by the retailer.

CONCLUSION AND PROBLEMS

In conclusion we can draw some theoretical and practical implications from the analysis. As theoretical implications, it is possible to

TABLE 15. Correlation Coefficient of Profit, Buying and Selling Trade for Direct Trade Wholesaler

	Ordinary profit	Synchronization Buying	Synchronization Selling
Ordinary Profit R	1		
N	355		
Synchronization Buying R	0.092	1	
Significant probability	0.086		
N	349	355	
Synchronization Selling R	0.138*	0.361**	1
Significant probability	0.01	0	
N	348	350	353

*p < .005   **p < .001

TABLE 16. Correlation Coefficient of Profit, Buying and Selling Trade for Sole Wholesaler

	Ordinary profit	Synchronization Buying	Hardware Selling
Ordinary Profit R	1		
N	83		
Synchronization Buying R	0.296**	1	
Significant probability	0.008		
N	80	83	
Hardware Selling R	0.227*	0.142	1
Significant probability	0.044	0.203	
N	79	82	82

*p < .005   **p < .001

TABLE 17. Correlation Coefficient of Profit, Buying and Selling Trade for Final Wholesaler

	Ordinary profit	Synchronization Buying	Controlled Selling
Ordinary Profit R	1		0.056
N	84		80
Synchronization Buying R	0.161	1	
Significant probability	0.154		
N	80	83	
Controlled Selling R	0.056	0.368**	1
Significant probability	0.624	0.001	
N	80	83	83

**p. < .001

identify the wholesale business format based on the trade-relationship perspectives in terms of buying trade and selling trade. There are differences in the trade relationships of the three wholesale business formats: direct trade wholesaler, sole wholesaler, and final wholesaler. Practical implications are also presented. In Japan, wholesalers tend to undertake trade synchronization as a whole to suppliers in the buying trade, whilst in selling relationships the focus is on synchronization, commitment to the trade in the hardware aspects, and being controlled. The trade behaviour of the wholesaler depends upon the business format and stage in the channel.

There are several areas for future study in this research area. Whilst, it is possible to describe the change of wholesale business format by using trade-relationships and linkage of trade concepts, this approach is not able to explain the changing nature of relationships. The three types of wholesalers in this study are representative of wholesale business formats. Whilst they can be described as the different stages of distribution channel it is likely that other formats could be identified.

REFERENCES

Brouthers, K.D., Brouthers, L.E. and Werner, S. (2003), Transaction Cost-Enhanced Entry Mode Choices and Firm Performance, *Strategic Management Journal*, Vol. 24 No. 12, pp. 1239-1248.

Brown, S. (1987), Institutional Change in Retailing: A Review and Synthesis, *European Journal of Marketing*, Vol. 21 No. 6, pp. 3-36.

Ishihara, T. (1999), The kind of business and type of business in retailing, *Ryutsukenkyu*, 2-2, pp. 1-14.

Japan Agriculture Newspaper, 24 Jan 2004.

Japan Food Industry Newspaper, 22 Jun 2001.

Nikkei Newspaper, 21 Oct 2000.

Nishimura, J. (2002), Trade Selection by Wholesaler and the Change of Distribution Channel, *Ryutsujoho*, 402, pp. 4-12.

Nishimura, J. (2003), Wholesale Business Format and the Shift of Wholesaler Type, *Marketing Journal*, 89, Vol. 23 No. 2, pp. 34-47.

Nishimura, J. et al. (2004), *Cultivation of Marketing Science*, Chikura Syobou.

Shelanski, H.A. and Klein, P.G. (1995), Empirical Research on Transaction Cost Economics: A Review and Assessment, *Journal of Law, Economics and Organization*, Vol. 11 No. 2, pp. 335-361.

Shimaguchi, M. (1984), *Theory of Strategic Marketing*, Seibundoshinkosya.

Suzuki, Y. (1980), The Shift of Retail Management Technology, *Quarterly Journal of Consumption and Distribution*, 4-1, pp. 11-16.

Weekly Toyokeizai, 9 Dec 2000.

Wiliamson, O.E. (1991), Comparative Economic Organization: The Analysis of Discrete Structural Alternatives, *Administrative Science Quarterly*, Vol. 36, pp. 269-296.

Yhagi, T. (1994), *Innovation of Convenience Store System*, Nihonkeizaishinbusya.

Yhagi, T. (1997), *The Origin of Retail Innovation*, Nihonkeizaishinbusya.

Yomiuri Newspaper, 21 Oct 2000.

The Characteristics
of the New Retail Competition in Asia
and the Research Agenda

Masao Mukoyama

SUMMARY. Research on international retailing has generally emanated for Europe and North America. A recent trend has been an increase in interest from Asian researchers who have been looking at the effects on Asian economies of international activity. International activity by large western retailers in Asia is characterised by rapid development in multi-country and multi-format strategies. This approach has provided little time for local retailers to adapt to the new competition. New research initiatives are suggested to consider format changes and store image of western retailers as they become established in Asian markets. *[Article copies available for a fee from The Haworth Document Delivery Service: 1-800-HAWORTH. E-mail address: <docdelivery@haworthpress.com> Website: <http://www.HaworthPress.com> © 2004 by The Haworth Press, Inc. All rights reserved.]*

KEYWORDS. International retailing, competition, entry times, multi-format strategy

---

Masao Mukoyama is Professor of Retailing and Dean of the Graduate School of Marketing and Distribution Sciences, UMDS, 3-1 Gakuen Nishi-Machi, Nishi-Ku, Kobe 651-2188, Japan (E-mail: Masao_Mukoyama@red.umds.ac.jp).

[Haworth co-indexing entry note]: "The Characteristics of the New Retail Competition in Asia and the Research Agenda." Mukoyama, Masao. Co-published simultaneously in *Journal of Global Marketing* (International Business Press, an imprint of The Haworth Press, Inc.) Vol. 18, No. 1/2, 2004, pp. 187-198; and: *International Retailing Plans and Strategies in Asia* (ed: John Dawson, and Jung-Hee Lee) International Business Press, an imprint of The Haworth Press, Inc., 2004, pp. 187-198. Single or multiple copies of this article are available for a fee from The Haworth Document Delivery Service [1-800-HAWORTH, 9:00 a.m. - 5:00 p.m. (EST). E-mail address: docdelivery@haworthpress.com].

Digital Object Identifier: 10.1300/J042v18n01_11

187

INTRODUCTION

Interest in the internationalisation of retailing reached increased rapidly from the late 1980s onwards and through the 1990s this area has become a major focus of retail research. The interest of researchers has concentrated on the intense activity of global movements by large scale retailers from Europe and America. Naturally, because European and American retailers were the main retail companies taking part in internationalisation European and American researchers were the first to explore this phenomenon. Their interest was simple. The main questions centered on "when did internationalization start," "where and to what extent have the retailers penetrated different markets," "why have they chosen particular countries" and "how have they moved into those countries" (Brown and Burt 1992; Dawson 2003).

At the same time research effort was also applied to analyses of the international strategies of retail operators (e.g., Treadgold 1988; Salmon and Tordjman 1989; Pellegrini 1994; Tordjman 1995). These areas of research were developed mainly by Western researchers. Recently, however, a new wave of research is coming from Asian based researchers who are exploring Asian distribution systems.

The trend of researching internationalisation as an activity looked at from the outside has changed to one of looking at internationalisation from the perspective of the countries being internationalized. The reason is clear. It is because the area being targeted by Western retailers has shifted from Europe to Asia. This shift has been both swift and dynamic. As a result, Asian retail systems have been subjected to large influences. Concern over what is happening in the Asian countries as a result of the internationalisation of Western international companies has given rise to a new wave of research. It is the researchers in these areas that are being internationalized that are forming the core of this research. This is clearly seen in the papers in this publication

This special issue focuses on Asian countries, especially South Korea and Japan, but it is also pointing to research findings in other Asian countries (Davies and Yahagi 2000; Davies 2002; Dawson, Mukoyama, Choi and Larke 2003). As a conclusion of the special edition, this paper describes the effects of retail competition on Asian counties from this shift of interest by Western international retailers and investigates the new research questions towards international retailing based in the Asian field.

CHARACTERISTICS OF RETAIL COMPETITION IN ASIA

Change of Leaders

The change from targeting the European markets, which were seen as mature, to targeting the growing Asian markets was a logical move for Western retailers. The Asian region is not only the world's production center but is now also positioned as the consumer center. It is the Japanese retail enterprises that have been first to focus on these markets. For example, the Daimaru department store opened in Hong Kong in 1960 and then in Thailand in 1964. In the 1970s Isetan (1973) and Matsuzakaya (1975) opened in Hong Kong. Since then specialty stores and general merchandising stores have continued to open and by the end of the 1980s there were over 100 stores in the Asian area (Mukoyama 1996; Kawabata 2000).

The reason that Asia was chosen by the Japanese was its proximity to Japan both geographically and culturally as pointed out by Treadgold and Davies (1988) and Burt (1993). However, moving into the 1990s the situation changed dramatically. Japanese retailers started to withdraw from their foreign operations in the Asian market. The main reasons for this were a shift to concentrating capital in order to stimulate the domestic market after the collapse of the property market bubble and also there were regional changes in Asia such as rises in wages and rent. It was now the turn of the Western retailers to move into the Asian market in the vacuum that was left.

Table 1 shows the state of penetration into Asia by major international retailers. Western retailers started moving into China in 1992 with the approval for foreign retail investment and in 1995 approval for establishing experimental chain stores. All of the retailers moved into Taiwan because of the deregulation of restrictions on foreign retailers in 1986 and also into Korea because of similar deregulation in 1996. As for movements into Japan, these came later around 2000 because of the complexity and maturity of the market. By the middle of the 1990s the leading retailers in Asia had shifted totally from being Japanese to being Western.

THE STATE OF RETAIL COMPETITION

By the end of the 1990s the rapid influx of Western retailers had a big impact on the traditional Asian distribution system led by small and me-

TABLE 1. The Year of Entry and Number of Stores in 2003 of Main International Retailers in Asia

	Carrefour	Tesco	Ahold	Auchan	Wal-Mart	Metro	Costco
China	1995 (35)		1996 (1999*)	1999 (7)	1996 (34)	1996 (16)	
Taiwan	1989 (28)	2000 (3)		2000 (17)			1997 (3)
Korea	1996 (25)	1999 (21)			1998 (15)		1995 (5)
Thailand	1996 (17)	1998 (52)	1997 (49)			1989 (**)	
Malaysia	1994 (6)	2002 (3)	1996 (2003*)			1993 (**)	
Japan	2000 (8)	2003 (0)			2002 (0)	2002 (2)	1999 (4)
Vietnam						2002 (2)	
Singapore	1997 (1)		1997 (1999*)				
Indonesia	1998 (10)		1997 (2003*)				

Notes: *Indicates a year of withdrawal.
          **Indicates withdrawal with lack of the year.
Source: Annual report of each company.

dium retailers. The following is a summary of the factors that show the competition in retail sectors in Asia.

Simultaneous Influx

Why did Western retailers enter foreign markets and establish fixed positions there? That was because they had a superiority over their competitors in the countries they moved into. Asian countries were still developing their distribution systems. The retail markets in each region were essentially made up of small and medium sized retailers in the existing markets. There were no large scale retailers and underdeveloped distribution systems were the norm. Western retailers moved into these situations. They had the ability to operate innovative formats which were supported by innovative retailing technologies and management systems. In effect a battle took place in Asian countries between modern equipped operations and simple technologies.

The entry was not of a single retail firm. Multiple enterprises appeared with their favored and innovative formats. For example, the technologies they possessed were different in both form and ability. Technologies never seen before began to appear. Faced with this situation, many Asian retailers were probably stunned and lost the will to compete.

There was yet another problem–these new innovative formats appeared in rapid succession. For example, in China the first department store opened in the early 20th century when Sincere was established in Shanghai (Huang 2002). However, department stores in China were run on completely different methods from department stores elsewhere because of the planned economic system. For a while the Chinese retail market had only one form of large scale retail format-the department store. The next introduction of an innovative format was the supermarket in the 1990s. From then on, through the influx of Japanese and Western retailers, GMS, hypermarkets, warehouse stores, discount stores, wholesale clubs, cash and carry and convenience stores were introduced. Stated simply, in China over a period of just 10 years all these new formats were introduced. In America it took 70 years from the first department store opening to the introduction of supermarkets, and a further 20 years from supermarkets to discount stores. In other countries the introduction of new formats was similarly gradual. But in Asia the time span was very short. As a result, by the time the Asian retailers realized what was happening they were surrounded by strong rivals.

This kind of multiple and rapid influx by Western retailers that had a strong competitive advantage meant there was no time for Asian retailers to copy and learn. They faced new innovations one after another without having time to respond. McNair (1958) theorized that innovative retail formats eventually trade up and the next innovative format enters into a low cost low price vacant market. However, in Asia is it true to say that the "Wheel of Retailing" proposed by McNair applies?

Diversification of Competitive Relations

Due to the influx of Western retailers it is highly likely that a fierce competition will emerge between Western retailers and existing traditional small and medium retailers based on fresh foods and daily goods. Hypermarkets brought in by Western retailers provide a one stop shopping function selling fresh foods and non-foods at low prices. This form of business is in direct competition with the business form of traditional retailers. In developed countries, with the introduction of supermarkets and GMS, fierce competition broke out between them and small and medium retailers, and as is now known it led to a decrease in the number of retail stores. It is highly likely that the same thing will happen in Asian countries. Regulations on the expansion of large scale stores that are being developed by Western companies are recently emerging (Yahagi 2003).

The competition that arises, however, is not just between the incoming Western companies and the local operators. As shown in Table 1

Western companies are competing against each other in Asian markets. For example, Carrefour, Auchan, Walmart, and Metro are competing in China and also another four companies are competing in Taiwan and Korea. It is not the case that these companies all have the same retail formats. When the retail formats are different the target consumers are different too and this does not mean that competition on all fronts occurs. This is because there is a difference in the positioning in each market. However, at the present time it is not clear how consumers in Asia view these differences in retail formats. As will be discussed later, this is one new research topic. The retail formats of the Western companies are targeting the daily needs of the middle consumer layer that is beginning to expand in Asia. In this respect we can say that although their formats differ they are targeting the same broad segment.[1] In that sense, competition between Western companies will become fiercer. Furthermore, this competition will break out between local companies. For example, in China at the end of 2000 state owned companies were grouped into 425 large scale companies. These companies are planning for competition with Western firms but on the other hand as a result of targeting a common consumer segment the state owned companies are escalating competition amongst themselves (Huang 2002).

In Korea, in the discount market, local companies such as E-Mart, Lotte Mart, Magnet, and Hanalo Club are in competition and the department store battle in Taiwan is also fierce. Furthermore in Asian countries there are many cases where 100% foreign ownership is not allowed and so Western companies are joining with local companies. These local partners are planning to develop their own stores. In Asian countries Chinese backed capital plays a major role. As can been seen from the above a complex battle is being played out between the Western retailers, local small and medium retailers, local large scale retailers and Chinese merchants residing abroad.

Multiple Formats

Table 2 summarizes the retail formats and store names of representative international retailers around the world. We can see that each enterprise is developing a diversified business approach giving unique names to their stores. However, in Asian countries Western retailers are opening stores based on limited retail formats. For example, Wal-Mart operates supercenters and Tesco and Carrefour operate hypermarkets in Asia conducting concentrated investment with clear positioning. However, recently they have started to open multiple retail formats aimed at

TABLE 2. Multiple Formats of International Retailers

	Metro	Carrefour	Tesco	Wal-Mart
C&C	Metro	Docks Market/ Gossiper/ Prompcash, etc.		Sam's Club
Hypermarket	Real	Carrefour	Extra	Walmart Supercenter
Supermarket	Extra	Norte/ Champion/ GS/ GB, etc.	Superstore/ Metro	Neighbourhood Market
Discount Store		Dia		Walmart Store
Convenience Store		Di per Di/ Proxi/ Shopi, etc.	Express	
Others	Praktiker (home improvement/ DIY) Kaufhof (department store) Media Market and Saturn (electronics)			

Source: Annual report of each company.

offering market adapted services that fit the lifestyles of consumers against the backdrop of expanding Asian market and a deepening of experience in the Asian market. Already Metro in new emerging European markets such as Poland and Hungary are carrying out multiple retail formats, and Carrefour are operating 3 formats in Argentina and Brazil and 4 formats in Spain, Greece and Italy. Carrefour declared in an Annual Report 2002 as follows:

> The Long-term objective is to supplement the network of hypermarkets by installing other formats so as to offer consumers a wide range of sales spaces and product lines that suit their lifestyles. Expanding through multiple formats also speeds up the penetration into a country by profiting from the complementarity of the various formats.

Western retailers are moving towards a strategy of all-out penetration of the retail markets in Asia. The competitive structure in Asia is getting more complex.

NEW AREAS OF RESEARCH
IN INTERNATIONALISATION OF RETAILING

Given the developments in the Asian markets, there are new research topics that have not been previously been explored by research on international retailing.

Construction of Format-Formula Theory

In this paper the term "format" has been used. Table 2 lists the formats of several Western retailers. These include Cash and Carry, Hypermarkets, Supermarkets, Discount Stores, Convenience Stores, etc. We have used this term format unconsciously but this is a very abstract term and is interpreted in many ways. Needless to say Format is a fundamental concept in the theory of retailing which is fixed by retail mix (Levy and Weitz 2001). However, is the image presented by the term format as used by different researchers a common one? Take for example the term Department Store. British researchers base their idea of department stores on the department stores that have been developed in Britain. Japanese researchers base their concept on Japanese department stores and the same applies to American researchers. While we use the same concept of "Department Store" they are very different in reality. This applies to all types of formats. This has extremely deep implications for international retail research. This leads us on to ask the following questions.

- Why do hypermarkets being developed by Carrefour in China have a different image to those hypermarkets seen in France? Can we regard the Carrefour hypermarkets in Taiwan as being different also?
- Why is it that hypermarkets being developed by Carrefour and Tesco in Thailand just do not seem the same?
- Why do we get the impression that the cash and carry stores being opened in China by Metro are also slightly different?

It is not possible to answer these questions with currently available research findings. It is easy to propose that "there are reasons for differences in strategies for international retailers." However, if we go one step further, it is not possible to find convincing arguments for what factors and what influences are being exerted on questions such as "do differences emerge when the same company develops hypermarkets in different countries" or "do the same hypermarkets cause different business forms among the different companies?" If we call these subtle differences between countries and companies Formula, we can perhaps restate it as "Why and how Format changes to Formula."

Retail internationalisation research has focused on retailers' entries abroad. Therefore, it has looked at "when, where, how much, how, why?" rather than looking at the main subjects which are carried overseas by retailers. The reality in Asian countries shows that it is possible to reach a greater understanding of retail competition and retail internationalisation strategies only by focusing on "what is internationalized," that is, "what contents of Format retailers transfer overseas."

Store Image Research

There is considerable research on store image. This image research measures the evaluation of consumers towards specific stores. The subject of evaluation is not the retail company but the consumers who use those stores on a daily basis and research has focused on questions such as "what is store image" (Lindquist 1974-75; Amirani and Gates 1993) "what variables do consumers use to evaluate stores" (Martineau 1958; Doyle and Fenwick 1974-75; Oppewal and Timmermans 1997; Burt 2000) and "why do differences of evaluation emerge" (Marcus 1972; Pathak, Crissy and Sweitzer 1974-75; Joyce and Lambert 1996; Birtwistle, Clarke and Freathy 1999).

Western retailers have opened multiple format stores in various Asian markets. These stores are all based on a definite strategy of these Western retailers. In other words, these stores project a message (or in a wider sense, some information). However, these messages are not necessarily recognized by the consumers according to the original intention. In some cases, the images are interpreted in completely different ways.

In the case of internationalisation of retailers they open stores based on a certain format. If there is congruence between retailer intention and consumer image this usually leads to increased profits. However, if the intentions of the store are not recognized a gap in image emerges. Retailers may recognize this gap and carry out refinements to the stores to close the gap. By researching how the gap has changed the stores are refined more and become more adapted to the markets. Looking at the changes in stores that have opened in the Asian markets, we can see the refinements in strategies that come about through international experience.

In order to understand this process of refinement there is a need to carry out comparative research on retailers and consumers that looks at questions such as "what are the intentions of the stores" and "how are those intentions seen by the consumers?" There are already signs of such comparative research being carried out between countries (McGoldrick and Ho 1992; McGoldrick 1998; Burt and Carralero-Encinas 2000). It is likely that store image research will become more important in order to make clear the process of internationalisation in local markets after market entry.

Internationalisation by Retailers in Emerging Markets

Distribution systems in emerging countries including Asia have been regarded as "backward" and being dependent on traditional small and medium retailers. The emerging markets have been seen by advanced Western retailers as potential new markets. Because of simultaneous penetration by Western retailers local retailers in these new markets do not have enough time to learn and respond to the innovations being introduced.

There are signs, however, that the local retailers have not been passive bystanders. For example, in China, Taiwanese RT-Mart and Hy-Mall have opened a supermarket, Trust Mark, a discount store and Grand Pacific, a department store. Parkson of Malaysia opened a department store in China and Parknshop has also opened a supermarket there. The Korean E-Mart has started to move into China as well as competing with Western retailers in home market.

Research on retail internationalization has regarded Western retailers as possessing a competitive strength that makes it possible to move into offshore markets. In these emerging markets, what kind of competitive advantages do retailers, irrespective of origin, possess? How have they gained these advantages? The international strategies can be expected to differ greatly between Asian and Western retailers. This is likely due to a difference in the resources that are held. Different strategies result from these different resource bases. The advent of new actors on a stage of retail internationalisation makes possibly to explore aspects of internationalisation research that previously have been ignored. Research on international retailing and retail business in the 21st century can be advanced further by building research combining Western and Asian researchers with retailers in both Western and Asian cultural domains.

NOTE

1. In Korea, "Discount Store" is often used as a general term to describe all large scale retail formats, for example hypermarket, superstore, discount store, and GMS.

REFERENCES

Amirani, S. and Gates, R. (1993) An Attribute-Anchored Conjoint Approach to Measuring Store Image, *International Journal of Retailing and Distribution Management*, 21 (5): 30-39.

Birtwistle, G., Clarke, I. and Freathy, P. (1999) Store image in the UL fashion sector: Consumer versus retailer perceptions, *The International Review of Retail, Distribution and Consumer Research*, 9 (1): 1-16.

Brown, S. and Burt, S. (1992) Conclusion–Retail Internationalisation: Past Imperfect, Future Imperative, *European Journal of Marketing*, 17 (4/5): 80-84.

Burt, S. (1993) Temporal Trends in the Internationalisation of British Retailing, *The International Review of Retail distribution and Consumer Research*, 3(4): 391-410.

Burt, S. and Carralero-Encinan, J. (2000) The role of store image in retail internationalization, *International Marketing Review*, 17 (4/5), 433-453.

Davies, R. (ed.) (2002) *Full Proceedings of the Asian Pacific Retail Conference 2002*, Templeton College, University of Oxford.

Davies, R. and Yahagi, T. (eds.) (2000) *Retail Investment in Asia Pacific: Local Responses and Public Policy Issues*, Templeton College, University of Oxford.

Dawson, J.A. (2003) Towards a model of the impacts of retail internationalisation, in Dawson, J.A., Mukoyama, M., Choi, S.C. and Larke, L. (2003) *The Internationalisation of Retailing in Asia*, London: Routledge Curzon: 189-209.

Dawson, J.A., Mukoyama, M, Choi, S.C. and Larke, R. (eds.) (2003) *The Internationalisation of Retailing in Asia*, London: Routledge Curzon.

Doyle, P. and Fenwick, I. (1974-75) How store Image Affects Shopping Habits in Grocery Chains, *Journal of Retailing*, 50 (4): 39-52.

Huang, Lin (ed.) (2002), *Chinese Market after WTO Entry* (WTO Kamei go no Chugoku Shijyo), Tokyo: Sososha.

Joyce, M.L. and Lambert, D.R.(1996) Memories of the way stores were and retail store image, *International Journal of Retail & Distribution Management*, 24 (1): 24-33.

Kawabata, M. (2000) *The Overseas Expansion and Strategy of Retailers* (Kourigyo no Kaigai Shinshutsu to Senryaku). Tokyo: Shinhyoron.

Levy, B.A. and Weitz, B. (2001) *Retail Management (4th edition)*, McGraw-Hill/Irwin.

Lindquist, J.D. (1974-1975). A Survey of Empirical and Hypothetical Evidence, *Journal of Retailing*, 50 (4): 29-38.

Marcus, B.H. (1972) Image Variation and the Multi-Unit Retail Establishment, *Journal of Retailing*, 48 (2): 29-43.

Martineau, P. (1958) The Personality of Retail Store, *Harvard Business Review*, 47-55.

McGoldrick, P.J. (1998) Spatial and Temporal Shifts in the Development of International Retail Image, *Journal of Business Research*, 42 (2): 189-196.

McGoldrick, P.J. and Ho, S.S.L. (1992) International Positioning: Japanese Department Stores in Hong Kong, *European Journal of Marketing*, 26 (8): 61-73.

McNair, M.P. (1958) Significant Trends and Development in the Postwar Period, in A.B. Smith (ed.) *Competitive Distribution in a Free, High-Level Economy and its Implications for the University.*

Mukoyama, M. (1996) *Toward the Landing of Pure Global* (Pyua Gurobaru he no Chakuchi), Tokyo: Chikura-Shobo.

Oppewal, H. and Timmermans, H. (1997) Retailer self-perceived store image and competitive position, *The International Review of Retail, Distribution and Consumer Research*, 7 (1): 40-59.

Pathak, D.S., Crissy, W.J.E. and Sweitzer, R.W. (1974-1975) Consumer Image versus the Retailer's Anticipated Image: A Study of Four Department Stores, *Journal of Retailing*, 50 (4): 21-28.

Pellegrini, L. (1994) Alternatives for Growth and Internationalisation in Retailing, *The International Review of Retail, Distribution and Consumer Research*, 4 (2): 121-148.

Salmon, W.J. and Tordjman, A. (1989) The Internationalization of Retailing, *International Journal of Retailing*, 4 (2): 3-16.

Tordjman, A. (1995) European Retailing: Convergence, Differences and Perspectives, in McGoldrick, P.J. and Davies, G. (eds.) *International Retailing: Trends and Strategies*, London: Pitman Publishing: 17-50.

Treadgold, A. (1988) Retailing Without Frontiers: The Emergence of Transnational Retailers, *International Journal of Retail and Distribution Management*, 16 (6): 8-12.

Treadgold, A. and Davies R.L. (1988) *The Internationalisation of Retailing*, Harlow: Longman.

Yahagi, T. (ed.) (2003) *Retailing Innovation in China and Asia* (Chugoku-Ajia no Kourigyo Kakushin), Tokyo: Nikkei.

Index

BOOK ORDER FORM!

Order a copy of this book with this form or online at:
http://www.haworthpress.com/store/product.asp?sku=5583

International Retailing Plans and Strategies in Asia

_____ in softbound at $19.95 ISBN-13: 978-0-7890-2889-1. / ISBN-10: 0-7890-2889-1.
_____ in hardbound at $39.95 ISBN-13: 978-0-7890-2888-4. / ISBN-10: 0-7890-2888-3.

COST OF BOOKS _____

POSTAGE & HANDLING _____
US: $4.00 for first book & $1.50
for each additional book
Outside US: $5.00 for first book
& $2.00 for each additional book.

SUBTOTAL _____

In Canada: add 7% GST. _____

STATE TAX _____
CA, IL, IN, MN, NJ, NY, OH, PA & SD residents
please add appropriate local sales tax.

FINAL TOTAL _____
If paying in Canadian funds, convert
using the current exchange rate,
UNESCO coupons welcome.

❏ BILL ME LATER:
Bill-me option is good on US/Canada/
Mexico orders only; not good to jobbers,
wholesalers, or subscription agencies.

❏ Signature _____

❏ Payment Enclosed: $ _____

❏ PLEASE CHARGE TO MY CREDIT CARD:
❏ Visa ❏ MasterCard ❏ AmEx ❏ Discover
❏ Diner's Club ❏ Eurocard ❏ JCB

Account # _____

Exp Date _____

Signature _____
(Prices in US dollars and subject to change without notice.)

PLEASE PRINT ALL INFORMATION OR ATTACH YOUR BUSINESS CARD

Name	
Address	
City	State/Province	Zip/Postal Code
Country	
Tel	Fax
E-Mail	

May we use your e-mail address for confirmations and other types of information? ❏ Yes ❏ No We appreciate receiving
your e-mail address. Haworth would like to e-mail special discount offers to you, as a preferred customer.
We will never share, rent, or exchange your e-mail address. We regard such actions as an invasion of your privacy.

Order from your **local bookstore** or directly from
The Haworth Press, Inc. 10 Alice Street, Binghamton, New York 13904-1580 • USA
Call our toll-free number (1-800-429-6784) / Outside US/Canada: (607) 722-5857
Fax: 1-800-895-0582 / Outside US/Canada: (607) 771-0012
E-mail your order to us: orders@haworthpress.com

For orders outside US and Canada, you may wish to order through your local
sales representative, distributor, or bookseller.
For information, see http://haworthpress.com/distributors

(Discounts are available for individual orders in US and Canada only, not booksellers/distributors.)

Please photocopy this form for your personal use.
www.HaworthPress.com

BOF05